Caroline Orton · Carolyn Brophy

FIELDS
OF VISION

English for Work and Study

PEARSON

Montréal Toronto Boston Columbus Indianapolis New York San Franc͏   ͏dle River
Amsterdam Le Cap Dubaï Londres Madrid Milan Munich Paris
Delhi México São Paulo Sydney Hong-Kong Séoul Singapour Taipei Tōkyō

Managing Editors
Christine Cozens
Patricia Hynes

Editor
Lucie Turcotte

Copy Editor
Jeremy Lanaway

Proofreader
Katie Shafley

Coordinator, Rights and Permissions
Pierre Richard Bernier

Photo Research
Interscript
Marie-Chantal Masson

Rights and Permissions
Marie-Chantal Masson

Art Director
Hélène Cousineau

Graphic Design Coordinator
Lyse LeBlanc

Cover Design
Frédérique Bouvier

Book Design
Catapulte
Interscript

Book Layout
Interscript

Illustrations
Volta

© ÉDITIONS DU RENOUVEAU PÉDAGOGIQUE INC. (ERPI), 2012
ERPI publishes and distributes PEARSON ELT products in Canada.

1611 Crémazie Boulevard East, 10th Floor
Montréal, Québec H2M 2P2
CANADA
Telephone: 1 800 263-3678
Fax: 1 866 334-0448
infoesl@pearsonerpi.com
pearsonelt.ca

Registration of copyright: Bibliothèque et Archives nationales du Québec, 2012

Registration of copyright: Library and Archives Canada, 2012

Printed in Canada   3456789   II   17 16 15
ISBN 978-2-7613-3846-2   133846 ABCD   0F10

Acknowledgements

I'd like to thank my writing partner on this book, Carolyn Brophy, for making my life easier at every turn.

To my husband, Pano, my daughter, Anna, and my son, Demetrios. All my love and thanks.

Caroline Orton

I'd like to thank my mentor, Caroline Orton, for her patience and strength, and for having faith in my abilities.

To Teresa Mycyk, for her words of encouragement.
Thanks Biff.

To my husband, Murray, and my daughters, Renee and Erika. Thanks for your love and support.

Carolyn Brophy

Credits

Unit 1, p. 2 Audio text "Motivation 3.0" © Canadian Broadcasting Corporation. pp. 7-8 "Retrain Your Brain from 'Left' to 'Right' to Fit into New Economy" by Marco R. della Cava, © Copyright 2009, USA TODAY, a division of Gannett Co., Inc.; reprinted with permission. p. 13 Video segment "Interview with Sean Aiken" © CTV. pp. 19-20 "Putting Ideas to Work" by Scott E. Page reprinted by permission of Princeton University Press.

Unit 2, pp. 28-29 "Digital Natives" reprinted with permission. p. 32 Video segment "Audacity of Tech," courtesy of Global News. pp. 38, 39-41 "Mental and Well-Being of Ontario Students" and "STUDY: Teens Spending Seven Hours a Day in Front of TVs, Computers" by Tralee Pearce, © The Globe and Mail Inc. All rights reserved. p. 43 Audio text "Twitter Love" © Canadian Broadcasting Corporation.

Unit 3, p. 61 Video segment "Mentors and Protégés" © Fashion Television, a division of CTV Ltd. All rights reserved.

Unit 4, pp. 81-83 "Great Expectations: Do Millennials Expect Too Much Too Soon?" by Caroline George reprinted with permission. p. 85 Audio text "Interview with Don Tapscott" © Canadian Broadcasting Corporation. pp. 89-90 "Brand You" by Simon Payn reprinted with permission.

Unit 5, p. 107 "Science of Origami: Mathematicians and Artists Use Algorithms to Make Complicated Paper Sculptures" © Invanhoe Broadcast News. All rights reserved; reprinted with permission. p. 110 Video segment "Weather Becomes Artistic Expression"© CTV. pp. 114-115 "Body Art or Body Parts?" reprinted with permission. p. 116 Audio text "Twaiku Poetry" © Canadian Broadcasting Corporation. pp. 121-122 "When Science Met Art: Fermenting the Future of Fashion" by Lauren Day reprinted with permission. p. 122 "Artist Makes Fabric with Voice" reprinted with permission.

Unit 6, pp. 129-130 "Marketing Lessons from the Grateful Dead" from "Jerry Bears, Doobage and the Invention of Social Networking" by Jordan Timm, *Canadian Business* 83(13-14): 74-75; reprinted with permission. p. 134 Video segment "Old Spice's Popularity Reborn," courtesy of Global News. pp. 139-140 "The Best-Ever Social Media Campaigns" by Victoria Taylor reprinted with permission. p. 143 Audio text "Interview with Dan Ackerman Greenberg" © Canadian Broadcasting Corporation.

Unit 7, pp. 159-161 "How Ideas Are Born" by Kathryn Blaze Carlson reprinted with permission. pp. 164, 165 Audio texts "Inside the *Dragons' Den* Auditions" and "'Green Over Grey' Makes Its Pitch" from *CanadExport*, the official e-magazine and podcast of the Canadian Trade Commissioner Service. Used with permission from the Government of Canada (Foreign Affairs and International Trade Canada) www.canadexport.qc.ca. pp. 169-170 "Take Aim at Your Target Market" reprinted with permission. pp. 175-177 "Lessons from *Dragons' Den*: What Dragons Want" by Prof. Sean Wise, Ryerson University & Industry Advisor to CBC's *Dragons' Den*, reprinted with permission. p. 180 Video segment "Peer FX in the Den" © Canadian Broadcasting Corporation.

Introduction

Fields of Vision: English for Work and Study provides English as a Second Language (ESL) teaching material and themes specifically developed to help you meet the requirements of a course for English students at the intermediate to high-intermediate level.

College-oriented and filled with Canadian content, *Fields of Vision: English for Work and Study* offers a unique approach to field-specific English for both pre-university and technical students. The units contain Field Work assignments that tie in with students' various fields of study, but they are also designed to be appropriate to all students.

Although *Fields of Vision: English for Work and Study* covers topics that are deemed to be essential in a technical program curriculum, such as résumés, cover letters, funding proposals and research reports, it also explores academic topics and interesting themes of a more general nature.

Fields of Vision: English for Work and Study offers a variety of activities to help students progress in the four main skills of reading, writing, listening and speaking. Each unit also maintains a strong focus on vocabulary, containing a high percentage of words from the Academic Word List and General Service List, as well as many "working words." The units also provide extensive explanations and practice of reading, listening, vocabulary and revision strategies. The revision strategies and text lengths comply with the new MELS *devis* to help students become more autonomous in their English comprehension and production.

Fields of Vision: English for Work and Study was created with flexibility in mind. You can complete the units in order, or you can move around within the book to fit your teaching approach.

Unit 7 is a special, project-based unit—in one sense, it is the culminating point of the book. You can treat Unit 7 as any other in the book, or you can allot more time to it— the choice is yours. Although all the units in the book call for some teamwork, Unit 7 centres on teamwork, with activities designed to prepare students to write and present a funding proposal.

The last unit in the book is a specially designed Field Guide that includes checklists and templates to which the other units in the book are cross-referenced. This handy reference tool will help students understand, step-by-step, how to do assignments related to the four main skills, with a particular focus on pre-university and technical writing needs.

Fields of Vision: English for Work and Study is complemented by an audio and a video program. The *Fields of Vision: Grammar Guide* is also available and includes grammar point explanations, charts, exercises, communicative activities and online self-grading exercises.

The *Fields of Vision My eLab* provides a variety of added-value activities and self-grading exercises to give students additional practice and encourage them to pursue the topics in depth. In My eLab Documents, teachers will find additional project ideas as well as testing materials, notes and answer keys. We are confident that you will enjoy using this book.

Caroline Orton and Carolyn Brophy

Highlights

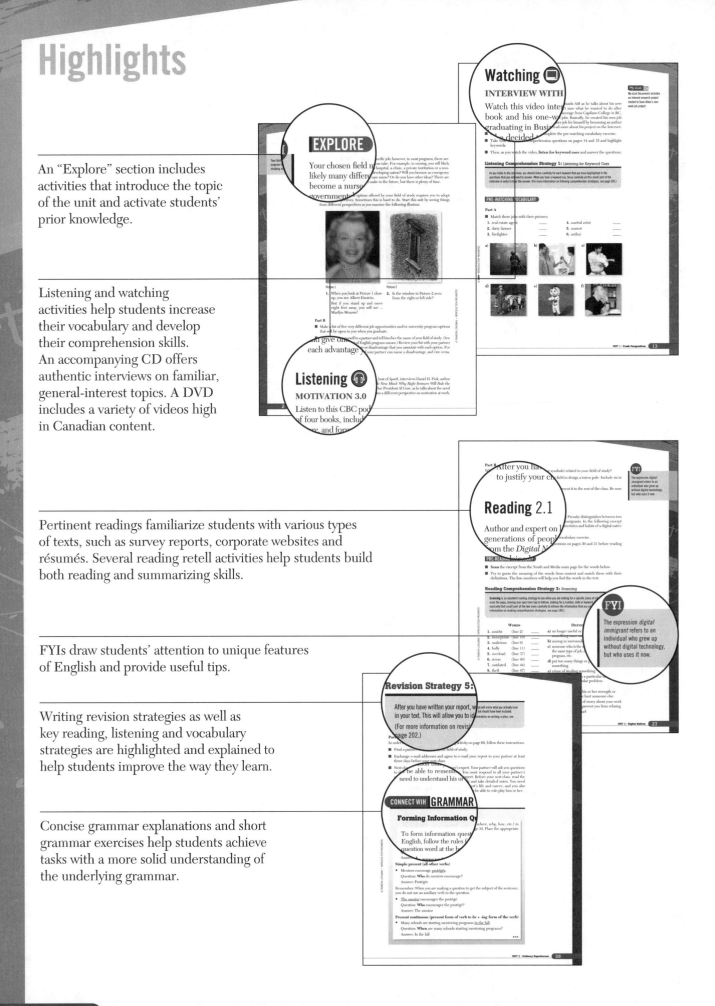

An "Explore" section includes activities that introduce the topic of the unit and activate students' prior knowledge.

Listening and watching activities help students increase their vocabulary and develop their comprehension skills. An accompanying CD offers authentic interviews on familiar, general-interest topics. A DVD includes a variety of videos high in Canadian content.

Pertinent readings familiarize students with various types of texts, such as survey reports, corporate websites and résumés. Several reading retell activities help students build both reading and summarizing skills.

FYIs draw students' attention to unique features of English and provide useful tips.

Writing revision strategies as well as key reading, listening and vocabulary strategies are highlighted and explained to help students improve the way they learn.

Concise grammar explanations and short grammar exercises help students achieve tasks with a more solid understanding of the underlying grammar.

A general vocabulary list allows students to consolidate their knowledge of newly acquired vocabulary, including words from the Academic Word List and the General Service List as well as working words related to unit contents.

My eLab offers additional project ideas and practice that build on the themes of the units.

Each unit ends with a Field Work section containing individual field-of-study vocabulary activities and increasingly difficult writing and speaking assignment choices.

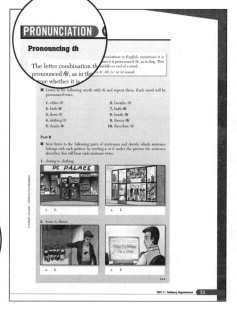

Each unit contains a pronunciation exercise that is specifically geared to Québec CEGEP students' needs.

A special Field Guide offers checklists and templates as well as sections on researching, referencing and revising to help students understand step-by-step how to do assignments in all four skills, with particular focus on both pre-university and technical writing.

An appendix provides a list of CEGEP programs.

Scope and Sequence

UNIT	READING	WRITING	SPEAKING
1. Fresh Perspectives	• Identify main ideas and specific details • Conduct research • Retell short reading texts **Strategies:** 1. Activating your prior knowledge – 2. Visualizing	• Summarize • Describe a familiar subject • Describe from different perspectives • Practise free-writing • Invent a job description **Strategies:** 1. Editing your work – 2. Emphasizing the positive – 3. Obtaining feedback	• Discuss questions with a partner • Describe yourself and present personal information • Discuss a topic from different perspectives • Create a new job in teams, using group brainstorming
2. Digital Natives	• Identify main ideas and specific details • Retrieve key information • Match subtitles to texts • Understand graphs and surveys • Identify transition words to order ideas • Comprehend overall meaning and synthesis of ideas • Conduct research • Recognize support • Retell a reading **Strategies:** 3. Scanning – 4. Skimming	• Summarize • Write personal statements and questions • Prepare a survey • Write a survey report • Design a social networking homepage • Prepare a graph **Strategy:** 4. Peer reviewing	• Discuss questions in a small group • Express opinions • Come to a consensus • Present familiar information • Role-play • Present a graph, survey results and/or a homepage • Describe technologies, devices or instruments
3. Ordinary Superheroes	• Identify main ideas and specific details • Comprehend overall meaning • Locate information and interpret/analyze data • Synthesize information • Recognize citation techniques • Conduct research and take notes • Recognize transition words • Scan for discrete information	• Summarize • Write descriptions • Write autobiographical information • Write a request letter/e-mail • Write Twitter updates • Research and write a basic technical field report • Prepare and conduct a survey • Write a survey report **Strategies:** 5. Writing a reverse plan – 6. Proofreading	• Discuss questions in a small group • Discuss advantages and disadvantages • Express opinions, concern or necessity • Ask for and give advice • Role-play • Create and present an avatar-mentor
4. Millennials @ Work	• Identify main ideas and specific details • Comprehend overall meaning • Retrieve key information • Matching subtitles to texts • Focus on form • Retell a reading • Scan for discrete information	• Summarize • Write a branding statement • Use action verbs • Create a checklist of dos and don'ts • Write a résumé and a cover letter	• Discuss questions in a small group • Express opinions • Role-play • Create your brand • Give a presentation
5. Fielding Creativity	• Identify main ideas and specific details • Comprehend overall meaning • Make logical deductions • Locate information and interpret/analyze data • Identify and order steps in a process • Synthesize information • Retrieve key information • Conduct research	• Summarize • Write main ideas and support them • Write a descriptive paragraph • Write a haiku poem • Research and write an essay **Strategy:** 7. Examining paragraphs	• Discuss questions in a small group • Express opinions and discuss likes and dislikes; passions • Brainstorm • Give instructions • Describe a technique or process
6. Viral Marketing	• Identify main ideas and specific details • Comprehend overall meaning • Retrieve key information • Make logical deductions, analyzing positive and negative information • Synthesize information • Recognize references • Conduct research • Retell a reading • Scan and skim **Strategy:** 5. Inferring	• Summarize • Write main ideas • Brainstorm ideas • Prepare a target audience profile • Write advertising/promotional messages • Write a complaint or request letter • Write a request letter • Explain how you will use marketing strategies • Write a dialogue for a viral video	• Discuss questions in a small group • Express opinions • Exchange personal information • Debate • Create and present a viral video
7. The Pitch	• Identify main ideas and specific details • Compare facts to make choices • Retrieve key information • Retell a reading • Matching subtitles to texts • Synthesize information • Scan for discrete information	• Summarize • Brainstorm using the brainwriting technique • Write a mission statement • Describe an innovation • Prepare survey questions • Develop an action plan • Write feedback • Write a proposal	• Brainstorm • Discuss questions in a small group • Give suggestions in a small group • Describe a product • Ask questions and give feedback • Analyze, come to a consensus; negotiate; plan • Present a pitch

LISTENING/WATCHING	PRONUNCIATION	GRAMMAR	VOCABULARY
• Identify main ideas and factual details • Understand keywords, expressions and a few idioms **Strategy:** 1. Listening for keyword cues	• Minimal pairs: /I/ versus /i:/	• Using the simple present tense versus the present continuous tense	• Guess the meaning of words and expressions • Look up words in a dictionary • Classify parts of speech • Create a list of words that help you describe and discuss your field of study **Strategies:** 1. Guessing the meaning from context – 2. Looking up words
• Identify main ideas and factual details • Understand keywords, expressions and a few idioms **Strategy:** 2. Activating your prior knowledge	• Pronouncing *sh*	• Forming simple present and present continuous yes/no questions	• Guess the meaning of words and expressions • Fill in the missing letters • Write extended definitions • Look up words in a dictionary • Recognize prefixes • Create a list of technologies, devices, instruments and/or instruments related to your field of study **Strategy:** 3. Breaking up words
• Identify main ideas, factual details and opinions • Understand keywords, expressions and a few idioms **Strategy:** 3. Note-taking	• Pronouncing *th*	• Forming information questions	• Guess the meaning of words and expressions • Look up words in a dictionary • Find synonyms • Recognize prefixes and suffixes • Recognize transition words • Create a list of personality traits valued in your field of study **Strategy:** 4. Finding synonyms
• Identify main ideas and factual details • Understand keywords, expressions and a few idioms • Listen for specific information • Recognize power verbs and cognates	• Pronouncing the simple past of regular verbs	• Using the simple past tense	• Guess the meaning of words and expressions • Look up words in a dictionary • Recognize power verbs and cognates • Identify parts of speech • Create a list of positive adjectives for use in the résumé or cover letter **Strategy:** 5. Identifying parts of speech
• Identify main ideas and factual details • Understand keywords, expressions and a few idioms • Listen for specific information **Strategy:** 4. Skimming	• Pronouncing *ch*	• Using the future tense (*will* and *to be + going to*)	• Guess the meaning of words and expressions • Look up words in a dictionary • Fill in the missing letters • Identify parts of speech • Create a list of tools of the trade related to your field of study
• Identify main ideas and factual details • Understand keywords, expressions and a few idioms • Skim for main idea	• Pronouncing *h*	• Using the present perfect tense	• Guess the meaning of words and expressions • Look up words in a dictionary • Do a crossword puzzle • Combine words • Recognize suffixes • Recognize synonyms • Invent a list of field-related neologisms
• Identify main ideas, important details and opinions • Understand keywords, expressions and a few idioms • Synthesize information	• Pronouncing multi-syllabic words	• Using modal auxiliaries	• Guess the meaning of words and expressions • Choose dictionary definitions from context • Recognize antonyms and synonyms • Create a list of field-related terms that you will use in your proposal **Strategies:** 6. Finding antonyms – 7. Playing with words

Table of Contents

Fresh Perspectives

Now that you have chosen your field of study, all your decisions are made. You have no more questions about your future career. That's one perspective.

lawyer mechanic news anchor journalist ecologist jewellery maker

Here's another one.

In this unit, you will discuss and write about some of the various job or university options available to graduates in your field of study, and examine them from a variety of different viewpoints. You will use these fresh perspectives to challenge and expand the beliefs that you and your classmates may hold about your programs. You will learn to use the differences that each of you brings to the table to your advantage because, according to Scott E. Page,[1] diversity can lead to creative new ideas and solutions.

---

1. Page, Scott E. *The Difference: How the Power of Diversity Creates Better Groups, Firms, Schools, and Societies*. Princeton: Princeton University Press, 2007. Print.

EXPLORE

Your chosen field may lead directly to a specific job; however, in most programs, there are likely many different directions that you can take. For example, in nursing, you will likely become a nurse, but will you work for a hospital, a clinic, a private institution or a non-governmental organization (NGO) in a developing nation? Will you become an emergency nurse, a pediatric nurse or a palliative care nurse? Or do you have other ideas? There are many decisions that you will need to make in the future, but there is plenty of time.

Part A

■ Weighing the different options offered by your field of study requires you to adopt different perspectives. Sometimes this is hard to do. Start this unit by seeing things from different perspectives as you examine the following illusions.

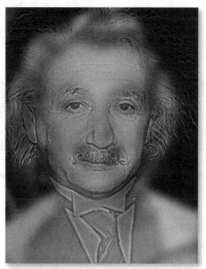

Picture 1

Picture 2

1. When you look at Picture 1 close up, you see Albert Einstein.

But if you stand up and move eight feet away, you will see ... Marilyn Monroe!

2. Is the window in Picture 2 seen from the right or left side?

Part B

■ Make a list of five very different job opportunities and/or university program options that will be open to you when you graduate.

■ Now introduce yourself to a partner and tell him/her the name of your field of study. (See pages 208–209 for a list of English program names.) Review your list with your partner and give one main advantage or disadvantage that you associate with each option. For each advantage you give, see if your partner can name a disadvantage, and vice versa.

Listening 🎧

MOTIVATION 3.0

Listen to this CBC podcast as Nora Young, host of *Spark*, interviews Daniel H. Pink, author of four books, including *Drive* and *A Whole New Mind: Why Right Brainers Will Rule the Future*, and former speech writer to then-Vice President Al Gore, as he talks about the need for creativity in today's economy and explains a different perspective on motivation at work.

- Before you listen to the interview, complete the pre-listening vocabulary exercise.
- Then take the time to read the comprehension questions.

FYI

The word 'cause is slang for because.

PRE-LISTENING VOCABULARY

- Match these words and expressions with their definitions.

My eLab

Answer additional questions for "Motivation 3.0."

WORDS		DEFINITIONS
1. drive	____	**a)** examination of something in a very specific way
2. root	____	**b)** simple and easy to understand; not complex
3. throwing out	____	**c)** discipline in which the actions and reactions of humans and animals are studied through observational and experimental methods
4. behavioural science	____	
5. straightforward	____	
6. task	____	
7. reward	____	**d)** getting rid of something; not using something anymore
8. backfire	____	**e)** autonomous control
9. narrow focus	____	**f)** base, origin or cause
10. self-direction	____	**g)** job; piece of work to be done
		h) motivating force
		i) have a negative effect, often opposite to what was intended
		j) give someone something because he or she has worked hard or done something well

EXPRESSIONS		DEFINITIONS
1. sand off the rough edges	____	**a)** non-traditional strategy
2. radical approach	____	**b)** smooth something; make it nicer
3. a hotbed of	____	**c)** place where lots of exciting activity happens

COMPREHENSION

- Answer the following questions.

1. Which of the following are examples of Daniel Pink's third drive?
   Circle the letter(s) of the correct answer(s).

   a) I like to do things just to do them.

   b) I find it interesting.

   c) I get paid at the end of the week.

   d) It's the right thing to do.

   e) My boss will fire me if I don't do it.

   ...

Daniel H. Pink

2. A carrot motivator

    a) rewards.   **b)** punishes.

3. A stick motivator

    a) rewards.   **b)** punishes.

4. a) Give an example of a carrot motivator.

_____

    b) Give an example of a stick motivator.

_____

5. a) Do carrot and stick motivators work?   ☐ Yes   ☐ No

    b) Do they work under all circumstances? Explain.

_____

6. a) According to Daniel Pink, what kind of work are most people doing nowadays?

_____

    b) Give an example of this type of work.

_____

_____

7. What is the best way to get people to do creative work?

_____

8. How does Pink define

    a) "autonomy"? _____

    b) "mastery"? _____

    c) "purpose"? _____

_____

9. What is an example of a self-directed motivational approach?

_____

_____

10. a) Describe a FedEx day.

_____

_____

    b) What is the purpose of a FedEx day?

_____

_____

11. What is the main idea of the listening?

_____

_____

_____

DISCUSSION

■ Answer these questions in a small group.

1. Which motivational approach would work best for you at work: the carrot, the stick or Motivation 3.0? Why?

2. Do you think FedEx days would be motivating? Why or why not?

3. Which approach is generally used at school? Does this approach work well for you?

4. Brainstorm some Motivation 3.0-type approaches that your school could use to motivate students to learn.

Reading 1.1

Experts say merging left-brain, analytical traits with right-brain, creative ones might make employees much more marketable in the job markets of the future. The following text discusses how the way that you think can help you succeed at school or at work, and suggests that if you can access both left and right ways of thinking when you analyze problems—in other words, if you can see things from different perspectives—you will become a valued employee in today's new economy.

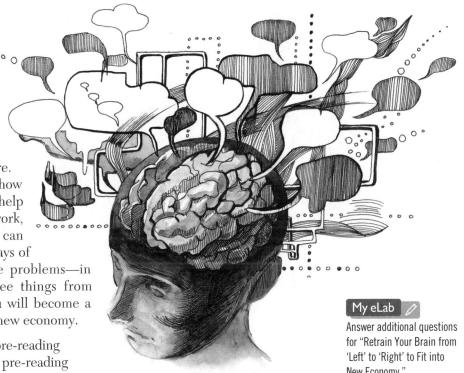

My eLab

Answer additional questions for "Retrain Your Brain from 'Left' to 'Right' to Fit into New Economy."

■ Before you read, do the pre-reading activity and complete the pre-reading vocabulary exercise.

■ Then take time to read the comprehension questions on pages 10 and 11.

■ After you finish reading the text, answer the vocabulary and comprehension questions.

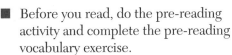

PRE-READING ACTIVITY

■ Take this short brain quiz and share your results with a partner in order to **activate your prior knowledge** on the subject.

Reading Comprehension Strategy 1: Activating Your Prior Knowledge

Reflecting and talking about a subject before you read more about it helps you activate topical information and key vocabulary that you already know and makes it easier and faster for you to access your prior knowledge as you read. (For more information on reading comprehension strategies, see page 189.)

BRAIN QUIZ: IS YOUR BRAIN A LEFTY OR A RIGHTY?

■ Circle *Yes* or *No* to determine whether your thinking is more left- or right-brain focused. Then use the answer key to calculate your score.

1. I am a very optimistic person in general.	Yes	No
2. I believe there is a right and a wrong way to do everything.	Yes	No
3. When I talk, I move my hands.	Yes	No
4. I plan what I will wear each day in advance.	Yes	No
5. In a play, I would rather direct than act.	Yes	No
6. Sometimes other people think I'm psychic.	Yes	No
7. When I plan a party, I plan every detail.	Yes	No
8. I always read the directions before I build something.	Yes	No
9. I like to make lists.	Yes	No
10. I believe that there could be more than one right answer.	Yes	No
11. I like to draw.	Yes	No
12. I hate following directions.	Yes	No

Answer key: Each *Yes* is worth one point and each *No* is worth zero points. Add up the *Yes* scores for questions 1, 3, 6, 10, 11, 12. Now subtract the *Yes* scores (one point each) for questions 2, 4, 5, 7, 8, 9. If your score is still positive, you are a right-brained thinker. Six is the highest possible right-brained score. If your score is negative, you are a left-brained thinker. Minus-six is the highest left-brained score. If your score is zero, you use both sides of your brain equally.

Source: Adapted from: Right Brain / Left Brain Quiz. Intelliscript. N.d. Web. 20 June 2010. <http://www.intelliscript.net/test_area/questionnaire/questionnaire.cgi>; Right Brain vs Left Brain Creativity Test. The Art Institute of Vancouver. N.d. Web. 14 July 2010. <http://www.wherecreativitygoestoschool.com/vancouver/left_right/rb_test.htm>.

PRE-READING VOCABULARY

■ Match these jobs mentioned in the reading with their pictures.

1. real estate investment banker ___b___
2. attorney/in-house counsel ___e___
3. management consultant ___d___
4. physician ___a___
5. interior designer ___c___

a)

b)

c)

d)

e)

Retrain Your Brain from "Left" to "Right" to Fit into New Economy

By Marco R. della Cava, *USA Today*

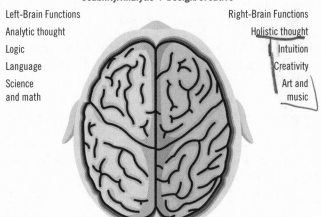

Experience =
Usability/Analytic + Design/Creative

Left-Brain Functions
Analytic thought
Logic
Language
Science
and math

Right-Brain Functions
Holistic thought
Intuition
Creativity
Art and
music

The Old Economy developed out of the Industrial Revolution and our ability to mass-produce goods. The value of a product was simply determined by the value of its parts; for example, the amount and quality of metal or wood used. In the New Economy, a product's value can also include less quantifiable aspects, such as how people feel or react to a product because of how it is designed, branded and marketed.

1   As stars of the Old Economy go, Shu Kim and Khanh Pham sparkled. Working for a **storied** finance firm—Kim, 40, as in-house counsel and Pham, 33, as a real estate investment banker—the two women deployed classic analytical left-brain skills to keep a seemingly **well-oiled machine** [going].
5   A machine called Lehman Brothers [Corp]. Lehman is [now bankrupt], but the two New Yorkers [, Kim and Pham,] are alive and optimistic, thanks to a simple yet significant shift. They embraced their right brains, the bold, creative **lobe** that in the New Economy can make the difference between reinvention and extinction.

2 10   "Those old jobs are just not there anymore, so to survive you have to think outside the box," says Pham, who, along with her former colleague, recently launched *Shustir.com*, a marketing website for small businesses. Now, instead of [preparing] legal and financial documents, the two brainstorm innovative ways to bring their new **brand** to the masses, relying on **flights of**
15 **creative fancy** rather than **rote** skills.

3   "It's funny—our parents were entrepreneurs," Kim says. "So we're going back to right-brain thinking." And not a moment too soon. As companies continue to **triage** their way through this economic war, a growing chorus of cultural observers argue that recovery is contingent on the marriage of right-
20 brain innovations with left-brain skill sets. [...]

4   [Daniel] Pink [, author of *A Whole New Mind: Why Right-Brainers Will Rule the Future*,] says the shift to right-brain thinking can already be found in companies that welcome well-rounded employees, medical schools that push art studies and classrooms that encourage collaborative problem-solving.
25 "We're realizing that our economy is not about standardization," he says. [...]

   ...

storied: talked about a lot

well-oiled machine: something that works very well

lobe: part of the brain

brand: logo, name or design associated with a company

flight of creative fancy: thinking creatively

rote: learned through repetition with no thinking required

triage: help people survive in an emergency

An *app* is an application program that helps you perform a specific task, like finding a restaurant on your telephone. A *killer app* is an application program that is so great that everybody wants it.

fusing: combining different qualities, ideas or things

well-versed: knowing a lot about something

internist: doctor who generalizes and does not perform surgery

steeped: having a lot of a particular quality

think tank: group of experienced people who work to produce ideas and give advice

powerhouse: strong force

broadly: widely; in general, overall terms

backbone: most important part; the basis

5   In fact, **fusing** left-brain skills with right-brain insights is considered the killer app in a new economy that will put a premium on creative breakthroughs, says Laszlo Bock, vice president of people operations at Google. "We're convinced true innovation comes at the intersection of
30   different fields," he says.

6   When Bock and his team look to hire new talent, they assess a candidate's "Googliness"—the ability to solve problems in unique ways, lead co-workers and thrive in a loose organizational structure. "If you have those skills, you can learn any job we give you," he says.

7   35   In Cambridge, Massachusetts, Joel Katz has spent the past six years proving that doctors will be better at their left-brain craft if they're **well-versed** in art. First- and second-year Harvard Med students now vie to get into Katz's ten-week course that uses Boston's Museum of Fine Arts to teach future physicians how to critically analyze famous paintings.

8   40   Those who take the art course typically show "a 50 percent improvement" in assessing a patient's symptoms, says Katz, himself an **internist**. "Usually doctors are not trained in humanism. Students usually say this has expanded their way of thinking, which benefits the patient."

9   But that doesn't mean those **steeped** in quantitative skills need an arts-
45   major makeover. Unique solutions often come from pairing people with complementary skills, says Darrell Rigby, Boston-based head of global innovation practices for management consulting firm Bain & Company, citing fashion as a prime example of how right-brain types can thrive within a financially driven matrix. "Brain transplants are not as successful as simple
50   teamwork," he jokes.

10   Seeking out creative solutions is now the prime directive for many companies, says Ross DeVol, director of regional economics at the Milken Institute, a Los Angeles-based non-profit **think tank**." If [we are] going to remain an economic **powerhouse**, it will be due to value-added ideas. That
55   means employees have to think more **broadly** about their job than ever before." [...]

11   For ex-Lehman employees Kim and Pham, their ability to [move] away from their left-brain comfort zone into uncharted right-brain waters has resulted in not just employment, but innovative work that could prove the
60   **backbone** of a resurgent economy.

12   "I [have] liked putting people together ever since I was a little girl, but I just went ahead and became a lawyer," says Kim, whose website connects local entrepreneurs with a national marketplace. "Who knew that what I loved doing as a kid could be a job?"

(683 words)

Source: Adapted from della Cava, Marco R. "Retrain Your Brain from "Left" to "Right" to Fit into New Economy." *USA Today*. 13 July 2009. Web. 10 June 2010. <http://www.usatoday.com/life/lifestyle/2009-07-13-right-vs-left-brains_N.htm>.

■ **Guess the meaning** of the following words **from context** and match them with their definitions. The line numbers will help you find the words in the text.

Vocabulary Strategy 1: Guessing the Meaning from Context

One of the strategies that most of us use when we don't understand a word in our first language is to guess the meaning by examining the word in the surrounding context of the reading. (For more information on vocabulary strategies, see page 190.)

Part A

WORDS			DEFINITIONS
1. shift	(line 7)	c	a) taught the skills of a particular job or activity
2. benefit	(line 43)	b	b) give an advantage; improve life
3. non-profit	(line 53)	e	c) change in the way people do something or think about something
4. solve	(line 32)	d	d) find a solution
5. cite	(line 48)	h	e) when money is used to help people and not to gain financially
6. insight	(line 26)	g j	f) solution to an important problem
7. breakthrough	(line 28)	f	g) sudden, clear understanding
8. firm	(line 2)	i	h) refer to something as an example
9. craft	(line 36)	j g	i) business; company
10. trained	(line 42)	a	j) job involving skills in which you make things with your hands

Part B

■ **Look up these expressions** in the dictionary and write their definitions. The line numbers are provided so that you can find the expressions in the text.

Vocabulary Strategy 2: Looking Up Words

Sometimes the best way to learn a word is to use a dictionary. Remember that a word can have several definitions, so it is important to use the context to help you decide which definition is best. When you have to find the meaning of an expression, look under the main word(s) and see if the expression is listed below the main meaning. (For more information on vocabulary strategies, see page 190.)

1. think outside the box (line 11): _Think differently_

2. well-rounded (line 23): _Well-balanced in a large or variety of aspects._

3. value-added (line 54): _Value has been increase_

4. uncharted waters (line 58): _Situation that's unfamiliar to you_

5. skill set (line 20): _Combination of skill that someone has_

COMPREHENSION

■ Answer the following questions.

1. What do Kim and Pham do now?

   a) They work for Lehman Brothers Corp. as a lawyer and a banker.

   b) They run their own website marketing business.

   c) They are unemployed, left-brain stars of the Old Economy.

2. The author states that Kim and Pham now need to be creative in their work, whereas before they could rely on skills they had learned at school. Are Kim and Pham currently using left-brain skills or right-brain skills in their jobs?

   Alors que They using both of them.

3. Finish this sentence: Many people believe that for long-term recovery to happen in the economy, people will have to learn to combine left and righ brain thinking.

4. What argument is Daniel Pink making when he gives the example of medical schools requiring their students to take art courses?

   paragraph 4.

5. Pink, Bock and Rigby all believe that in the New Economy people need to

   a) have a standard set of skills that they are very good at.

   b) use left-brain thinking strategies.

   c) work as a team to combine their skills sets.

6. "Googliness" is a newly coined word (a word that has just been invented). In your own words, say what it means.

   paragraph 6 leader, creative, nerd problem.

7. a) What does Bock do at Google?

   He is vice president of people operation

   b) Do you think Bock has Googliness himself? Explain.

   Yes, because he trust in the change.

8. According to Katz, how is an art course helping med students become better doctors?

   that expanded their way of thinking.

9. Explain the terms *Old Economy* and *New Economy* as they are used in the text. one side

   old economy = Revolution and mass product

   beside. New economy ± The value is less quantifiable

10. Explain what the text is saying about teamwork in the New Economy.

They say that combine R and L
is good because

DISCUSSION

■ Discuss these questions in groups.

1. Bock says, "We're convinced true innovation comes at the intersection of different fields." What do you think this means?

2. Rigby says that the answer to today's business needs lies in teamwork—pairing up people who have complementary skill sets. Do you agree or disagree? Who do they want to pair up, and why? What would this accomplish?

3. Do you think it is a good idea for companies to look for Googliness in their employees? Why or why not? Do you have Googliness?

4. Pink's right- and left-brain theory is really a metaphor to help us understand how to think from different perspectives. He states that we all obviously use both sides of our brains.[2] With this in mind, are you more of a left- or right-brain thinker? Explain.

5. Do you think that schools teach people to use both sides of the brain? Explain.

EXPANSION

What are your strengths? What can you do that no one else can do? Are you a left- or right-brain thinker? Or are you somewhere in the middle? Do you make decisions emotionally or logically? Are your views generally optimistic or pessimistic? Do you have Googliness? Can you think outside the box?

■ Free writing helps to develop right-brain skills. Write 150 to 200 words about yourself and what makes you unique. Try to answer some of the questions above. Don't worry about punctuation or spelling, and don't censure any of your ideas.

■ Your teacher may ask you to rewrite your text using a more formal paragraph structure. (For more information about writing paragraphs with topic sentences and support, see page 201.) As you revise your writing, make sure that you **edit your text** and carefully examine the present tense verbs you have used.

Revision Strategy 1: Editing Your Work

An important step in the revision process is editing, which is done as soon as you finish writing. Reread your writing to make sure the content is clear, well-organized and complete. Check that your paragraphs are well-structured. Look for error patterns in verb tenses and verb forms. (For more information on revision strategies, see page 204. For more information on verb tenses, see the Grammar Guide.)

2. Handler, Richard. "Does the Future Belong to Right-brained Humans?" CBC. 4 Nov. 2008. Web. 14 June 2010. <http://www.cbc.ca/canada/story/2008/11/04/f-vp-handler.html>.

Using the Simple Present Tense versus the Present Continuous Tense

The Simple Present

Ask yourself these questions to determine if the verb is in the simple present tense and if it is formed correctly.

- Can you add one of these time expressions without changing the meaning: *usually, generally, always, nowadays, sometimes, never*?

- Is the verb formed correctly, e.g., *I work* (not *I'm work*), *they work* (not *they're work*), etc.?

- Have you remembered the third person singular *-s*, e.g., *He work**s**?*

The Present Continuous

Ask yourself these questions to determine if the verb is in the present continuous tense and if it is formed correctly.

- Can you add one of these time expressions without changing the meaning: *at the moment, as we speak, right now, today*?

- Is the verb formed correctly, e.g., *I am working* (not *I did working*), *he is working* (not *he is work*), etc.?

■ Underline the correct verb forms below, choosing between the simple present and present continuous tenses. Use the time expressions (where provided) as context clues. Refer to the information above on the differences between the simple present and the present continuous tenses.

Right now, as you [1](are working / work) on this exercise, ask yourself whether you [2](are relying / rely) more on the left or right side of your brain. Certain activities seem to call for the use of one side of the brain more than the other. Yet, according to Daniel H. Pink, some people are more left-brain thinkers and some people are more right-brain thinkers. However, this does not necessarily mean that we always [3](are using / use) only one side of our brains. Of course not!

Still, it's a fact that left-brain thinkers [4](are focusing / focus) more on logical and analytical tasks, and right-brain thinkers [5](are concentrating / concentrate) more on tasks that require a creative component.

In *A Whole New Mind* (2005), Pink [6](is suggesting / suggests) that in today's new economy, employers [7](are looking / look) for employees who are both analytical and creative thinkers. Employers want* employees who are versatile, and [8](are making / make) big changes to accommodate these employees. Likewise, employees [9](are asking / ask) for more than just money. "Meaning is the new money," says Pink, and meaning [10](is coming / comes) from a workplace that is fun and rewarding to be in.

* The verb *want* is a stative verb. For more information on stative verbs, see the Grammar Guide.

Refer to Unit 1 of Grammar Guide for further explanations and practice on the simple present and present continuous verb tenses.

Watching 🖥

My eLab 🗁
My eLab Documents includes an Internet research project related to Sean Aiken's one-week job project.

INTERVIEW WITH SEAN AIKEN

Watch this video interview with Sean Aiken on *Canada AM* as he talks about his new book and his one-week job project. Aiken wasn't sure what he wanted to do after graduating in Business Administration with a 4.0 average from Capilano College in BC, so he decided to try out many different types of jobs. Basically, he created his own job opportunities for a year and then created another job for himself by becoming an author and writing about his experiences. You can read more about his project on the Internet.

■ Before you watch the interview, complete the pre-watching vocabulary exercise.

■ Take time to read the comprehension questions on pages 14 and 15 and highlight keywords.

■ Then, as you watch the video, **listen for keyword cues** and answer the questions.

Listening Comprehension Strategy 1: Listening for Keyword Cues

As you listen to the interview, you should listen carefully for each keyword that you have highlighted in the questions that you will need to answer. When you hear a keyword cue, focus carefully on this small part of the interview in order to hear the answer. (For more information on listening comprehension strategies, see page 205.)

PRE-WATCHING VOCABULARY

Part A

■ Match these jobs with their pictures.

1. real estate agent _____   4. martial artist _____
2. dairy farmer _____   5. mascot _____
3. firefighter _____   6. author _____

a)

b)

c)

d)

e)

f)

Part B

■ Match these words and expressions with their definitions.

WORDS		DEFINITIONS
1. donate	_____	**a)** look for something carefully
2. search for	_____	**b)** not less than a certain number or amount of something; minimum
3. at least	_____	**c)** event held to raise money
4. last	_____	**d)** money made at a job
5. fundraiser	_____	**e)** organization that asks for money to help people
6. journey	_____	**f)** desire to do something
7. earnings	_____	**g)** continue for a certain length of time
8. figure out	_____	**h)** give money to an organization to help people
9. charity	_____	**i)** trip; travel experience
10. willingness	_____	**j)** think about something until you find the answer

We can say "a trip," meaning "a journey," and sometimes this means a vacation or a business trip, but we cannot say "a travel." *Travel* is a verb or an adjective, but not a noun, so you can say "I travel a lot" and "a travel experience," but not "I went on a travel."

Experience is knowledge you gain from going places, meeting people and doing things, whereas an experiment is a trial of different procedures, often done in a science laboratory, in order to see which one works best, what the results are, etc.

EXPRESSIONS		DEFINITIONS
1. blast through	_____	**a)** quit
2. put the feelers out	_____	**b)** go into a situation gradually and easily
3. put it out there	_____	**c)** check / explore the available options
4. jump ship	_____	**d)** let people know something
5. make a smooth transition	_____	**e)** do / experience at a rapid pace

COMPREHENSION

■ Answer the following questions.

1. What did Sean Aiken do?

_____

_____

2. Why did he do this?

_____

_____

3. Where did he do this?

_____

4. What did he do with the money he was paid?

_____

5. What surprised him during the project?

_____

_____

_____

_____

6. Where did he most often stay?

_____

7. Sean says that the worst job he did was picking cattails in the wilds outside of Montréal for a company that processes them and sells them to high-end restaurants. Why did he dislike this job?

_____

_____

Cattails

8. Name one of the jobs that he liked.

_____

9. What did he learn from his experience?

_____

_____

_____

10. Summarize the watching in two to three sentences.

Sean Aiken _____

_____

_____

_____

_____

_____

_____

DISCUSSION

■ Answer these questions with your group.

1. Not only has Sean completed this year-long project, but he has also written a book and starred in a documentary about it. Now he is helping others to recreate his experience. In a sense, Sean has created a new job for himself. He says that he wants to become a teacher, but what do you think he should do?

2. Does Sean think outside the box? Do you think he is a left- or right-brain thinker? Does he have Googliness? Explain your answers.

3. Sean tried out some very unusual jobs, such as his first job as a bungee jumping instructor. Tell the group about your most unusual job experience.

PRONUNCIATION

Minimal Pairs: /I/ versus /i:/

Many students of English have difficulty distinguishing between the sounds /I/ (as in *filled*) and /i:/ (as in *field*). The /i:/ sound can be made with several different letter combinations, such as: *e, ee, ie, ei* and *ea*.

Part A

■ Listen to these words with the short /I/ sound and repeat them after the speaker. You will repeat each word twice.

1. filled
2. grin
3. pitch
4. risen
5. sit

6. slips
7. will
8. live
9. is
10. fill

Part B

■ Now listen to these words with the long /i:/ sound and repeat them after the speaker. You will repeat each word twice.

1. field
2. green
3. peach
4. reason
5. seat

6. sleeps
7. we'll
8. leave
9. ease
10. feel

Part C

■ Listen to the words and circle the word that you hear by determining if it is the short /I/ sound or long /i:/ sound that you hear. The first two are done for you.

Short /I/ Sound	Long /i:/ Sound
1. (live)	leave
2. grin	(green)
3. filled	field
4. pitch	peach
5. risen	reason
6. sit	seat
7. is	ease
8. slips	sleeps
9. will	we'll
10. fill	feel

Speaking

ROLE-PLAYING AND BRAINSTORMING FROM DIFFERENT PERSPECTIVES

This speaking activity will introduce you to a unique group brainstorming and decision-making technique.

You will be working in groups of six. Each team member will be assigned a "hat" of a different colour.

Part A

■ Carefully read the description associated with the colour of your hat (paragraphs 1 to 5 below and paragraph 6 on page 18). You may take point-form notes as you read. Then explain it to the other members of your team with your book closed.

1. White Hat

As a white-hat thinker, you must try to be neutral and not give your own personal opinions or feelings on a subject. Focus on information that is known about a topic. Be objective and present the facts to your group. Ask the other group members what information is needed in order to make a decision.

2. Red Hat

As a red-hat thinker, you must try to be emotional and intuitive. Rely on your instinctive feelings. It is not necessary for you to explain or provide a justification for your responses in any way. Focus on how you feel about a subject and the ideas expressed by the others. Ask other people for their gut reactions.

3. Black Hat

As a black-hat thinker, you must try to see a subject in a pessimistic light. Be cautious; don't just agree with the ideas or direction of the group. Be judgmental and critical. Focus on the negative features of the group's ideas and try to identify the flaws of the subject. List the drawbacks for your group.

4. Yellow Hat

As a yellow-hat thinker, you must be a voice of optimism in your group. Be sure to look on the bright side. Look at the positive features of the subject. Evaluate the merits of the group's ideas and decide which parts of the subject have value. List the benefits for your group.

5. Green Hat

As a green-hat thinker, you must channel the creative spirit inside of yourself. You are responsible for bringing new and original ideas to the group discussion, as well as energy and possibility. Focus on lateral thinking (making unusual connections between ideas). Don't worry about expressing "crazy" ideas. Who knows where they might lead you?

6. Blue Hat

As a blue-hat thinker, you must lead your group. It is your job to control the process. Think about what the others are saying. Make sure each member gives their perspective about each new idea. If you think the group needs a new idea, ask the green hat, for example. Provide a summary for the group.

Source: Adapted from De Bono for Business. N.d. Web. 2 June 2010. <http://www.debonoforbusiness.com/asp/six_hats.asp?gclid=CN638sb5gaICFRRM5QodeFa5GA>.

Part B

■ Working as a group, you will analyze a job or university program open to one of you through your field of study, discussing its advantages and disadvantages. To do so, each group member must put on his or her thinking hat and adopt the perspective (way of thinking) that is associated with that hat only. For example, if you are wearing the yellow hat, you must analyze the job from a very positive perspective, whereas if you are wearing the blue hat, you should lead your group and give a summary of the group's discussion at the end.

■ Then, switch hats with another team member and repeat this exercise until you have, as a group, analyzed one job or program from each of your fields of study in this unique way.

Reading 1.2

When a company is hiring, do they look for people who are similar to the employees they currently have? Or do they look for divergent personalities and varied backgrounds and ethnicities? Do schools expect all graduates to learn the same things, or do they encourage them to follow their interests and learn a more personal curriculum? Read one of the two excerpts below taken from *The Difference: How the Power of Diversity Creates Better Groups, Firms, Schools, and Societies*, by Scott E. Page, to find out.

■ Work with a partner. Read only one of the two excerpts below while your partner reads the second one. Read the text you are assigned slowly and try to **visualize** what Page is saying.

■ Then retell your text and listen as your partner retells his or her text.

■ Working with your partner, complete the vocabulary and comprehension exercises on pages 20 and 21.

Scott E. Page

Reading Comprehension Strategy 2: Visualizing

After you read each paragraph, close your eyes for a minute and try to create a visual image of the paragraph. This excellent, right-brain strategy will help you better understand the text. (For more information on reading comprehension strategies, see page 189.)

Putting Ideas to Work

By Scott E. Page

Excerpt 1 *François*

1   Google can hire almost anyone it likes. If it wanted, Google could hire just the top students from top-ranked engineering schools. These people would all be smart, but they might be trained similarly. They also might have had similar college experiences. Like many modern corporations, Google

5   organizes itself in work teams that solve problems. For these teams to be successful, people must be able to communicate, and they must also be diverse. That's why Google doesn't pursue a strategy of hiring only the people with the best grades from the best schools. In its own description of "Who we're looking for," Google's first criterion is diversity—"people with **broad**

10 knowledge and expertise in many different areas of computer science and mathematics"—as is their last [criterion], "people with diverse interests and skills." People who think alike get **stuck**, so Google samples widely. It looks for diversity in training, experience and identity. Computer science graduates

15 work alongside **former** math professors. But Google is also aware of the **Calculus Condition**. It seeks diverse people with knowledge in mathematics and computer science. It [doesn't seek] poets. Though, if a good mathematical **epidemiologist** showed up at Google's

20 door, it would hire her because she might possess novel understandings of how diseases spread across populations and how these understandings might inform Google's efforts to organize information flows.

(222 words)

broad: including many things

stuck: unable to move forward or find a solution

former: before now

Calculus Condition: process stating that people hired as the possible problem solvers must have the ability to solve the problem in the first place (i.e., the correct training)

epidemiologist: disease specialist

Excerpt 2

1   As firms and universities seek more diversity, they encourage the creation of even more diversity. Students believe—sometimes mistakenly and sometimes correctly—that employers and **graduate programs** place enormous emphasis on grades. As a result, students shy away from difficult classes. Surveying a

5   random selection of undergraduate **transcripts** reveals that few students take extra physics, organic chemistry or advanced mathematics courses. These classes demand lots of time and effort and earning a good grade in any one of them is difficult. Yet if someone wanted to be a good lawyer, wouldn't an upper-level mathematical logic class or some basic economic theory be

10 beneficial? Of course. But it is hard work compared to taking a course that the student can **ace**. The history of Elvis course might be difficult (really, dude, it has, like, lots of readings!), but it may not help the student develop relevant perspectives, interpretations, **heuristics** or predictive models. It may just be a way for the student to apply existing tools to a new subject area and maintain

graduate program: university program where you study for a master's or doctorate degree

transcript: official paper from a school detailing a student's grades

ace: do exceptionally well

heuristics: thinking tools (i.e., models or rules) that are used to find solutions to problems

...

grade point average
(GPA): average of all
subject grades

15 that **grade point average** above 3.5 [(on 4)]. The cost to society of students
pursuing high grades rather than accumulating knowledge is enormous. We
would all prefer that our doctor knew a bit more chemistry or physics, or that
our elementary school teacher knew a bit more math.

(219 words)

Source: Page, Scott E. *The Difference: How the Power of Diversity Creates Better Groups, Firms, Schools, and
Societies*, Chapter 14. Princeton: Princeton University Press, 2007. Print.

VOCABULARY

■ **Look up these words** in a dictionary. With your partner, clarify the context of words
for which the dictionary offers more than one meaning. (For more information on
vocabulary strategies, see page 190.)

■ Then organize the words into the parts of speech in the chart below.

1. hire (**Part A**, line 1): _To engage soreove_
2. skill (**Part A**, line 12): _talent or ability_
3. alike (**Part A**, line 12): _Similar_
4. aware of (**Part A**, line 16): _Well informed_
5. seek (**Part A**, line 16): _Search for_
6. widely (**Part A**, line 13): _____
7. grades (**Part A**, line 8; **Part B**, line 4): _a degree_
8. mistakenly (**Part B**, line 2): _____
9. random (**Part B**, line 5): _____
10. earning (**Part B**, line 7): _____
11. tools (**Part B**, line 14): _____
12. relevant (**Part B**, line 12): _____

NOUNS	VERBS	ADJECTIVES	ADVERBS
Skill	hire	alike	Widely
grade	Seek	Aware	

COMPREHENSION

■ Ask your partner questions in order to determine the answers to questions involving your partner's text.

1. Google doesn't like to hire only the top graduates from top schools. Why not?

_____

2. According to Page, what is the main thing Google looks for when hiring?

a) A strong educational background with top grades

b) Similarity in interests and expertise

c) Differences in interests and expertise

3. Page states that "Google is also aware of the Calculus Condition." What does this mean in regards to the company's hiring practices?

_____

_____

4. According to Page, a student might avoid certain classes because

a) it might lower their grade point average.

b) it might teach them relevant perspectives that would help them in university or on the job.

c) they don't like them.

5. According to Page, what is the argument against taking only easy classes in which you can get a higher GPA?

_____

_____

6. What does Page imply is the cost to society of students pursuing high grades?

_____

7. Both texts address the concept of diversity. Work with your partner to write one sentence that combines the ideas about diversity from both texts.

_____

_____

_____

DISCUSSION

■ Answer these questions with your partner or in a small group.

1. What are some strengths you can offer your group or future employer that you have not learned during the course of your studies? How are you different? What makes you stand out?

2. Have you ever chosen not to take a difficult course because it might affect your GPA? If so, do you think this hurt or helped you?

3. What are some future implications of Google-style hiring practices?

4. If students avoid taking difficult courses, what could be the future implications for both the students and society?

GENERAL VOCABULARY LIST

My eLab
Review the vocabulary from this unit.

These are words and phrases that you should know after completing this unit. Remind yourself of their meanings by writing down their definitions or translations.

DEFINITIONS/TRANSLATIONS
1. at least
2. benefit
3. breakthrough
4. charity
5. cite
6. craft
7. donate
8. earnings
9. field
10. figure out
11. fundraiser
12. insight
13. journey
14. last
15. marketable
16. random
17. relevant
18. search
19. shift
20. skills
21. solve
22. strengths
23. tools
24. trained
25. willingness

"True innovation comes at the intersection of different fields."
—Laszlo Bock, VP, Google

Vocabulary Assignment

■ First read the speaking and writing assignments below.

■ Find ten words that are related to your field of study and necessary to help you discuss and describe the new job that your group is creating in this Field Work assignment. Make sure that the words you choose aren't cognates in your own language.

■ Write your words in the Field-Specific Vocabulary List below and include an English definition for each. Make sure your words are spelled correctly.

Field-Specific Vocabulary List

	ENGLISH DEFINITIONS
1. _____	_____
2. _____	_____
3. _____	_____
4. _____	_____
5. _____	_____
6. _____	_____
7. _____	_____
8. _____	_____
9. _____	_____
10. _____	_____

■ Exchange your list with another student and test each other for meanings and spelling.

Speaking Assignment

Part A: Group Work

■ Work with five other students from different fields of study. Combine your complementary skill sets and use both left- and right-brain thinking to create one new job that all of you would like to do. This job should combine at least one unique feature from each of your fields of study.

■ To do this successfully, you must each wear one of the six different hats from the Speaking activity on page 17, and the hat you wear must influence your perspective and the way you respond to the group as you work as a team to invent the new job.

Part B: Individual Presentations

■ Present your newly created job to another group or the class in a two- to three-minute presentation. (For more information about presenting, see page 206.)

FIELD WORK

Writing Assignment

1. Description

■ Write 150 to 200 words describing the new job that your group created in the speaking assignment. You should adopt only the perspective of the hat you are wearing.

■ Form a small group with two other students. Read your partners' texts and comment on them. When you comment on another student's text, it is a good idea to **emphasize the positive**. Another good revision strategy is to **obtain feedback** from partners who read your own text. These revision techniques teach you to see your work from different perspectives and help you to notice **strengths** and **weaknesses** in your writing.

Revision Strategy 2: Emphasizing the Positive

Work with a partner and read each other's texts. As you read one of your partner's texts, highlight an idea in it that you think is well-written and important to the meaning of the text. Then ask your partner to read it out loud and explain why it is well-written and important to the text.

Revision Strategy 3: Obtaining Feedback

Work in a group of three. Each student should take a turn and read another student's text out loud to the group. Then the writer of the text should listen carefully as the other two students comment on the strengths and weaknesses of his or her text. (For more information on revision strategies, see page 204.)

2. Research

■ Conduct research on one job or university program option in your field that you are not very familiar with (perhaps a non-standard option). You may be able to find your program described at various college or university websites, and you will certainly be able to find job descriptions online at any job search website.

■ First, write a 150- to 200-word description of this option *from the perspective of the white hat*—the factual perspective (see the Speaking activity on page 17). Be sure to paraphrase the information you have found and not to plagiarize (copy word for word from another). Write this description as if you are preparing to promote your particular university program or selected job to students in your class.

■ Next, rewrite your 150- to 200-word description from a different perspective: red, yellow or black. Be careful not to say which of the perspectives you have chosen. (Do not choose green or blue.)

■ Now you will give your two paragraphs to another student and you will be given another student's texts. Read both texts and guess which hat the student was wearing when he or she wrote his or her second text.

FYI

Technique is a noun that refers to a learned skill or system for doing something, whereas *technical* is an adjective that describes the type of knowledge related to how systems work.

strength: quality or ability that someone has that gives them an advantage

weakness: fault in someone's character that gives them a disadvantage

My eLab Documents includes additional research assignments to help you learn more about your field of study.

Digital Natives

Today's world is filled with a new and exciting interconnectedness. Technology has the capacity to change not only what we do, but how we do it. It can alter our awareness of ourselves and our understanding of others. Today's youth live with technology like no generation before them. They are wired, online, checked in, logged on 24/7. They are "digital natives." In this unit, you will create a survey, write a report and design a homepage for a social networking site for your field of study.

A totem consists of one or more objects thought to have a special connection with a particular tribe.

EXPLORE

Part A

The naming of things has a place of importance in all native cultures. How much do you know about the names of objects associated with your digital tribe?

■ Answer the following questions by circling the letters of the correct answers.

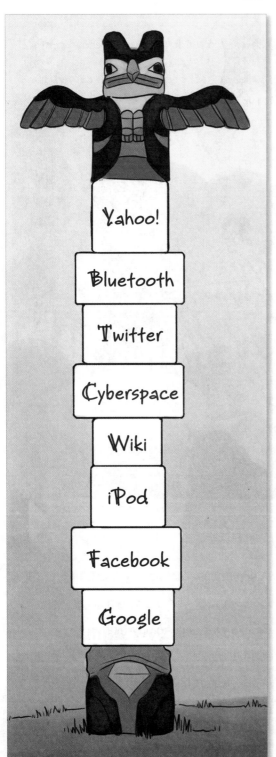

1. *Yahoo!* is
   a) named after a famous Japanese novel.
   b) the name of a character in the Stanley Kubrick film *A Clockwork Orange*.
   c) an acronym for "Yet Another Hierarchical Officious Oracle."

2. Bluetooth's name refers to the
   a) second King of Denmark, King Harold Bluetooth.
   b) fact that it is the size and shape of a blue shark's tooth.
   c) wireless link uniting PC and cellular technologies.

3. The expression *twitter* originated from the
   a) word *twit*, meaning "a silly person."
   b) sound that birds make when they chirp.
   c) word *wit*, meaning "quick and funny."

4) The term *cyberspace* originated from
   a) the *Star Trek* TV series.
   b) William Gibson's novel Neuromancer.
   c) the word *Siberia*, which is thought to be vast and impenetrable.

5. The expression *wiki* comes from
   a) the Hawaiian word for "quick."
   b) Rudolph Wikinson, the creator of Wikipedia.
   c) the scientific expression for "stem or place of origin."

6. The word *iPod* comes from the
   a) Latin language, meaning "one leg."
   b) movie *2001: A Space Odyssey*.
   c) name of the first robot created in Japan.

7. The term *Facebook* has its origins in a
   a) publication of digital portraits produced in 1995.
   b) book used by police to identify suspects in crimes.
   c) college publication given to students to help them get to know each other.

8. The word *google* means
   a) "an infinite number."
   b) "online information."
   c) "search."

© **ERPI** • REPRODUCTION PROHIBITED

(handwritten notes at top: "Celeris Paribus", "Duo tang", "π")

Part B

What are some totems (special objects or symbols) related to your field of study?

■ Work alone or with other students in your field to design a totem pole. Include six to eight totems on your pole.

■ After you have completed your totem pole, present it to the rest of the class. Be sure to justify your choice of totems.

Reading 2.1

Author and expert on learning and education, Marc Prensky distinguishes between two generations of people: digital natives and digital immigrants. In the following excerpt from the *Digital Natives Wikipedia* page, the characteristics and habits of a digital native are explained.

■ Before you read, complete the pre-reading vocabulary exercise.

■ Take time to read the comprehension questions on pages 30 and 31 before reading the text.

PRE-READING VOCABULARY

■ **Scan** the excerpt from the Youth and Media main page for the words below.

■ Try to guess the meaning of the words from context and match them with their definitions. The line numbers will help you find the words in the text.

Reading Comprehension Strategy 3: Scanning

> **Scanning** is an excellent reading strategy to use when you are looking for a specific piece of information. Slowly scan the page, moving your eyes from top to bottom, looking for a number, date or keyword. When you find it, read only that small part of the text more carefully to retrieve the information that you are looking for. (For more information on reading comprehension strategies, see page 189.)

WORDS			DEFINITIONS
1. amidst	(line 2)	b	**a)** no longer useful or effective because something more modern exists
2. susceptible	(line 10)	f	**b)** among or surrounded by things
3. malicious	(line 9)	*(j)*	**c)** someone who is the same age as you, who has the same type of job, or who is in the same program, etc.
4. bully	(line 11)	h	**d)** put too many things or people on or into something
5. overload	(line 37)	d	
6. stress	(line 40)	i	**e)** crime of stealing something
7. outdated	(line 44)	a	**f)** likely to suffer from a particular illness or be affected by a particular problem
8. theft	(line 47)	e	**g)** happening soon
9. peer	(line 51)	c	**h)** someone who uses his or her strength or power to frighten or hurt someone else
10. upcoming	(line 52)	g	**i)** continuous feelings of worry about your work or personal life that prevent you from relaxing
			j) very unkind and cruel

Digital Natives

The word *Internet* is always preceded with *the* unless it is being used as an adjective.

assert: state firmly that something is true

bad ware: software designed to infiltrate a computer system without the owner's consent

medium: way of communicating information and news to people, such as newspapers, television, etc.

hinder: make it difficult for something to develop or succeed

posterity: future generations

1. Subtitle: _____ b _____

1 Amidst a digital landscape that offers up a constant explosion of information and influence, natives **assert** their personal thoughts and experiences, as well as their own political beliefs. Digital natives carry this theme of personalization into their wider lives by creating and showing their own
5 personalities in order to, among many other reasons, assert themselves amongst a sea of information and influence.

2. Subtitle: _____ p _____

2 The digital world is inherently more vulnerable to malicious intent via **bad ware**, viruses, hackers, etc. Some argue that youth are also more susceptible
10 to sexual predators and bullies online. However, often new dangers are real world threats encountered through different **media**. There is a history of panic surrounding the introduction of new media forms, and a careful, objective strategy is needed to protect our young people without **hindering**
15 their development.

3. Subtitle: _____ i _____

3 Most digital natives live online, 24/7, where everything done is recorded for **posterity**. Some digital natives call it expression. Some digital immigrants feel it is shifting our notions of privacy. Forums for education
20 and discussion around online sharing practices, as well as legal dialogue about the documentation and availability of private information, have become crucial considerations for our society.

4. Subtitle: _____ e _____

4 Just as an artist may create a sculpture from
25 materials found in the wild, digital natives view the media landscape as their natural habitat from which they can pull resources for creativity, expression and commerce. The future balance of expression and property issues will be an
30 important legal discussion in the years ahead.

5. Subtitle: _____ c _____

5 Every day, the Internet becomes more important for society. The Internet revolution is fundamentally and significantly changing politics, education and
35 the nature of human interactions.

6. Subtitle: _____ d _____

6 Information overload refers to the increasingly frequent state of having too much information to make a decision or remain informed about a topic. This problem can lead to low productivity,
40 frustration, stress and poor decision making.

...

7 **7. Subtitle:** _____ h _____

As opposed to reading books and magazines, digital natives largely **draw** information from the Internet. Since everybody with Internet access can be a publisher on the Internet, such information can be incorrect, outdated or
45 inconsistent. Digital natives should base their knowledge on high-quality information that is fit for its intended use.

8 **8. Subtitle:** _____ a _____

Most adults recognize the consequences of theft. To them, illegally downloading a song carries the same weight as walking out of the grocery
50 store with an unpaid gallon of milk. Digital natives, on the other hand, are growing up in a post-Napster world where most of their peers **condone** casual **piracy**. From watching uploaded TV shows to getting an upcoming album (CD) before the rest of the neighbourhood, the youth's incentives to pirate media significantly **outweigh** the possible consequences.

9 55 **9. Subtitle:** _____ g _____

Technology has always been an important factor for education, but the rapid development of Internet and digital technology over the past decade is changing more than just the equipment used in the classroom. Learning styles and school behaviour are constantly being shaped by the growing
60 presence of the Internet.

(486 words)

Source: "Main Page." *Youth and Media.* N.p., 5 Oct. 2010. Web. 1 Nov. 2010. <http://www.youthandmedia.org/wiki/Main_Page>.

as opposed to: unlike; instead of

draw: get something that you need or want from someone or something

condone: accept or forgive behaviour that is illegal or in a moral grey zone

piracy: the crime of copying and selling books, tapes, videos, computer programs, etc.

outweigh: to be more important or valuable than something else

My eLab 🖉

Read about a recent study exploring the connection between Facebook and self-esteem. Do the online pre-reading exercise and answer the comprehension questions.

Part A

■ Answer the following questions.

1. Fill in the blank. The constant explosion of information and influence on the Internet has led to natives asserting their personalities when they are ___c___ the Internet. (Choose the letter of the correct answer.)
   a) on
   b) off
   c) both a) and b)

2. Digital natives are more susceptible to __b__ when they are online.
   a) malicious intent from hackers and viruses
   b) bullies
   c) neither a) nor b)

3. True or false? A sense of panic always accompanies the introduction of a new medium.
   ☒ True   ☐ False

4. Being online 24/7 has led to a change in the way digital natives
   a) express themselves.
   b) view the notion of privacy.
   c) see themselves in relation to others.

5. True or false? While the Internet is a source of creative material and inspiration for digital natives, the issue of creative ownership still needs to be explored.
   ☒ True   ☐ False

6. Information overload has
   a) increased.
   b) decreased.
   c) remained unchanged.

7. True or false? The more information you have, the more you can get done.
   ☐ True   ☒ False

8. Digital natives need to be careful about the information they get from the Internet because
   a) anybody could have written it.
   b) it may be untrue.
   c) both a) and b)

9. True or false? Most digital natives do not regard media piracy as theft.
   ☑ True   ☐ False

10. Many digital natives commit piracy because
    a) their friends think it is OK.
    b) it is cheaper than buying CDs.
    c) they think it is cool.

Part B

■ Reread *Digital Natives* and match the following subtitles with the paragraphs that they describe. Write the letters of the correct answers in the spaces provided in the reading.

a) Digital Piracy

b) Digital Identity

c) Digital Opportunities

d) Digital Information Overload

e) Digital Creativity

f) Digital Safety

g) Digital Education

h) Digital Information Quality

i) Digital Privacy

DISCUSSION

■ Discuss the following questions with a partner or in a small group.

1. How is the Internet changing the way humans interact?

2. What are some ways to ensure the information you are getting off the Internet is correct?

3. What is your opinion about casual piracy? Justify your opinion.

4. Do you agree with the way the article represents your generation overall? Why or why not?

VOCABULARY

If you **break up the words** *inherent* and *inconsistent*, you will notice that the prefix *in-* has two different meanings.

inherent(ly) (line 9): inside something else; part of something

inconsistent (line 45): not consistent

Vocabulary Strategy 3: Breaking Up Words

Breaking up a word into its smaller parts, like its prefix, root word and suffix, can help you learn its meaning. It can also help you learn the meanings of many other words with the same prefixes or suffixes. (For more information on vocabulary strategies, see page 190.)

■ Decide which meaning the prefix *in-* has in these sentences. Place a check mark in the appropriate column.

	"Not"	"In/Inside"
1. The CEGEP is *install*ing new computer software.	_____	_____
2. Check your *inbox* to see if you have any new messages.	_____	_____

•••

	"Not"	"In/Inside"
3. This password is *inactive*.	_____	_____
4. It is *inappropriate* to talk on your cellphone in class.	_____	_____
5. Digital natives *inhabit* the blogosphere.	_____	_____

Watching

AUDACITY OF TECH

Imagine your world without digital technology. In this *Global News 16x9* video, *Audacity of Tech*, digital native Sarah Prevette and digital immigrant Nancy Kendrew participate in a twenty-four-hour experiment to see how they manage with or without technology.

■ Before you watch the video, complete the pre-watching vocabulary exercise.

■ Then take time to read the comprehension questions and highlight the keywords in the questions.

■ While you watch the video, **listen for keyword cues** and answer the questions. (For more information on listening comprehension strategies, see page 205.)

PRE-WATCHING VOCABULARY

■ Match the following words and expressions with their definitions. If necessary, use a dictionary to help you, or work with a partner.

WORDS		DEFINITIONS
1. audacity	____	a) someone born between 1946 and 1960
2. Neanderthal	____	b) state of thinking about something or someone much more than is necessary or sensible
3. premise	____	
4. obsessed	____	c) quality of having enough courage to take risks or say impolite things
5. invaluable	____	d) all the ordinary people in society
6. fuelling	____	e) sleeping lightly for a short time
7. dozing	____	f) statement or idea that you accept as true and use as a base for developing other ideas
8. Boomer	____	g) extremely useful
9. masses	____	h) extremely unhappy and without hope
10. despondent	____	i) early type of human being
		j) making something, especially something bad, increase or become stronger

EXPRESSIONS		DEFINITIONS
1. make a switch	____	a) avoid punishment or criticism for something
2. jot things down	____	b) get involved in something that has recently become very popular
3. off the hook	____	c) so frightened that you cannot think clearly or behave sensibly
4. jump on the bandwagon	____	d) change places
5. panic-stricken	____	e) take note of or write down quickly

COMPREHENSION

■ Answer the following questions.

1. Explain the experiment that *Global News 16x9* is conducting?

_____

_____

2. What do Nancy Kendrew and Sarah Prevette represent?

_____

_____

3. What is Twitter?

_____

_____

_____

_____

4. How does Sarah define a laggard or luddite?

_____

5. What is Nancy's challenge?

_____

6. What is Sarah's challenge?

_____

_____

7. What is Sarah's final question?

_____

8. What does Nancy find surprising during the experiment?

_____

9. What example does Sarah use to explain how challenging it is to go twenty-four hours without technology?

_____

_____

10. By the end of the experiment, how many followers did Nancy end up with?

_____

EXPANSION

■ Write a tweet-like summary of the video *Audacity of Tech* in 140 characters or less.

■ Exchange your summary with a partner and **peer-review** each other's work.

■ Then return your partner's summary and explain what you found. (For information on writing summaries, refer to page 203.)

Revision Strategy 4: Peer Reviewing

Exchange your writing with a partner and read through your partner's paper. Check to see if your partner used the correct verb tense. Is the verb tense consistent or does your partner switch between the past and the present? Are the pronouns consistent? Do the verbs agree with their subjects? Does the piece of writing have a title? Finally, use a pencil and underline or circle any errors that you notice in the verb tenses, pronouns, spelling, etc. (For more information on revision strategies, see page 204.)

CONNECT WITH GRAMMAR

Forming Simple Present and Present Continuous Yes/No Questions

Rule Number 1: Use subject-verb inversion with the verb *to be* in the simple present tense.

Example:

| Statement: | Nancy | is | a | luddite. |
| | subject | verb | | |

| Question: | Is | Nancy | a | luddite? |
| | verb | subject | | |

Answer: No, not anymore.

Rule Number 2: All other verbs in the simple present tense use *do* or *does* as an auxiliary verb in questions and follow the pattern below.

Examples:

Auxiliary	Subject(s)	Verb	Rest of the sentence
Do	Sarah and Nancy	live	in Toronto?
*Does	Sarah	have	a Blackberry?

*Note: The first verb always agrees with the subject in the sentence. *Does* is the first verb in the sentence, so it takes the third-person –s. The main verb goes back to its root form.

■■■

Rule Number 3: Verbs that already have an auxiliary use this auxiliary in the question form. This rule is true for the present continuous tense.

Examples:

Auxiliary	Subject(s)	Verb	Rest of the sentence
Is	Nancy	tweeting	at the moment?
Are	Nancy and Sarah	chatting	on Facebook?

■ Nancy, a digital immigrant, and Sarah, a digital native, are chatting. Form simple present or present continuous questions to get the required response.

1. Sarah: *Are you on* IS Nancy chatting on fb?

   Nancy: No, I'm not on Facebook.

2. Sarah: Do you want to join?

   Nancy: Yes, I want to join.

3. Sarah: Are you doing special right now?

   Nancy: No, I'm not doing anything special right now.

4. Sarah: Does your cegep have a fb account.

   Nancy: Of course, my CEGEP has a Facebook account. LOL!

5. Sarah: IS the site are working now?

   Nancy: Yes, the site is working now.

Refer to Unit 6 of the Grammar Guide for further explanations and practice on yes/no question formation.

Reading 2.2

This reading includes a chart and three graphs that accompanied a recent newspaper article discussing the effects that the Internet is having on the health of Ontario students.

■ First, do the pre-reading activity and discussion.

■ Then complete the pre-reading vocabulary exercises.

■ Finally, make sure you read the instructions to the comprehension activity on page 38 before you begin the reading.

■ Take this short quiz and then compare your answers with those of a partner in order to **activate your prior knowledge** on the subject. Check your answers at the end of the quiz. (For more information on reading comprehension strategies, see page 189.)

TEENS AND THE INTERNET		
1. College students love the Internet ... but spend far less time *browsing* than older adults.	Yes	No
2. Over 76 percent of Canadian youth belong to a social networking site.	Yes	No
3. Fifty-five percent of the time college students use two or more media or digital devices at the same time.	Yes	No
4. A typical college student sends and receives ninety-six messages per day.	Yes	No
5. Twenty-five percent of young women and 33 percent of young men said they have had **nude** or semi-nude images— originally meant for someone else—shared with them.	Yes	No
6. Approximately 65 percent of all college students **surveyed** said that they had heard or seen other students using mobile telephones to **cheat** at school.	Yes	No
7. College students spend approximately two hours and twenty minutes a day on the Internet. Most of that time is spent working on schoolwork.	Yes	No
8. Only 15 percent of young adults felt that they couldn't survive without their cellphone.	Yes	No

Answers: 1. True; 2. True; 3. False—They do this 23 percent of the time; 4. True; 5. True; 6. True; 7. False—They do spend two hours and twenty minutes a day on the Internet, but they spend most of this time accessing social networking sites; 8. False—Thirty-seven percent of young adults said that they couldn't survive without their cellphone.

Sources: Kamibeppu, Kiyoko. "Impact of the Mobile Phone on Junior High School Students' Friendships in the Tokyo Metropolitan Area." *Cyberpsychology & Behavior* 8.8 (2005). Print; Lemhart, Amanda. "Teens and Social Media : An Overview." Pew Internet and American Life Project. New York Department of Health and Mental Hygiene. 10 Apr. 2009. Web. 2 July 2010. <http://isites.harvard.edu/fs/docs/icb.topic786630.files/>; Nielson Report. "How Teens Use Media." June 2009. Web. 2 July 2010. <http://blog.nielsen.com/nielsenwire/reports/nielsen_howteensusemedia_june09.pdf>; Sachoff, Mike. "More Teens Using Social Networking Sites." 22 June 2009. Web. 2 July 2010. http://www.webpronews.com/topnews/2009/06/22/more-teens-using-social-networking-sites; The National Campaign to Prevent Teen and Unplanned Pregnancy. "Sex and Tech: Results form a Survey of Teens and young Adults." N.d. Web. 3 July 2010. <http://www.thenationalcampaign.org/sextech/PDF/SexTech_Summary.pdf>; PhysOrg.com. "US Teens Use Smart Phones for Cheating: Study." 19 June 2009. Web. 2 July 2010. <http://www.physorg.com/news164627196.html>.

■ Discuss the following questions with a partner or in a small group.

1. Which of the statistics above surprises you the most? Why?

2. Name five ways you think teens' use of digital technologies is getting negative press.

3. Name five positive uses of digital technology.

browsing: searching for information on the Internet

FYI

When you use a number at the beginning of a sentence, you need to spell it out.

nude: not wearing any clothes

survey: ask a large number of people questions in order to find out their attitudes or opinions

cheat: behave in a dishonest way in order to win or get an advantage, especially in a competition, game or examination

FYI

The nouns *data* and *research* refer to information or facts. They are both non-count nouns (no plural form).

Part A

■ Below are some words used in the reading. Match each word with its definition.

WORDS		DEFINITIONS
1. conduct	_b_	a) spending a lot of time sitting down, not moving or exercising
2. mental	_e_	b) carry out a particular activity or process, especially in order to get information or prove facts
3. sedentary	_a_	
4. obese	_d_	c) when there is not enough of something, or none of it
5. lack	_c_	d) overweight in a way that is unhealthy
		e) relating to the health or state of someone's mind

Part B

■ Below are some words used when describing graphs and surveys. Look up each word in the dictionary and write down its definition and part of speech (noun, verb or adjective).

1. respondent

Part(s) of speech: _noun_

Definition(s): _A person who answer question_

2. bias

Part(s) of speech: _noun_

Definition(s): _Opinion that we have without a fact knowing._

3. increase

Part(s) of speech: _verb, noun_

Definition(s): _An augmentation of something. bigger_

4. decrease

Part(s) of speech: _verb, noun_

Definition(s): _the opposite of augmentation lesser, smaller_

5. stable

Part(s) of speech: _Adjective_

Definition(s): _____

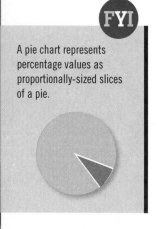

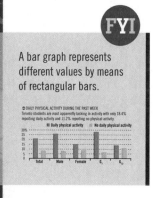

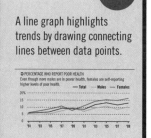

Mental Health and Well-Being of Ontario Students

Ontario students are spending more time in front of screens than ever before, according to a recent CAMH study. In addition, more of them are reporting poor health and less daily activity compared to the past. The study, conducted between November, 2008 and June, 2009, involved students from grades 7 to 12 across the province.

↪ SEDENTARY BEHAVIOUR
Percentage of Ontario students who spend more than seven hours in front of a TV or a computer

Total	Gender	Grade	Region	
	Male 11.4%	G_7 4.9%	Toronto 14.5%	West 8.7%
9.7%	Female 7.8%	G_{12} 12.8%	North 8.3%	East 8.8%

↪ OVERWEIGHT OR OBESE
Estimated weight
30% of males are overweight compared to females at 20.1%

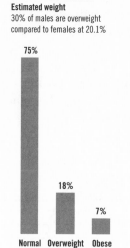

Normal	Overweight	Obese
75%	18%	7%

↪ DAILY PHYSICAL ACTIVITY DURING THE PAST WEEK
Toronto students are most apparently lacking in activity with only 18.4% reporting daily activity and 11.2% reporting no physical activity.

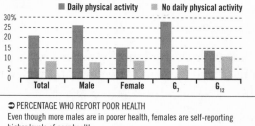

■ Daily physical activity   ■ No daily physical activity

Total   Male   Female G_7 G_{12}

↪ PERCENTAGE WHO REPORT POOR HEALTH
Even though more males are in poorer health, females are self-reporting higher levels of poor health.

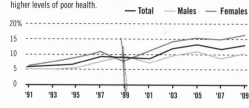

— Total   — Males   — Females

'91 '93 '95 '97 '99 '01 '03 '05 '07 '09

CARRIE COCKBURN / THE GLOBE AND MAIL. SOURCE: CENTRE FOR ADDICTION AND MENTAL HEALTH, ONTARIO STUDENT DRUG USE AND HEALTH SURVEY.

COMPREHENSION

■ **Skim** the information in the chart and the graphs above.

Reading Comprehension Strategy 4: Skimming

Look at the title, subtitles, captions, graphs and charts to get a general idea of the topic and the main direction of the text. (For more information on reading comprehension strategies, see page 189.)

■ Using that information, complete the exercise on page 39. Fill in the blanks in the sentences with the letters of the appropriate phrases below.

■ Once you have completed the exercise, compare your answers with a partner's.

a) increased by 7.9 percent   d) more physical activity

b) 92 percent of female students   e) 75 percent of Ontario students

c) poorer health   f) being overweight   ...

g) a slight decrease

h) are not obese

i) a dramatic decrease

j) 0.1 percent difference

k) approximately 89 percent

l) in good health

1. The percentage of Ontario students who spend time in front of a computer screen or TV _____ as they got older.

2. As the bar graph indicates, 93 percent of Ontario students _____ .

3. As the line graph indicates, in 2007, there was _____ in the percentage of Ontario students who reported poor health.

4. As indicated in the bar chart, there is _____ in the amount of daily physical activity Ontario students engage in as they get older.

5. In Toronto, _____ of students participate in some form of physical activity.

6. The study appears to equate poor health with _____ .

7. According to the line graph, approximately _____ felt that they were _____ in 1999.

8. Male students do _____ yet are in _____ than female students.

9. There is only a _____ in the proportion of Ontario students living east and west of Toronto who spend more than seven hours per day online.

10. The survey indicates that _____ maintain a healthy weight.

Reading 2.3

Have you thought about the impact digital technology will have on the next generation of students? Below is the newspaper article entitled *Study: Teens Spending Seven Hours a Day in Front of TVs, Computers*, in which the graph in Reading 2.2 was published.

■ Read the article and complete the vocabulary exercise on page 41.

■ Then answer the comprehension questions on page 42.

STUDY: Teens Spending Seven Hours a Day in Front of TVs, Computers

By Tralee Pearce

1   For parents who fret about the amount of time their kids **devote** to electronic media, consider this: in Ontario, hundreds of thousands of teens spend nearly seven hours a day staring at a computer or TV screen.

2   The number surprises even researchers familiar with this growing trend
5   and is likely to take a serious **toll**, not only on adolescents' physical health, but also on their emotional and mental well-being as well.

devote: use all or most of your time, effort, etc., in order to do something or help someone

toll: bad effect that something has on something or someone over a long period of time

...

causal: relating to the connection between two things, where one causes the other to happen or exist

log: use a computer

attention span: period of time during which you continue to be interested in something

taboo: custom that says you must avoid a particular activity or subject because it is considered offensive or because your religion does not allow it

3   "That's a lot of time spent in front of a screen being sedentary," said Robert Mann, a senior scientist at Toronto's Centre for Addiction and Mental Health, whose study revealed the new screen-time data. "That's almost a
10   third of the day."

4   Public health officials such as the Canadian Paediatric Society recommend no screen time for children under two years of age and a maximum of two hours for children older than two.

5   The new statistic—9.7 percent of kids in Grade 7 to 12, or about 327,000
15   students, spend at least seven hours a day in front of a TV or computer—was released Monday as part of CAMH's annual Ontario Student Drug Use and Health Survey. (The drug data was released in November.) Dr. Mann, the study's co-principal investigator, says he was surprised by the results of the screen-time question, the first time it was included in the survey.

6   20   The study does not make a direct **causal** link between screen time—or "sedentary behaviour," as it is sometimes called—and health issues, but in an interview, Dr. Mann said it is no coincidence that various indicators of physical health are simultaneously on the decline.

7   The survey found that the number of students who rate their health as
25   poor has increased significantly over the past two decades, to 14.5 percent from 8.9 percent in 1999. More than a quarter of the students are either overweight or obese. And 8.5 percent of students reported no physical activity in the seven days before the survey.

8   The study also did not connect screen-time and long-term effects on
30   mental health and cognitive function, but Dr. Mann noted that many of the students who **logged** long hours in front of a screen expressed feelings of unhappiness and experienced loss of sleep.

9   Other recent studies have linked screen-time to adverse effects on social skills and attachments to peers and parents. (Speaking of parents, they are
35   not in the clear either—emerging research has found that parents' use of technology is creating negative emotional effects in their children.) Just last week, a study published in the journal *Pediatrics* found TV and video-game use is associated with **attention-span** problems in schools.

10   There may also be a parallel between extreme electronic-media use and
40   Internet addiction, says screen-time expert Dimitri Christakis, a professor of pediatrics at the University of Washington School of Medicine. The 10 percent of adolescent heavy users is about the same percentage as estimates of North Americans who suffer from true Internet addiction, he says.

11   While there are social **taboos** around other addictive substances, such as
45   alcohol and drugs, there is no such constraint on technology.

12   "If there is a genetic predisposition, which there probably is, because we're reaching a level of such high saturation ... we are going to in fact ensure that everybody who's susceptible goes on to develop an addiction," he said.

13   But researchers admit science is having a hard time tracking these risks,
50   because the technology is moving so fast. (Dr. Christakis's current research is looking at whether changing the television diet of preschoolers can affect their behaviour and levels of aggression.) "We're not able to keep up with it. It takes us years to get a study funded, then years to conduct it, and in the meantime, Twitter comes out," he said.

14 55   Nevertheless, he says, the emerging picture does give parents a reason to be cautious about how teens use media and to question exactly what they are not doing while they are staring at a screen. Chances are it is connecting with their families, reading books, being active and getting enough sleep.

●●●

15   Yet parents and researchers alike have to resist **lumping** all technology
60 use together. Texting is not the same thing as playing *World of Warcraft*, says Dr. Christakis.

16   There is nothing wrong with teenagers communicating with each other, he says. Much of the research on negative cognitive effects of screen time is linked to the **pacing** of the media; more stimulating, rapidly sequenced content is
65 associated with delayed attention spans across the age spectrum.

17   "If you're writing long e-mails online, if you're **penning** ten-page love letters, there's nothing wrong with that. It's just displaced putting pen to **parchment**," he said. "That's fundamentally different in the way that it engages your brain and the effects it has than playing four hours of *StarCraft*."

18 70   All of which makes it a challenge when it comes to both parenting and public policy.

19   In a way, it would be easier if it were all bad, says Dr. Christakis. "If media were like cigarettes, we could just say, 'Don't do it.' But we can't."

(850 words)

Source: Pearce, Tralee. "Teens Spending Seven Hours a Day in Front of TVs, Computers." *Globe and Mail*. 12 July 2010. Web.

lump: put two or more people or things together and consider them as a single group

pace: speed

pen: write something, such as a letter, a book, etc.

parchment: thick, yellow-white writing paper, sometimes used for official documents; *putting pen to parchment*: writing on ordinary paper

FYI

The abbreviation *'s* can stand for *is* or *has*. In line 67, *there's* is short for *there is*, whereas *It's* is short for *It has*.

VOCABULARY

■ Working with a partner, look at the following definitions and fill in the missing letters of the words that they define. Paragraph numbers are given to help you find the words in context.

DEFINITIONS	WORDS
1. worry about something, especially when there is no need (paragraph 1)	F r e t
2. being in an early state of development (paragraph 9)	E m e r g i n g
3. looking at something or someone for a long time without moving your eyes (paragraph 1)	S t a r i n g
4. way of doing something that has been officially agreed upon (paragraph 18)	P o l i c y
5. not good or favourable (paragraph 9)	ad v e r s e
6. let news or official information be known and printed (paragraph 5)	re l e a s e d
7. recording or studying the behaviour or development of someone or something over time (paragraph 13)	t r a c k i n g
8. decrease in quality, quantity or importance (paragraph 6)	D e c l i n e
9. mentioned something because it was important or interesting (paragraph 8)	N o t e d
10. provided money for an activity, organization, event, etc. (paragraph 13)	F u n d e d

■ Read the text a second time to find answers to these questions.

1. a) How many students in Ontario spend approximately seven hours a day staring at a computer or television screen? _327 000 Students_

   b) What is the percentage? _9.7%_

2. What is Robert Mann's title?
   Senior scientist at Toronto's _Center for addiction and mental health_

Sen dantary behavi·our

3. What link did Mann's study investigate?
   Health and Time on screen

4. Was Mann's research successful? In other words, did he establish a link?
   ☐ Yes   ☑ No

_P.8_

5. What did Mann's research reveal?
   That kid who rate them health as _poor as increase of 5.6% and 8.5%_ _quint they did not make sport in_ _the last seven days._

6. What percentage of North Americans are Internet addicts? _10%_

7. Why is it difficult for science to research risks associated with the Internet?
   Because technology is moving so fast.

8. What are students likely *not* to be doing while they are staring at a screen?
   Time with family, reading book, sleep _being active._

9. What two online activities does Dr. Christakis consider to be acceptable?
   Texting and write a text online

10. How is texting for four hours different from playing *World of Warcraft* or *StarCraft* for four hours?
    The way it engage your brain and _the effect is different._

DISCUSSION

■ Discuss the following questions with a partner.

1. Look at your answers to question 1. In your opinion, which of the two figures sounds most dramatic? Why?

2. Look at your answers to questions 2 and 3. In your opinion, is Robert Mann qualified to investigate this link? Explain.

3. Look at your answer to question 5. In your opinion, what factors could explain these results?

4. Look at you answer to question 6. In your opinion, how does this information relate to Mann's research?

5. Look at your answers to questions 8 and 9. In your opinion, is the amount of time students spend looking at a screen the problem, or is the problem how the student is engaged with the screen?

Listening 🎧

TWITTER LOVE

Don't be surprised if you hear Mathieu Murphy Perron and Jacqueline Turner start tweeting when asked how they first met and fell in love. As *Daybreak* host Steve Rukavina discovers, these two love birds have Twitter to thank for a lot more than just the occasional update.

Who is at the centre of your twitterverse?

■ Before you listen to the interview, complete the pre-listening discussion and vocabulary exercises in order to **activate your prior knowledge** on the subject.

Listening Comprehension Strategy 2: Activating Your Prior Knowledge

Reflecting and talking about a subject before you hear more about it can help you activate and remember topical information and key vocabulary that you already know. It can also make it easier and faster for you to access your prior knowledge as you listen because you can understand it in a context. (For more information on listening comprehension strategies, see page 205.)

■ Take time to read the comprehension questions on pages 44 and 45 and to highlight the keywords in those questions.

■ While you listen to the interview, **listen for keyword cues** and answer the questions. (For more information on listening comprehension strategies, see page 205.)

PRE-LISTENING DISCUSSION

■ Discuss the following questions with a partner or in a small group.

1. What are some different ways you connect with members of the opposite sex on the Internet?

2. Have you or someone you know ever been on a date arranged through an Internet dating site? If so, what was the experience like? If not, would you try Internet dating in the future? Why or why not?

3. What are some of the advantages and disadvantages of Internet dating?

4. Do you follow anyone on Twitter?

5. Do you think it is possible to fall in love with someone based solely on what they have written on a site like Twitter or Facebook or in a blog? Explain.

■ Match these words and expressions with their definitions.

WORDS		DEFINITIONS
1. endearing	____	**a)** not having a clear purpose or reason
2. dunk	____	**b)** very similar to
3. sweet	____	**c)** making someone love or like you
4. wandering	____	**d)** quick action of opening and closing one eye, usually as a signal to someone else
5. aimless	____	**e)** kind, gentle and friendly
6. wink	____	**f)** put something into a liquid quickly and take it out again, especially something you are eating
7. obvious	____	**g)** go to a bar or other public place and look for a sexual partner
8. neither ... nor	h	
9. akin to	____	~~h)~~ not one or the other
10. cruise	____	**i)** walking slowly and without a clear direction or purpose
		j) easy to notice or understand

My eLab 🖊

Answer additional questions for "Twitter Love."

COMPREHENSION

■ Answer the following questions.

1. How long have Mathieu and Jacqueline been together? _____

2. What is a hashtag?

_____

_____

3. What is a popular hashtag during the hockey season? _____

4. What was it about Jacqueline's initial tweet that Mathieu found endearing?

_____

_____

5. How did Mathieu respond to Jacqueline's initial tweet?

_____

6. What was Jacqueline's location name at the time? _____

7. How is Mathieu connected with the Montréal art scene?

_____

_____

8. How did Mathieu offer to help Jacqueline with her art work?

_____

_____

9. Why did Mathieu and Jacqueline meet for the first time? Where did they meet?

_____

_____

10. What does Twitter allow people to do?

_____

11. Who else do Mathieu and Jacqueline know who have met through Twitter?

_____

12. What is the name of the baby's Twitter account? _____

13. Would they recommend Twitter as a way of meeting others?

_____

14. According to Mathieu, how is meeting through Twitter different from meeting through an online dating website?

_____

_____

15. On a separate sheet of paper, summarize the listening in your own words (50–100 words). (For more information on how to write a summary, refer to the summary checklist on page 203.)

refer to the summary checklist on page 203.

EXPANSION

■ Below are icons affiliated with popular Internet sites. How many of the sites can you identify?

Answers:
Top row: Twitter; Google; MySpace; RSS; Facebook; Technoradi.
Bottom row: Digg; Furl; Stumbleupon; Flickr; Del.icio.us; YouTube; Favourites.

■ Get into small groups and design an icon representing each of your fields of study.

■ Present your icons to your classmates. Explain your design.

Pronouncing *sh*

Part A

> The *sh* sound /ʃ/ has several spelling forms: *sh, ci, ce, si, ssi, su, ssu* and *ti*.
>
> **Example:**
>
> The *ci* in the word *social* is pronounced as *sh* (transcribed as /ʃ/), so we say "*so-shal*," not "~~so-si-al~~."

■ Listen to the following words. You will hear each word twice. The first time you hear a word, pronounce it after the speaker. When you hear it a second time, write it in the appropriate column according to the way the *sh* sound is spelled.

sh	*ci/ce*	*si/ssi*
_____	_____	_____
_____	_____	_____
_____	_____	_____
_____	_____	_____

su/ssu	*ti*
_____	_____
_____	_____
_____	_____
_____	_____
_____	_____

Part B

> Sometimes *su* and *si* are pronounced as the voiced /ʒ/ *zh* sound.
>
> **Example:**
>
> The *su* in *leisure* and the *si* in *decision* have the voiced /ʒ/ *zh* sound.
>
> *Si* is pronounced *zh* after a vowel sound or the consonant *r*.

■ Listen and repeat the following words. Each word will be pronounced twice.

1. pleasure
2. measure
3. usual
4. unusual
5. conclusion
6. immersion

GENERAL VOCABULARY LIST

These are the words and phrases that you should know after completing this unit. Remind yourself of their meanings by writing down their definitions or translations.

	DEFINITIONS/TRANSLATIONS
1. akin to	
2. audacity	
3. bias	
4. conduct	
5. decline	
6. decrease	
7. digital immigrant	
8. digital native	
9. increase	
10. lack	
11. luddite	
12. masses	
13. medium	
14. mental	
15. neither ... nor	
16. outdated	
17. piracy	
18. respondent	
19. sedentary	
20. stable	
21. sweet	
22. theft	
23. track	
24. upcoming	
25. wander	

My eLab

Review the vocabulary from this unit.

"An invasion of armies can be resisted, but not an idea whose time has come." —Victor Hugo, *Histoire d'un crime*, 1852

Vocabulary Assignment

■ Create a list of ten technologies, instruments or devices related to your field of study, such as a computer, test tube, compass, etc. Make sure the words you choose aren't cognates in your own language and that you have spelled them correctly.

Provide a definition for each item on your list. Your definitions can include

a) a description of the item's appearance;

b) a description of what it is made of; and

c) an explanation of its principle of operation or how it works.

Field-Specific Vocabulary List

	ENGLISH DEFINITIONS
1. _____	_____
2. _____	_____
3. _____	_____
4. _____	_____
5. _____	_____
6. _____	_____
7. _____	_____
8. _____	_____
9. _____	_____
10. _____	_____

■ Exchange your list with another student and test each other for meanings and spelling.

Writing Assignment

1. Designing a Survey on Technology Use in Your Field of Study

In this assignment, you will design a survey to determine

a) which kinds of technologies, instruments or devices are used by students in your field of study; and

b) students' reasons for using these technologies, instruments or devices.

Part A: Preparing to Write Your Survey

■ Create six to eight yes/no questions about your objective. (Refer to page 34 and to Unit 6 of the Grammar Guide for more information on yes/no questions.)

■ ■ ■

- Incorporate a minimum of six vocabulary words from your Field-Specific Vocabulary List on page 48. If you are working with a partner, you should each contribute three words. If you are working in a group, each group member should contribute two words.

- Get at least five students from your field of study to answer the questions. Be sure to record the results.

Note: Generally speaking, a survey of this size is too small to be considered accurate. If this bothers you, you may wish to prepare additional copies of your survey and ask as many people as you and your fellow group members are prepared to take the time to analyze. (For more information on how to write a survey report and for a sample template, see pages 197 and 199.)

Part B: Writing Your Survey Report

- Write a 200- to 250-word survey report including

   a) the objective of the survey;

   b) the questions on the survey;

   c) the results of the survey;

   d) an analysis of the results;

   e) a graph illustrating your results.

2. Designing a Homepage for a Social Networking Site for Your Field of Study

In this assignment, you will play the role of web designer and design a social networking homepage for a social networking site devoted to your field of study. If you are working with a partner or in a group, you will share this role.

Part A: Preparing to Write

- Consider what other students in your field of study might want in a social networking site. Create six to eight yes/no questions to ask students in your field. (Refer to page 34 and to Unit 6 of the Grammar Guide for more information on yes/no questions.)

- Get at least five students from your field of study to answer the questions. Be sure to record the results.

Part B: Writing

- Create the name, web address, logo or slogan of your site and determine the things that it will offer (to be listed on your homepage).

- Then design your homepage. Consider the basic concept and look of the homepage: toolbars, login, colours, advertising, images, etc.

- Write the content of your homepage and insert it in your homepage. On a separate sheet of paper, justify your homepage's design and content in detail (200-250 words). Be sure to include your survey results to help you in your justification. If you worked with a partner or in a small group, then each member should write their own justification.

Speaking Assignment

1. Presenting Your Survey

■ If you did Writing Assignment 1, present your survey illustrating the results of your research. If you worked in a group, everyone in the group must take part in this presentation. Each person should try to speak for two to three minutes. (For more information on preparing an oral presentation, see page 206. If you are using PowerPoint, see page 207 for information on how to create an effective PowerPoint presentation.) Your presentation should include

a) a statement of your objective;

b) a list of the questions that you asked and justification for the questions;

c) an explanation of what you predicted the results would be;

d) an explanation of what your actual results were and how they were the same or different from what you had predicted;

e) a short list of things that you would change or do differently the next time you do a survey;

f) a graph illustrating the results of your survey.

2. Presenting Your Field-of-Study Homepage

■ If you did Writing Assignment 2, present your field of study homepage to the rest of the class. Explain the different parts of your homepage. If you worked in a group, everyone in the group must take part in this presentation. Each person should speak for two to three minutes. (For more information on preparing an oral presentation, see page 206. If you are using PowerPoint, see page 207 for information on how to create an effective PowerPoint presentation.) Your presentation should include

a) a list of the questions that you asked students and justification for the questions;

b) an explanation of the content on your homepage;

c) an explanation for the design of your homepage;

d) a short list of things you would do differently the next time you create a homepage.

My eLab

My eLab Documents includes additional research assignments to help you learn more about your field of study.

FIELD WORK

Ordinary Superheroes

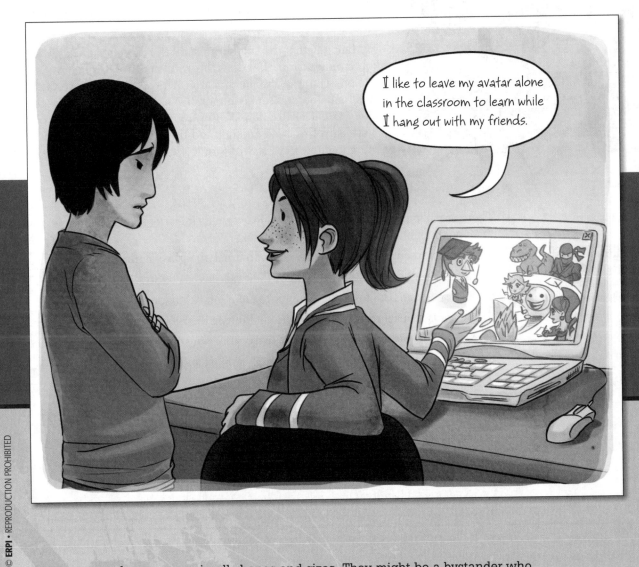

Ordinary superheroes come in all shapes and sizes. They might be a bystander who courageously saves someone's life in an emergency, a volunteer who generously gives his or her time to people in need or a mentor who advises the up-and-coming in his or her field. Anyone can be an ordinary superhero. They are simply people who inspire others in their daily lives. In this unit, you will examine the role of one type of ordinary superhero: the mentor. You will look at education and workplace mentors, and conduct research on an expert in your field of study. Finally, you will create an avatar for your field of study.

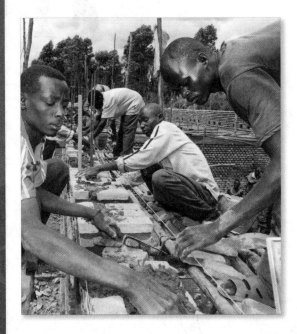

EXPLORE

Mentors are wise and trusted counsellors or teachers. Some say that the original concept of mentoring comes from the ancient Greek storyteller Homer. In his famous story, *The Odyssey*, Homer tells how the Goddess Athena, acting as a mentor, advised Telemachus to search for his father, Odysseus (or Ulysses), who was lost at sea. She counselled Telemachus to avenge his father by helping to kill the traitors who were trying to usurp the king and gain control of Ithaca.

Many say that the "modern use of the term *mentoring* more likely comes from the work of 18th century French writer Fenelon, who was also an educator. African scholars have [also] noted that mentors were commonplace in Africa, long before the ancient Greek civilization ..."[1] For example, African stonemasons would learn from one another and then, in turn, teach the next generation how to work with stone.

■ Answer the following questions.

1. There are all types of mentors in society. Place a check mark (√) beside the roles that you think involve some kind of mentoring.

   glass ceiling: expression referring to the attitudes and practices that prevent women from getting high-level jobs

   a) Women executives assist other women to break the **glass ceiling**. ☐

   b) Senior executives give 10 percent of their salaries to charity. ☐

   c) Senior citizens demonstrate hobbies to elementary students. ☐

   d) Business managers take new employees "under their wings." ☐

   e) Volunteers partner with students at risk of dropping out of school. ☐

   f) People managing life challenges provide support and wisdom to others. ☐

   g) Successful businesspeople help clean up the neighbourhood. ☐

   h) Older students help younger students cope with peer pressure. ☐

   i) University alumni provide guidance to students seeking business careers. ☐

   j) Second-year students sell cupcakes to raise money for a school trip. ☐

   k) Experienced faculty members assist their new colleagues. ☐

   l) Successful businesspeople help new entrepreneurs starting out. ☐

   m) Police officers coach basketball to teens at an inner-city community centre.[2] ☐

2. If you could have a mentor in your field of study, what role would you want him or her to play in your life? In other words, how could he or she help you?

   _____

   _____

1. "Mentors: Peer Resources." Web. 5 July 2010. <http://www.islandnet.com/~rcarr/mentorrationale.html>.
2. Correct answers adapted from: "Mentoring Rationale, Examples and Our Expertise." Peer Resources. Peer Systems Consulting Group. 2010. Web. 8 July 2010. <http://www.mentors.ca/mentorrationale.html>.

3. What personality **traits** do you think a mentor should have? Create a list of six to eight traits with a partner.

trait: characteristic

_____

_____

_____

_____

_____

Reading 3.1

How can a successful college student have an equally successful career or university experience? Nowadays, with our new economic reality to consider, it is important not to overlook any tools that may provide us with an edge. One tool that is overlooked with surprising frequency—although it can be extremely constructive when used properly— is mentoring. Read this article to find out more about mentoring.

■ Read the comprehension questions on pages 57 and 58 before you read the text.

■ After you finish reading the text, answer the vocabulary and comprehension questions.

Mentoring: Empowering or Overpowering?

1   Perhaps the issue of **whether or not** to find a mentor is often overlooked due to the amount of effort and difficulty people generally associate with finding a mentor. After all, many questions should ideally be asked and addressed, such as those involving suitability, availability and compatibility.
5   At first glance, it is true that the process may appear **daunting** and time-consuming. However, the advantages to be had from a productive mentor/ protégé relationship far **outweigh** these initial disadvantages.

2   Nowadays, there are many good reasons for having a mentor. The Peer Mentoring website lists these among the reasons why some people consider
10   a mentoring relationship: an enthusiastic young entrepreneur may receive expert advice on getting started from a well-connected, **savvy** business owner; a young woman's first tentative steps up the corporate ladder might be made easier if she has the support and encouragement of a highly placed woman executive in the company; and a new student in university may gain
15   confidence and understanding through the help of his or her peers.

3   According to David Clutterbuck, Ph.D., author and well-known authority on mentoring, the benefits of mentoring for the protégé include

- greater clarity about personal development and career goals;

- the opportunity to discuss issues about his or her career and development
20   in an open and **non-threatening** environment;

- improved **networking**;

whether or not:
if you should do something or not

daunting: frightening; making you feel less confident

outweigh: have more importance than something else

savvy: knowledgeable

non-threatening: not making someone worried or afraid

networking: the practice of meeting other people involved in the same kind of work for information and support

■■■

- practical advice on organizational politics and behaviour;
- the opportunity to be challenged constructively;
- the transfer of knowledge and, in particular, judgment;
- 25 • [having] a role model.*

4   In fact, having an excellent mentor in your life, who can coach you along in your career or university program, advise you on the ins and outs of your chosen field, and help you with goal setting, is almost as good as having your very own Greek god or goddess **waiting in the wings** to give you a hand up 30 whenever you need it. For example, a recent study by Blau, Currie, Croson & Ginther (2010) suggests that women in higher education receive more offers to publish and more federal **funding** when they have a mentor. However, keep in mind that not all mentor matches are made in heaven. It takes effort on both sides to make it work, and naturally, the more planning 35 and **legwork** you put into the initial search, the better.

Suitability

5   The first question to answer in your search for a mentor, if you wish to build a solid mentoring **bond**, is whether or not a prospective mentor is a suitable match to your requirements. When you are looking at a few different 40 potential candidates, ask yourself if they are in positions that interest you in your field of study. Are they well respected? Are their career goals similar to yours? Only once you are satisfied with your responses here, should you move on.

Availability

6 45 Even if you determine that a potential mentor is a suitable fit, he or she may simply not be available. Try not to become offended if you ask for a meeting and they **decline**. Many people feel that their lives are already busy enough and that they can't take on any more. You may have to try several possible candidates before one agrees to meet with you. Just tell yourself 50 that this is part of the process and keep trying.

Compatibility

7   In a study on mentoring in the workplace, Baker (2002) found that "... what was most highly valued by both protégés and mentors were those aspects of the mentoring relationship which were psychosocial in nature."** In other 55 words, feeling **nurtured** and supported, learning to reflect on one's own skills and processes, being helped with personal issues that **arose** and taught how to successfully navigate working relationships with co-workers and the boss were among the key issues that both protégés and mentors identified as among the most enriching aspects of mentoring.

8 60 These issues are more easily **dealt with** if the mentor and protégé are compatible to some extent. On the other hand, perfect compatibility is not always necessary, or even desirable. If you are too alike, then possibly no new ideas will develop from your discussions. You may, in this case, even end up reinforcing certain negative traits, rather than developing new, positive skills 65 and practices. After all, one of the reasons you want a mentor in theory is to gain a different perspective, which you will not do if you are too similar.

•••

waiting in the wings: waiting nearby

funding: money provided by an organization or government for a particular purpose

legwork: hard boring work that has to be done

bond: a sense of unity between two or more people

decline: say no; refuse

nurtured: helped to develop, grow, succeed, etc.

arise (past: arose): appear

dealt with: solved; resolved

9   If you, as protégé, control the mentoring experience from the outset, and do not allow the need for careful, advanced preparation and planning to overpower you, then the mentoring relationship that **ensues** may prove quite
70   successful and give you an edge in your field. On the other hand, if the mentoring trajectory is not carefully planned, and if the questions of suitability, availability and compatibility are not adequately considered, then the end result will not be as enriching and empowering for you as it could be.

ensue: happen after something else

(813 words)

* Clutterbuck, David. "The Benefits of Mentoring." International Associations of Business Website. Web. 19 July 2010. <http://www.iabc.com/cwb/archive/2009/0109/Clutterbuck.htm>.

** "Quality Conversations." Herdsa. 10 July 2002. Web. 16 July 2010. <http://www.herdsa.org.au/wp-content/uploads/conference/2002/papers/Baker.pdf>.

References: "Quality Conversations." Herdsa. 10 July 2002. Web. 16 July 2010. <http://www.herdsa.org.au/wp-content/uploads/conference/2002/papers/Baker.pdf>; Mentors: Peer Resources. Web. 5 July 2010. <http://www.islandnet.com/~rcarr/mentorrationale.html>; Jaschik, Scott. "Proof That Mentoring.Matters." Inside Higher Ed. 4 Jan. 2010. Web. 16 July 2010. <http://www.insidehighered.com/news/2010/01/04/mentor>; Clutterbuck, David. 'The Benefits of Mentoring." International Associations of Business Website. Web. 19 July 2010. <http://www.iabc.com/cwb/archive/2009/0109/Clutterbuck.htm>; Hansen, Katharine. "The Value of a Mentor." Quintessential Careers. Web. 2 July 2010. <http://www.quintcareers.com/mentor_value.html>.

VOCABULARY

Part A

■ Use the context to help you **find the correct synonym** for each of these words. The line numbers will help you to find the words in the text. (For more information on vocabulary strategies, see page 190.)

Vocabulary Strategy 4: Finding Synonyms

Learning a variety of synonyms can strengthen and enlarge your vocabulary base, and help you to fine-tune your knowledge of English word meanings.

1. nowadays (line 8)
   a) today   **b)** these days

2. overlook (line 1)
   a) notice   **b)** miss

3. well (line 41)
   a) in a good way   **b)** healthy

4. gain (line 66)
   a) achieve   **b)** arrive

5. a few (line 39)
   a) some   **b)** almost none

6. outweigh (line 7)
   a) determine how heavy something is   **b)** be of more value than something else

7. quite (line 69)

    a) very   **b)** not really

8. rather than (line 64)

    a) suggests an alternative   **b)** gives no alternative

9. suitability (line 71)

    a) appropriate and well-matched   **b)** inappropriate and ill-matched

10. behaviour (line 22)

    a) comfort   **b)** conduct

Part B

■ Match these expressions with their definitions.

EXPRESSIONS			DEFINITIONS
1. an edge	(line 70)	____	**a)** exact details of a complicated issue
2. goal setting	(line 28)	____	**b)** help
3. ins and outs	(line 27)	____	**c)** establishing objectives
4. give a hand up	(line 29)	____	**d)** advantage
5. keep in mind	(line 33)	____	**e)** remember

Part C

■ **Look up the** following two **words** in the dictionary to see how they are different in meaning. Write out their definitions. Then **break up the words** into their prefixes and roots. Write a definition for each of the prefixes. (For more information on prefixes, see Unit 32 of the Grammar Guide.)

1. Definition of *overpower*: _____

    Prefix: _____ Definition of prefix: _____

2. Definition of *empower*: _____

    Prefix: _____ Definition of prefix: _____

■ **Look up the** following **words** in the dictionary and write out their definitions. Then **break up the words** into their roots and suffixes. Provide a definition for the suffix *-ship*. What role does it play in word meaning? (For more information on suffixes, see Unit 32 of the Grammar Guide.)

3. relationship: _____

4. mentorship: _____

5. apprenticeship: _____

6. scholarship: _____

7. partnership: _____

8. internship: _____

Definition of *-ship*: _____

My eLab
Read about some not-so-ordinary superheroes and answer the comprehension questions.

1. Scan the text for two transition words that suggest that the author is looking at both sides of the issue (an important aspect of a well-balanced academic article). They will be synonyms for *nevertheless*, and are used to introduce a contrast.

   _____

2. Find one argument in the text that has an opposing argument. Write down both the argument and the opposing argument.

   _____
   _____
   _____
   _____
   _____
   _____
   _____

3. Underline four different citation techniques used in the text.

4. Why don't more people seek out mentors?

   _____

5. Why do people sometimes refuse to become mentors?

   _____

6. What is the thesis—or main premise—of the article?

   _____
   _____

7. Name one psychosocial aspect of mentoring.

   _____
   _____
   _____

8. Summarize what the article has to say about "suitability" in one sentence.

   _____
   _____

9. Summarize what the article has to say about "availability" in one sentence.

   _____
   _____

10. Summarize what the article has to say about "compatibility" in two sentences

_____

_____

_____

_____

My eLab 📁

My eLab Documents includes additional research assignments to help you learn more about mentoring.

DISCUSSION

■ Answer the following questions and then share your answers in a small group.[3]

1. What three things would you like to achieve if you had a mentor?

2. What three things about yourself and your personality might make it difficult for you to benefit from mentoring?

3. Prepare a brief, point-form autobiography that you could share with a mentor at a first meeting. Be sure to include your life and career goals.

EXPANSION

■ Conduct research on an expert in your field of study. Choose someone whom you think would make a good mentor and who works in a position that both interests and suits your field of study.

Note: It is not necessary for you to speak with the person or ask him or her to become your mentor—unless you eventually decide that you wish to do so on your own. At this point, it is just a learning exercise.

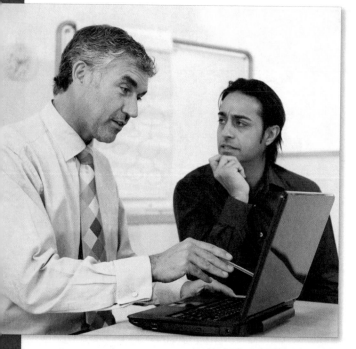

Part A

■ Find out as much about the expert as possible. Large companies may contain profiles of their high-level employees on their websites. News articles may be another source of information. Use quality, well-known sources. (For more information on evaluating your sources for credibility or how to use the CARS checklist, see pages 191 and 192.)

■ Take detailed notes on his or her personality traits, interests, personal history, educational background, career path, current situation and future goals. Try to determine—at first glance—if the person meets the requirements of suitability, availability and compatibility.

■ Use your notes to write a 200- to 250-word basic report about the expert. (For information on report writing and a sample template, see pages 195 and 196.)

■ Make sure that you have included all the necessary information by **writing a reverse plan**.

---

3. The discussion questions were adapted from: "Tips for Meeting with a Mentor." Peer Resources. Navigation Tools for the Heart, Mind and Soul. 2010. Web. 7 Oct. 2010. <http://www.islandnet.com/~rcarr/mentorpartnertips.html>.

Revision Strategy 5: Writing a Reverse Plan

After you have written your report, work backwards to create a "reverse" plan that will mirror what you actually have in your text. This will allow you to identify points that do not appear in your text but should have been included.

(For more information on revision strategies, see page 204; for more information on writing a plan, see page 202.)

Part B

In order to prepare yourself for the Speaking activity on page 60, follow these instructions.

■ Find a partner who is not in your field of study.

■ Exchange e-mail addresses and agree to e-mail your report to your partner at least three days before your next class.

■ Next class, you will become your partner's expert. Your partner will ask you questions to decide if you would be a good mentor. You must respond to all your partner's questions in the character of your partner's expert. Before your next class, read the information that your partner sent you carefully and take detailed notes. You need to be able to remember information on the expert's life and career, and you also need to understand his or her personality in order to be able to role-play him or her.

CONNECT WITH GRAMMAR

Forming Information Questions

To form information questions (*who, what, when, where, why, how*, etc.) in English, follow the rules for yes/no questions on page 34. Place the appropriate question word at the beginning of the question.

Simple present (verb *to be*)

- Mentors are <u>role models</u>.

  Question: **What** are mentors?

  Answer: Role models

Simple present (all other verbs)

- Mentors encourage <u>protégés</u>.

  Question: **Who** do mentors encourage?

  Answer: Protégés

Remember: When you are making a question to get the subject of the sentence, you do not use an auxiliary verb in the question.

- <u>The mentor</u> encourages the protégé.

  Question: **Who** encourages the protégé?

  Answer: The mentor

Present continuous (present form of verb *to be* + *-ing* form of the verb)

- Many schools are starting mentoring programs <u>in the fall</u>.

  Question: **When** are many schools starting mentoring programs?

  Answer: In the fall

  ...

■ Create information questions for the statements below. The underlined words are the answers to the questions.

1. Currently, the Big Brothers Big Sisters of Canada mentoring program is taking place <u>in schools throughout the country</u>.

   Where the mentoring program is taking place?

2. <u>In-school mentoring</u> makes a big difference in the life of a child.

   What makes

3. Mentors need to <u>be nineteen years of age or over</u> to mentor a child in a school.

   how old the

4. A mentor meets his or her protégé <u>one hour each week</u>.

   how long a   each week

5. The mentoring experience benefits <u>both the child and the mentor</u>.

   ~~How many~~ who does benefit of

6. It is possible to volunteer <u>by contacting the Big Brothers Big Sisters office in your area</u>.

   How is it possible to volounteer

Refer to Unit 6 of the Grammar Guide for further explanations and practice on information questions.

Speaking

ROLE PLAY: YOU'RE THE EXPERT

■ Prepare eight to ten information questions to ask your potential "mentor." (Refer to the "Connect with Grammar" section on page 59 for help forming information questions.) Remember that you are trying to determine if this expert would make a good mentor for you. Since you are the one who researched this expert, you know approximately what answers to expect from your partner.

■ Take turns playing the student and the expert. The student should ask the expert his or her prepared questions, and the expert should answer the questions using the information that he or she has read about the expert, and staying true to the character and personality of the expert at all times.

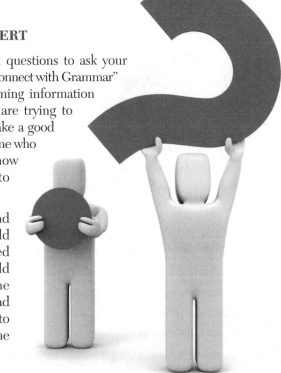

Watching 🖥

MENTORS AND PROTÉGÉS

"In pretty much every business, the relationship between a protégé and his or her mentor is an important one, and that is especially true in fashion, where young designers are often thrown into the limelight with very little time to learn the ropes." (from *Mentors and Protégés*.)

Mentors and Protégés will look at some ordinary superheroes who decided to do more than simply become successful in their own careers, choosing to help others become successful as well by sharing their knowledge and expertise as mentors.

■ Before you watch the interview, complete the pre-watching vocabulary exercise for help with expressions like those in the introduction above.

■ Then read the comprehension questions on pages 62 and 63 and highlight the keywords.

■ While you watch the video, **listen for keyword cues** and answer the questions. (For more information on listening comprehension strategies, see page 205.)

PRE-WATCHING VOCABULARY

■ Match the following words and expressions with their correct definitions.

WORDS		DEFINITIONS
1. protégé	____	**a)** someone who gets a prize
2. apprenticeship	____	**b)** advice and help
3. winner	____	**c)** give; donate money
4. guidance	____	**d)** someone, especially a young person, who is taught and helped by someone who has influence, power and experience
5. endow	____	
6. funding	____	**e)** internship where a person works without pay to learn a job
7. threatening	____	**f)** edge; farthest from the centre
8. fringe	____	**g)** skill (job-related)
9. craft	____	**h)** scary; frightening
10. delivery	____	**i)** the result of bringing goods to a location
		j) money given for a specific purpose

EXPRESSIONS		DEFINITIONS
1. thrown into the limelight	____	**a)** everybody benefits in this case
2. learn the ropes	____	**b)** become knowledgeable about a field
3. hands-off approach	____	**c)** visible to the public—even if not ready
4. up and comer	____	**d)** no one advises you in this type of situation
5. give-and-take situation	____	**e)** someone new who has potential

Sellin' is slang for *selling.*
Note that in the written form,
the word must include the *g*.

COMPREHENSION

Part A

■ Answer the following questions.

1. What type of person becomes a protégé in the fashion industry?

_____

2. Why is mentoring especially needed in the fashion industry?

_____

_____

3. Is mentoring common in the fashion industry? ☐ Yes ☐ No

How do you know? _____

4. Can a mentor help a fashion designer succeed, according to Anne Christensen?

☐ Yes   ☐ No

Why or why not? _____

_____

_____

5. What role has Ditty played in Zac Posen's career?

_____

6. How has Giorgio Armani helped young designers?

_____

7. How did Tom Ford recently help young designers?

_____

_____

_____

8. Why does Hal Rubenstein say fashion mentors are needed?

_____

_____

_____

_____

_____

9. What does Hilary Alexander of the *London Telegraph* mean when she says that mentoring in the fashion industry is "a give-and-take situation"?

_____

_____

_____

10. Summarize the listening in one or two sentences.

_____

_____

_____

_____

Part B

■ As you watch the video a second time, match the mentors in the first column with their protégés, according to what is said in the video. Hint: There are eleven matches. The first one is done for you. (Keep in mind that some of the mentors have had more than one protégé, and that one of the protégés has had more than one mentor.

My eLab

Match mentors and protégés from movies and sports and conduct research on mentoring relationships.

MENTORS		PROTÉGÉS
1. Narciso Rodriguez	_h_	a) Yves Saint Laurent
2. Christian Dior	____	b) Francisco Costa
3. Calvin Klein	____	c) Donna Karan
4. Donna Karan	____	d) Jean-Paul Gaultier
5. Ditty	____	e) Christopher Bailey
6. Pierre Cardin	____	f) Narciso Rodriguez
7. Karl Lagerfeld	____	g) Jeremy Scott
8. Anne Klein	____	h) Jason Woo
		i) Zac Posen
		j) Eddie Slaman

FYI

We say "so much knowledge" not "so many knowledge." (For more information on count/non-count nouns, see Unit 10 of the Grammar Guide.)

DISCUSSION

■ Discuss the following questions with a partner.

1. In this example of mentoring from the fashion industry, we see the concept of reciprocity: not only does the protégé benefit, but the mentor does too. Is reciprocity an important element in successful mentoring? Why or why not?

2. Think of at least three ways (big or small) in which you could be of benefit to a mentor, thus creating reciprocity in the relationship.

3. Think back to the Explore activity (page 52) where you and a partner made a list of personality traits that a mentor might have. Do you think that mentors in the fashion industry have these characteristics? Why or why not?

Reading 3.2

What if your field of study could offer you an online avatar as a mentor? You could simply go to your field of study's website, click on "Ask Your Mentor," and up would come an image of your avatar-mentor. He or she (or more appropriately, *it*) would answer any questions that you might have about your program and career path, thus helping you make better decisions about your personal career choices. While finding yourself a real-life mentor would clearly be best, read this article to find out why having an avatar-mentor for your program might work well for you.

An avatar

- Before you read, do the pre-reading discussion activity.

- Read the comprehension questions on pages 67 and 68 before you read the text.

- After you finish reading, answer the vocabulary and comprehension questions.

PRE-READING DISCUSSION

- Discuss the following questions with a partner in order to **activate your prior knowledge** on the subject. (For more information on reading comprehension strategies, see page 189.)

1. What is an avatar?

2. Do you have an avatar? If so, what do you use it for? If not, do you think you would ever want to have one?

3. How are avatars used on the Internet?

Virtual Mentoring: Avatars Make Great Mentors

user: someone who uses something

social networking site: website that focuses on building relationships between people

career path: direction a career develops in

1   An online avatar is a computer **user**'s alter ego, representation or extension of him- or herself. Many of us have seen or used an avatar to play a video game, where the character represents the user in the virtual world of the game. Some of us have even created avatars to act as our "virtual bodies" on **social**
5   **networking sites** like Facebook or in virtual worlds like Second Life. This article will examine the online potential of avatars to be used as mentors for students who may have questions about their **career paths**, course options or the requirements of their ultimate dream jobs. It will theorize that these
10   students would be more likely to go to a website that contained an avatar-mentor connected to their field of study than to take the time to find a real-life mentor. It will also demonstrate that even though nothing can completely match the benefit of a real-life mentor, the attention students would receive from an avatar-mentor would still respond well to their needs.

•••

2 15   There is no doubt that there are benefits to having **guidance** from a career mentor. Various researchers (Allen, et al. 2004; D'Abate and Eddy, 2008; Janasz et al., 2008) have described benefits, such as earlier promotion, higher pay, deeper social integration, increased network and job opportunities, better career satisfaction and improved academic performance. However,
20 finding a real-life mentor, while invaluable, poses certain challenges. Finding a mentor who is an expert in your field, who agrees to work with you and who is a good fit is not easy, and constraints due to busy **schedules** and differing geographical locations make meeting a mentor even more difficult. **According to** Ensher et al. (2003), mentoring over the Internet presents
25 none of the constraints of time, space or geography that real-life mentoring presents. Thus, providing students with the opportunity to go to an online mentor in their field would **address** these difficulties.

3   Moreover, in an experimental study of students learning with avatars, Falloon (2010) found that the **availability** of avatars, whose online characters
30 have been customized to be similar in background, age, looks and dress to their **intended** target audience, "added to [the users'] sense of **ownership** and identity" (114) with the avatars. This customization **boosted** the students' interest and motivation for interacting with the avatar, and led to "enhanced engagement in learning" (116). Consequently, a custom avatar that was
35 designed to appeal specifically to students in, for example, engineering, would theoretically hold a greater appeal for these students than a more generic-looking avatar, and this appeal might even **attract** these students and motivate them to ask more questions and learn more about their fields of study and future careers than otherwise.

4 40   In fact, students in Falloon's study were also less embarrassed to interact with the avatars than they were with real people and asked questions more easily. Dreyfus (2009) reminds us of the *Star Trek* episode where Kirk wants to remain in a virtual **holodeck** world and Picard changes his mind by pointing out that there is no real **risk** in a virtual world (95). Whereas this
45 might be a negative consideration if **one** were planning to live there, as Kirk was, if one was a student who needed answers but was too embarrassed to ask questions, then a low-risk environment would be encouraging.

5   Although mentor-avatar responses come from real-life people, such as mentor volunteers and teachers, having one avatar as the single interface that
50 all students in a field interact with **ensures** that the task of answering the questions doesn't sit too heavily on any one person's shoulders. The benefit to the behind-the-scenes real-life mentors is that any number of experts can share the mentor duties, thereby **splitting** the workload of answering the questions. A further benefit to the students is that the avatar would always
55 present the same, familiar image no matter which of the mentor experts was currently answering their questions.

6   In short, all these factors suggest that students would be more motivated and more likely to go to a website that contains an avatar-mentor specific to their field of study than to take the time to find a real-life mentor and arrange
60 meetings around both of their schedules. For busy students who need advice, having an online avatar-mentor who is an expert in their field of study, who is ready and willing to answer their questions and help them succeed in their fields of study, and who is available without geographical or time constraints, would, if not fully replace a real-life one-on-one mentor, then at least be of
65 much interest and benefit.

(769 words)

•••

guidance: help and advice

According to refers to something stated by someone (usually an expert). Do not say "according to me"; instead, say "in my opinion."

schedule: daily or weekly plan

address: try to solve a problem

availability: obtainability; accessibility

intended: planned for; expected

ownership: feeling or fact of having property

boost: increase

attract: make someone interested

holodeck: Star Trek room where you can view projected 3D holographic images

risk: chance; danger

one: any person; someone

ensure: make sure; make certain

split: divide

Sources: Allen, T.D., et al. "Career Benefits Associated with Mentoring for Protégés: A Meta-Analysis." *Journal of Applied Psychology* 89.1 (2004): 127–136. Print; Brooks, C. and C. McCulloch. "Teachers and other Mythological Creatures." *Networking 2000*. Web. 8 Oct. 2010. <http://nw2000.flexiblelearning.net.au/talkback/p42.htm>; D'Abate, Caroline P. and Erik R. Eddy. "Mentoring as a Learning Tool: Enhancing the Effectiveness of an Undergraduate Business Mentoring Program." *Mentoring & Tutoring: Partnership in Learning* 16.4 (2008): 363–378. Print; de Janasz, Suzanne C., Ellen A. Ensher and Christian Heun. "Virtual Relationships and Real Benefits: Using e-Mentoring to Connect Business Students with Practicing Managers." *Mentoring & Tutoring: Partnership in Learning* 16.4 (2008): 394–411. Print; Dreyfus, H.L. *On the Internet*, 2nd ed. New York: Routledge, 2009. Print; Ensher, E.A., C. Heun, and A. Blanchard. "Online Mentoring and Computer-Mediated Communication: New Directions in Research." *Journal of Vocational Behavior* 63.2 (2003): 264–288. Print; Falloon, Garry. "Using Avatars and Virtual Environments in Learning: What Do They Have to Offer?" *British Journal of Educational Technology* 41.1 (Jan. 2010): 108–122. *Academic Search Premier*, EBSCO host. Web. 11 Oct., 2010; Hillis, K. *Online a Lot of the Time: Ritual, Fetish, Sign*. London: Duke University Press, 2009. Print.

VOCABULARY

Part A

■ Match these transition words with their definitions. Note that some of the definitions work for more than one transition. The line numbers are provided to help you **guess the meaning from context**. (For more information on vocabulary strategies, see page 190.)

TRANSITION WORDS

1. moreover (line 28) ____
2. in fact (line 40) ____
3. although (line 48) ____
4. in short (line 57) ____
5. whereas (line 44) ____
6. consequently (line 34) ____
7. thereby (line 53) ____
8. thus (line 26) ____
9. even though (line 12) ____
10. however (line 19) ____

DEFINITIONS

a) used when you add information that contrasts what you have just said
b) used to emphasize what you have just said
c) used to introduce information that adds to or supports what has previously been said
d) used to introduce a summary and concluding statements
e) used to introduce a result
f) used to say that although something is true of one thing, it is not true of another

Part B

■ Match these expressions with their definitions.

EXPRESSIONS

1. one-on-one (line 64) ____
2. sit too heavily on someone's shoulders (line 51) ____
3. behind the scenes (line 52) ____
4. ready and willing (line 62) ____
5. alter-ego (line 1) ____

DEFINITIONS

a) opposite personality
b) interaction between two people
c) happy to do something
d) in the background; not visible
e) a burden; hard to deal with

Part C

■ Create sentences correctly using each of the following word groupings. The line numbers are provided to help you **guess the meaning from context**.

1. at least (line 64): _____

2. more likely ... than (lines 58–59): _____

3. more ... than otherwise (lines 38–39): _____

4. further (line 54): _____

5. more difficult (line 23): _____

COMPREHENSION

■ Answer the following questions.

1. Which of the following dictionary definitions for *avatar* is used in the article?

a) a person or animal who is really a god in human or animal form

b) a person who represents an idea or quality

c) a picture of a person or animal that represents someone in an online game, chat room, etc.

2. What is one of the benefits that researchers have found about mentoring?

_____

_____

3. What is one of the challenges of having a mentor?

_____

_____

_____

4. Which challenge does not present problems for online mentoring?

_____

5. Who is really giving the advice and answering the questions that the students ask their avatar-mentors?

_____

6. a) How should an avatar be designed to make it more interesting to students?

_____

_____

b) Why?

_____

_____

_____

7. Why does the author refer to Star Trek?

_____

_____

8. What is one benefit for students of using avatars as online mentors?

_____

_____

_____

9. What is one benefit for teachers of using avatars as online mentors?

_____

10. Summarize this article in two or three sentences.

_____

_____

_____

_____

_____

_____

DISCUSSION

■ Discuss the following questions with a partner or in a small group.

1. Have you ever used an online avatar-mentor? (They are often used to help you learn about a new virtual world.)

2. What would the positive aspects of having an online avatar-mentor be for you?

3. What would the negative aspects of having an avatar-mentor be for you?

4. Is it acceptable for teachers or other experts (volunteer mentors) to "hide" behind an avatar personality who may be very different from who they really are? Why or why not?

Listening 🎧

INTERVIEW WITH PROFESSOR JEAN-FRANÇOIS BELISLE

Listen to this interview with Professor Jean-François Belisle, a researcher from Concordia University's Molson School of Business, as he discusses his current exploratory research study on avatars and how people react to them.

■ Before you listen to the interview, do the pre-listening discussion activity and complete the vocabulary exercise.

■ Then read the comprehension exercise on pages 70 and 71 before listening to the interview.

■ Discuss these questions with a partner. This will help you to **activate your prior knowledge** on the subject. (For more information on listening comprehension strategies, see page 205.)

1. Can you think of any online avatars of famous people? Do their avatars have the same personality and physical traits as they do? In what ways are they the same or different? Why do you think certain traits are emphasized while others are minimized?

2. An example of an avatar of a famous person is the controversial *Guitar Hero* avatar of Kurt Cobain. Why do you think the makers of *Guitar Hero* created this avatar? Is his avatar a good representation of him or not? Why or why not?

3. What other reasons can you think of to explain why a company or a person would use an online avatar?

Guitar Hero avatar of Kurt Cobain.

PRE-LISTENING VOCABULARY

Part A

■ Match these words and expressions with their definitions.

WORDS		DEFINITIONS
1. perceive	____	a) having a confident, outgoing character
2. target	____	b) careful and responsible; wanting to do something properly
3. lead to	____	c) object that is being examined or studied
4. trendy	____	d) see or understand something in a particular way
5. bolster	____	e) results
6. extroverted	____	f) have something that belongs to you
7. cue	____	g) word, action or characteristic that signals or shows something
8. conscientious	____	h) up to date; fashionable
9. findings	____	i) improve or support
10. own	____	j) cause

EXPRESSIONS		DEFINITIONS
1. lay language	____	a) fashionable cut
2. stylish hairdo	____	b) person who participates in a specific virtual world
3. Second Life resident	____	c) simple so that someone who is not trained can understand it

Part B

Phrasal verbs are made up of verbs and prepositions. The addition of the preposition to the verb changes the meaning of the verb.

■ **Look up the** following **phrasal verbs** in the dictionary and write down the meanings of the verbs alone and the meanings of the phrasal verbs. (For more information on vocabulary strategies, see page 190.)

1. based on

   a) base: _____

   b) base on: _____

2. filled out

   a) fill: _____

   b) fill out: _____

My eLab

Answer additional questions for "Interview with Professor Jean-François Belisle."

COMPREHENSION

■ Read the headings and questions below. While you listen to the interview, **listen for keyword cues** and **take** clear and complete point-form **notes.**

Listening Comprehension Strategy 3: Note-Taking

Using subject headings helps you to organize and understand what you hear. In note-taking, you write key information under headings in point form and only include details if they help to explain or provide a clear example. You usually don't include small, unnecessary details, and you don't write too much. (For more information on listening comprehension strategies, see page 205.)

Note: In a true note-taking situation, you should determine the subject headings. In this exercise, headings and question prompts are provided to show you how effective note-taking can be when it is well organized.

EXPLORATORY RESEARCH STUDY

Subject

1. What was the subject of the research study? _____

Research questions

2. What questions was the research meant to answer?

   _____

   _____

Participants

3. How old were the participants in the study? _____

4. Who were the participants? _____

5. The participants in phase 1 of the field study were referred to as "targets." How many targets were in the study? _____

6. The participants in phase 2 of the field study were referred to as "perceivers." How many perceivers were in the study? _____

Methodology

7. What were the targets required to do?

_____

_____

_____

_____

8. What were the perceivers required to do?

_____

_____

Results (Findings)

9. The study found that people who are looking at an online avatar (perceivers) are able to perceive certain things about the personality of the avatar owner (target). How do the perceivers do this?

_____

10. What are some examples that Belisle gives to support these findings?

_____

_____

_____

_____

Implications

11. What implications does Belisle believe his research suggests for companies who are currently using different avatars and serving different segments of the market?

_____

12. What two examples does Belisle give to support these implications?

_____

_____

_____

_____

_____

> **FYI**
>
> In this study, Professor Belisle talks about the marketing concepts of segmentation and social demographic profiling. Segmentation is about dividing the market into segments according to the buying habits or personality traits of customers. For more information about social demographic profiling, see Unit 6 (page 137) and Unit 7 (page 172).

> **FYI**
>
> The interviewee, who speaks English as a second language, understandably has some trouble pronouncing the noun *conscientiousness*, which is pronounced with the emphasis on the second and third syllables: con/SHI/EN/shus/ness.

Pronouncing *th*

The letter combination *th* has two pronunciations in English: sometimes it is pronounced /θ/, as in *think*, and sometimes it is pronounced /ð/, as in *they*. This is true whether it is at the beginning, middle or end of a word.

Note: *th* is never pronounced with a /t/, /d/, /s/ or /z/ sound.

Part A

■ Listen to the following words with *th* and repeat them. Each word will be pronounced twice.

1. either /ð/
2. birth /θ/
3. those /ð/
4. clothing /ð/
5. thanks /θ/

6. breathe /ð/
7. both /θ/
8. booth /θ/
9. theory /θ/
10. therefore /ð/

Part B

■ Now listen to the following pairs of sentences and decide which sentence belongs with each picture by circling *a* or *b* under the picture the sentence describes. You will hear each sentence twice.

1. closing vs. clothing

a   b

a   b

2. team vs. theme

a   b

a   b

3. breed vs. breathe

a   b

a   b

4. boat vs. both

a   b

a   b

FYI

The expression *get the boot* means "to be fired from a job or kicked out of a relationship."

5. boot vs. booth

a   b

a   b

6. teary vs. theory

a   b

a   b

GENERAL VOCABULARY LIST

These are the words and phrases that you should know after completing this unit.
Remind yourself of their meanings by writing down their definitions or translations.

DEFINITIONS/TRANSLATIONS

1. apprenticeship
2. avatar
3. behaviour
4. conscientious
5. delivery
6. edge
7. endow
8. findings
9. funding
10. gain
11. goal setting
12. guidance
13. however
14. learn the ropes
15. mentor
16. overlook
17. own
18. protégé
19. rise
20. risk
21. threatening
22. trendy
23. up and comer
24. widespread
25. winner

Review the vocabulary from this unit.

"One can never consent to creep, when one feels an impulse to soar!"
—Helen Keller

"To get where you want to go, you should talk to someone who has been there." —Anonymous cited in tweet, Andrew G.R. "A Blog Mentor Is Hard to Find." *The Blog Herald.* 9 March 2010. Web. 29 Nov. 2010.

Vocabulary Assignment

■ Find ten personality traits (in adjective form) that are valued highly in your field of study. Note that they should be new words, not words that you already know. To do this, look up French adjectives that you believe are valued highly in your field of study, and then find their English translations. Make sure that the words you choose aren't cognates in your own language, and that you have spelled them correctly.

■ **Look up the definitions** of the adjectives in a dictionary and copy them down.

■ Exchange your list with another student and test each other on the spellings and/or meanings of the adjectives.

Field-Specific Vocabulary List

	ENGLISH DEFINITIONS
1. _____	_____
2. _____	_____
3. _____	_____
4. _____	_____
5. _____	_____
6. _____	_____
7. _____	_____
8. _____	_____
9. _____	_____
10. _____	_____

Writing Assignment

■ Choose one of the following topics to write about (or perhaps your teacher will assign one). Be sure to use at least five words from the General Vocabulary List on page 75 and five words from the Field-Specific Vocabulary List on this page, and highlight them.

1. Writing a Request Letter

■ Write a letter of request (approximately 200 words) to the expert you have researched and ask him or her to meet with you. Explain that you would like to explore a potential mentoring relationship and/or ask some questions about how he or she rose to the top of his or her field. Whether a request letter is mailed or attached to an e-mail, it should still be written in a formal letter structure. (For more information on writing a request letter and formal letter structure, see pages 193 and 194.)

2. Writing Time Tweets

■ Write regular Twitter updates on what your expert is doing and why he or she is doing it. Act as if you were the person—stay in character. Write at least ten tweets in total over a period of one week. Note that an actual Internet tweet cannot be more than 140 characters long, including spaces.

■ In addition to the ten tweets (each one with a date and time attached), provide a 200- to 250-word justification of your tweets, explaining how your research influenced the content of your tweets.

3. Writing a Survey Report

■ Conduct a survey in your field of study to see which mentor personality traits are most important in your field. The most important traits you find can be used in your Speaking assignment. Your survey should ask eight to ten questions (yes/no and multiple choice questions are best) of at least ten people. If you wish, you may ask your survey questions in an online forum related to your field of study.

Note: Generally speaking, a survey of this size is too small to be considered accurate. If this bothers you, you may wish to prepare additional copies of your survey and ask as many people as you and your fellow group members are prepared to take the time to analyze.

■ Write a 200- to 250-word survey report detailing your findings. (For more information on writing survey reports and a sample template, see pages 197 and 199.)

■ Make sure that your report writing is error-free by **proofreading your text**.

Revision Strategy 6: Proofreading

> Proofreading is the final stage in the editing process. After you write your text, put it aside for a day or two. Then proofread it carefully, looking for surface errors in capitalization, punctuation, verb tenses, articles and prepositions. Finally, check it for spelling errors and misused words. (For more information on revision strategies, see page 204.)

Speaking Assignment

1. Creating and Presenting an Avatar Mentor for Your Field of Study

In Reading 3.2 and in the Listening activity on page 68, you looked at some reasons for creating online avatars to represent yourself or another person and to help promote or sell a product or service.

■ Use your answers to the questions about personality and physical traits in the Expansion exercise on page 72 to create an avatar that will act as an online mentor for people interested in studying in your field. Also, if you did Option 3 of the Writing Assignment above, consult the results from your survey.

■ Draw a picture of your avatar or use an online website to help you build one. (Many online sites provide aid in designing avatars.)

■ ■ ■

- Be prepared to explain your avatar and how he or she relates to your field of study to your group in a two- to three-minute oral presentation. Make sure to describe each of your avatar's appearance and personality traits and to explain how he or she will behave. (For information on presenting oral presentations, see page 206.)

2. Presenting Your Research Information about an Expert in Your Field

Prepare a two- to three-minute oral presentation of your research findings on an expert in your field of study (from the Expansion exercise on page 58). Make sure to

- provide a brief introduction to your expert, including why you chose to research him or her;

- explain your expert's academic and career background as well as his or her current position in detail;

- conclude by explaining what you've learned about working in your field from researching your expert. (For information on preparing oral presentations, see page 206.)

3. Describing Avatars

The companies below want to have an avatar on their website to interface with a specific segment of the market. As the Listening activity on page 68 suggests, it is important for a company to choose the right personality or look for its avatar so that it gives people the right impression of their company. For example, a travel agency would probably not want to have an overly conservative-looking avatar who appears to be introverted and shy as its spokesperson. Think of a possible avatar for one of these companies and explain your choice in a two- to three-minute presentation. Make sure to describe each of the avatar's personality and physical traits. (For information on preparing oral presentations, see page 206.)

- Travel Canada
- The Design Centre
- Weight Lifters Incorporated
- Association of Safe Drivers of Canada
- Jeans and More
- Burger Heaven

My eLab

My eLab Documents includes additional research assignments to help you learn more about your field of study.

Millennials @ Work

Boomers and Gen-Xers, make way for the Millennials! Workers of this new generation born between 1981 and 2005 bring with them fresh insights, new skills and a few challenges. This generation is your generation and in this unit you will explore how you fit into the workplace. You will learn how to brand yourself for the job market, as well as how to apply some new trends to your résumé and cover letter.

The Millennials are also known as the Millennial Generation, Generation Next, Net Generation or Echo Boomers.

My eLab

Go to My eLab Documents for additional vocabulary exercises based on Constance Patterson's *Generation Stereotypes*.

EXPLORE

Psychologist Constance Patterson, PhD, in her article "Generation Stereotypes,"[1] indicates that there are differences in work ethics and values among Baby Boomers (born between 1946 and 1960), Gen-Xers (born between 1961 and 1980), and Millennials (born between 1981 and 2005).

■ Look at the following five statements. Which generational group do you think each statement refers to? Circle the letters of the correct answers.

1. They are often considered to be overly ambitious workaholics.
   a) Baby Boomers   **b)** Gen-Xers   **c)** Millennials

2. They are good multi-taskers, but they require supervision and structure at work.
   a) Baby Boomers   **b)** Gen-Xers   **c)** Millennials

3. If they feel that the work they are being asked to do is not meaningful, they will likely refuse to do it.
   a) Baby Boomers   **b)** Gen-Xers   **c)** Millennials

4. They reject the concept of "paying dues" and expect immediate rewards instead.
   a) Baby Boomers   **b)** Gen-Xers   **c)** Millennials

5. They tend to be skeptical and prefer to do things themselves rather than trust another person to get the job done.
   a) Baby Boomers   **b)** Gen-Xers   **c)** Millennials

■ Now that your teacher has shared the correct answers with you, discuss the following questions in groups.

1. Were you surprised by any of the answers to the statements? If so, which ones surprised you?

2. What characteristics do you think are shared by most Millennials? Try to come up with a list of 8 to 10 characteristics.

3. Look at the list of characteristics you came up with in question 2. Which of these characteristics describe you?

Reading 4.1

As the Baby Boomer generation is getting set to retire, the Millennial generation is preparing to enter the workforce. In *Great Expectations: Do Millennials Expect Too Much Too Soon?*, Caroline George looks at how the Millennial Generation is changing the workplace and how employers can prepare themselves for these changes.

■ First, complete the pre-reading vocabulary exercise.

■ Then read the comprehension questions on pages 83 and 84 before you read the text.

---

1. Patterson, Constance. "Generation Stereotypes." *Monitor on Psychology* 36.6 (2005). Print.

■ Try to **guess the meaning** of the words **from context** and match them with their definitions. The line numbers will help you find the words in the text. (For more information on vocabulary strategies, see page 190.)

WORDS			EXPRESSIONS
1. product of	(line 6)	____	**a)** person who is looking for employment
2. raise	(line 10)	____	**b)** decide the position of someone or something on a list based on quality or importance
3. openness	(line 44)	____	
4. goal	(line 40)	____	**c)** result of
5. co-founder	(line 30)	____	**d)** co-worker; classmate; associate
6. colleague	(line 29)	____	**e)** quality of being honest and willing to talk about things
7. jobseeker	(line 31)	____	
8. feedback	(line 46)	____	**f)** wanting a lot of love and attention
9. needy	(line 48)	____	**g)** opinion about the quality of someone or something
10. rank	(line 65)	____	
			h) one of a group of people who started a business
			i) something that you hope to achieve in the future
			j) look after your children and help them grow

Great Expectations: Do Millennials Expect Too Much Too Soon?

By Caroline George

1   **Money driven** or money conscious? Egotistical or self-confident? So-called Millennials are often criticized for having unrealistic expectations when it comes to their careers. They want a stable, well-paid job and they want it NOW! But for a generation **inundated** by stories about overnight successes like
5   Facebook's Mark Zuckerberg, are their expectations so unrealistic? "Millennial employees are just a product of their time," says Karyn Gordon, a leading North American authority on understanding and motivating Millennials. "They are very ambitious; have high expectations of themselves, and their parents have high expectations of them as well. Because of the culture they've
10   been raised in, Millennials tend to want things quickly and people may perceive this as impatience. But you must remember—this is a generation that has been basically raised on instant gratification, and like it or not, that **mindset** has been transferred into the workplace.

2   Max Valiquette, youth culture expert and president of Youthography, a
15   youth marketing consulting agency based in Toronto, attributes the

money driven: strongly motivated to make money

inundated: overwhelmed with too much of something

mindset: fixed mental attitude or inclination

•••

Millennials' "want it now" attitude to a lack of on-the-job experience. "Typically, an introductory salary for a recent college graduate ranges between $30,000 and $40,000. Graduates tell themselves they have just started and are maybe not 100 percent aware of how to adjust their expectations. It has less to do with any **sense of entitlement** than it does with a lack of real workplace experience." So if it is not about salary, what do Millennials want? "What they really want is a little respect," says Gordon. "We have to change our attitude and ask what we can learn from them and vice-versa. They did not choose to be born in this time. They are simply a product of the environment that they have been raised in. We should realize they are ambitious with fantastic goals, but one of the highest values they seek is respect—not just from their friends but also work colleagues and employers," Gordon says.

3 30   Ryan Healy, 25, co-founder of Brazen Careerist, a social networking site for Millennial jobseekers, agrees. "We are team players and grew up playing on sports teams and learned how to be in groups while in school. We were taught teamwork our entire lives and subsequently aren't just after salaries and promotions, but after feeling good about what we do."

4   In general, the media say they are selfish and want to **move up the ladder** fast, but really Millennials are just looking for a job that they enjoy and that matches their needs and goals. They are making their voices heard, more so than previous generations, and they're just asking for something everybody wants: a good job.

5   "But a good job isn't enough. **New hires** want openness and feedback too," adds Healy.

6 45   "Transparency is critical," he says. "Every time I speak to employers about Millennials, my main message is constant feedback. They want to know how they're doing, how the company they are working for is doing, and it's not because they're needy." "Young workers have lots to offer, despite their differences," adds Valiquette. "They're certainly a group that's grown up with very different work habits from their parent's generation. They are very **self-directed** and prefer to do their thing on their own schedule although they will always come back to a group environment, collaborate and connect with other people whether in real or virtual time," he says. "In reality, this generation is simply trying to choose what they think is the right path to financial and personal success," says Healy. So do Millennials expect too much too soon? Well, that all depends on who you talk to and what generation they are from. For what was *soon* twenty years ago, may not be *soon enough* today.

7

> **The Truth about Millennials**
>
> - Seventy percent are uncertain about where they want to work after they graduate.
>
> - Fifty-four percent would like to be hired into an organization where they could spend their entire career.

- Thirty-two percent expect to be promoted in one to 1.5 years.

65
- Fifty-two percent rank "good people to work with" as the number-one deciding factor for taking a job.

— Statistics from *Learning to Work Report 2008* (Brainstorm Consulting, *www.brainstorm.ca*)

(697 words)

Source: Adapted from George, Caroline. "Great Expectations." JobPostings.ca. 5 Oct. 2008. Web. 4 Nov. 2010. <http://www.jobpostings.net/article/great-expectations.>

COMPREHENSION

■ Answer the following questions using complete sentences.

1. In your opinion, is it realistic for a Millennial graduate to expect to get a stable, well-paid job upon graduation?

☐ Yes   ☐ No

Explain.

_____

2. What could explain the Millennials' high expectations?

_____

_____

3. What role does Karyn Gordon see culture playing in the Millennials' "want it now" attitude?

_____

_____

4. Does Max Valiquette agree with Gordon's explanation for why Millennials want things quickly?

☐ Yes   ☐ No

Explain.

_____

5. Rather than money, what do Millennials really want from their employers?

_____

6. According to Ryan Healy, what makes Millennials good team players?

_____

_____

_____

7. What do Millennials want that previous generations have also wanted?

_____

8. How were their parents' work habits different from their own?

_____

_____

9. Why do you think 70 percent of Millennials are uncertain about where they want to work after they graduate?

_____

_____

_____

_____

10. Think of a reason to explain why working with good people is more important to a Millennial than making lots of money.

_____

_____

_____

_____

DISCUSSION

■ Discuss the following questions in small groups.

1. Would you like to work for the same company or organization your entire career? Why or why not?

2. How long do you think it is reasonable to work at a place before you get a promotion?

3. What would be an appropriate name for the next generation in the workforce (those students born between 2005 and 2025)?

VOCABULARY

■ Working with a partner, **scan** the article again for qualities associated with the Millennial Generation. Determine which qualities are negative and which are positive and complete the chart below. The first quality has been done for you.

POSITIVE QUALITIES	NEGATIVE QUALITIES
money conscious	

Listening 4.1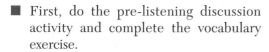

INTERVIEW WITH DON TAPSCOTT

What does it mean to grow up digital? CBC *Spark*'s Nora Young interviews Don Tapscott, leading Canadian business consultant and author of *Grown Up Digital: How the Net Generation Is Changing Your World* (2008). Young begins her interview by asking Tapscott about the notion of transparency in relation to the Millennial Generation. Note that instead of Millennials, Tapscott refers to the generation as Netgeners.

■ First, do the pre-listening discussion activity and complete the vocabulary exercise.

■ Then read the instructions in Part A of the comprehension exercise on page 86 before you listen to the interview.

Millennials are changing our world.

PRE-LISTENING DISCUSSION

■ Answer these questions with a partner or in a small group in order to **activate your prior knowledge** of this subject. (For more information on listening comprehension strategies, refer to page 205.)

1. Where do you want to work when you graduate?

2. What is your number-one consideration for accepting a job offer?

3. How do you think the workplace has changed over the last ten years?

PRE-LISTENING VOCABULARY

■ Guess the meaning of the following words and expressions and match them with their definitions.

WORDS	DEFINITIONS
1. ban _____	**a)** someone who has invested money into something and therefore is affected by its success or failure
2. cranky _____	**b)** say that something must not be done, seen, used, etc.
3. shift _____	**c)** important change in which the usual way of thinking or doing something is replaced by another way of thinking or doing something
4. wisely _____	**d)** doing something based on good judgment
5. stakeholder _____	**e)** bad-tempered

EXPRESSIONS		DEFINITIONS
1. coming of age	____	a) as a result of; because of
2. generational firewall	____	b) alert and eager
3. fissures and clashes	____	c) barrier that prevents understanding
4. in virtue of	____	d) reaching maturity
5. bright-eyed and bushy-tailed	____	e) arguments; disagreements

COMPREHENSION

Part A

■ Listen to the interview and **take notes** on what you hear as you listen. Use the following keywords to help you. (For more information on listening comprehension strategies, see page 205.)

Netgeners and work: _____

_____

Workplace transparency: _____

_____

Workplace tensions: _____

_____

Issue of privacy: _____

_____

Advice for generations: _____

_____

■ Now listen a second time. Before you listen, make sure you read the following questions and highlight keywords.

■ While you listen to the interview again, **listen for keyword cues** and answer the questions. (For more information on listening comprehension strategies, see page 205.)

■ Once you have answered the questions, compare your answers with a partner's.

My eLab ✎

Answer additional questions for "Interview with Don Tapscott."

1. Why is transparency a big deal for Netgeners?

_____

2. What three things can happen at the workplace when you increase transparency?

_____

_____

3. What do Netgeners bring with them to the job?

_____

_____

4. What is a generational firewall?

_____

5. According to Nora Young, what do Netgeners want or expect that could be contributing to tension at the workplace?

_____

6. What quality is important to our understanding of privacy?

_____

_____

7. Who is responsible for explaining the importance of privacy to Netgeners?

_____

8. What advice does Tapscott give to Boomers and Gen-Xers in the workforce?

_____

9. What advice does Tapscott have for Netgeners?

_____

_____

My eLab
Practise listening for French/ English cognates in Listening 4.1.

10. What three simple rules can you follow to help you get along in the workforce?

_____

_____

_____

DISCUSSION

■ Discuss the following statements in groups. Do you agree with the statements? Why? Why not?

1. Time-wasting websites such as Facebook and Twitter should be blocked at work.

2. Older, more experienced workers should be in positions of authority. After all, they have put in the hours and have the expertise to know what works and what doesn't work.

Reading 4.2

Who are you? What do you have to offer? What is your area of expertise? If you can confidently answer these questions, you are probably ready to create your own personal brand. Read this text to find out how to do it.

■ Complete the pre-reading vocabulary exercise on page 88.

■ Then take time to read the comprehension questions on page 91 before you read the text.

Part A

■ **Identify the part of speech** of the following words and **guess their meaning from** their **context** in the reading.

Vocabulary Strategy 5: Identifying Parts of Speech

Being able to recognize whether a word is a noun, a verb, an adjective or an adverb from its context will help you find the word's correct definition in the dictionary and assist your overall comprehension of a text. (For more information on vocabulary strategies, see page 190.)

■ Then **look up the words** in the dictionary to see if your guesses were correct. The line numbers will help you find the words in the text.

1. savvy (line 4)

Part of speech: _____

Definition: _____

2. guru (line 19)

Part of speech: _____

Definition: _____

_____

3. data (line 40)

Part of speech: _____

Definition: _____

4. exude (line 53)

Part of speech: _____

Definition: _____

5. sloppy (line 57)

Part of speech: _____

Definition: _____

Part B

■ The following words and expressions have more than one meaning. Try to **identify the part of speech** of the words from their context in the reading to help you determine their meaning. The line numbers will help you find the words in the text.

1. stand out (line 22)

Part of speech: _____

a) be stubborn or resistant   **b)** be very noticeable   **c)** be outside

2. shortcut (line 5)

Part of speech: _____

a) shorter way   **b)** short hairstyle   **c)** path
to achieve something

3. constant (line 15)

Part of speech: _____

a) continuing without pause   **b)** permanent   **c)** something that does not change

4. vacuum (line 65)

Part of speech: _____

a) use a vacuum cleaner   **b)** empty space   **c)** machine used to clean rugs

5. spin (line 68)

Part of speech: _____

a) cause to turn around rapidly   **b)** invent a story   **c)** bias

Brand YOU

By Simon Payn

1   Donald Trump equals money. Oprah equals empathy. Both have created successful personal brands—when you think of their name, you know immediately what they stand for. And now personal brands are moving into the workplace as savvy job hunters learn that associating their name with a
5   defined field of expertise is a shortcut to getting hired. So consider this: when a **recruiter** sees your name, what do they think of?

recruiter: person who finds new people to work in a company

2   **1. Subtitle:** _____
People are managing their own careers rather than having their career taken care of by an employer, according to William Aruda, executive coach and
10   author of *Career Distinction: Stand Out by Building Your Brand*.

3   "The speed at which we move through companies and the change that is happening in companies is accelerating. This is not to say job **stability** is decreasing. Rather, the length of time you may be working for a specific employer may be shorter than it was, say, a decade ago."

stability: condition of being steady and not changing

4 15   The one constant in the new world of work is your brand and your reputation, according to Aruda. And in this new world, we won't be the hunters looking for a new job—we are going to become the hunted. "So we need to make sure that our visibility is such that we are getting found."

5   Marketing guru Laura Ries, author of *The Origin of Brands*, says,
20   "What gets you ahead is having focus, being a specialist and being known for being very good in one thing. Being kind of OK in a few things is not going to help you stand out because most jobs today are extremely specific." So how can you find your brand and share it with the world? Aruda has a three-step process that jobseekers can use.

6 25   **2. Subtitle:** _____
First is the extraction phase, which is used to find what makes you different and what makes you compelling to others.

• • •

7

"Look at yourself from two angles," Aruda says. "Introspectively—who am I? What do I want? What are my passions, my vision and my career goals? Get an understanding of who you are and what motivates you."

8

At the same time, get an external perspective by asking people around you about your reputation—your strengths and weaknesses. What are your skills? "You need to understand the baseline brand you have before you **embark** on **aligning** it with who you really are and what it is that you want to communicate to the world," says Aruda.

9

3. Subtitle: _____

You need to choose a niche. The smaller you make your **target audience**, the larger your brand will be for them and the easier it will be for you to get your message to those people. Put the data you have collected into one sentence that says what your brand is all about. Next comes the express phase, which is all about getting your message out there. First, go back to your goal. Say, for example, you want to be working in sales for a major company, think of all the people you need to influence who are members of your brand community.

10

"You might know these people by name or job title," says Aruda. "Be clear about who they are; then say, 'here's my message— here are the people I need to get it to.'"

11

4. Subtitle: _____

The final phase of Aruda's three branding phases is the exude phase. This is when you really start to live and breathe your brand. "Everything that surrounds you should communicate your brand message," he says.

12

Your personal appearance needs to reflect your brand. "If you are all organized, structured and super dependable, looking sloppy or wearing wild, out-of-control clothes may not communicate the same brand message," Aruda says. Jobseekers also need to think of their brand identity system. "Have your name stylized as a logo; [create] a **tagline**, if it is appropriate. Think of a colour that represents your brand and use it consistently."

13

5. Subtitle: _____

"A **network** extends your brand for you," says Aruda. "None of us is successful in a vacuum… The more you give to members of your network what they need, the more they are going to be there for you when you need them."

14

Aruda says a brand must be based on authenticity—it's not spin or packaging. "It's about being yourself, understanding what makes you exceptional and compelling, and using that to stand out from everyone else who does what you do," he says. It's about creating your own unique promise of value. What more could an employer want?

(743 words)

embark: start something, especially something new, difficult or exciting

aligning: organizing or changing something so that it has the right relationship to something else

target audience: limited group, area, etc., that a plan or idea is aimed at

tagline: phrase associated with an individual, organization or product; a slogan

network: other people involved in the same kind of work

■ Answer the following questions.

■ Then compare your answers with a partner's.

1. How is today's workplace different from the workplace of the past?

_____

_____

2. What two things remain the same in the new world of work?

_____

3. How are jobs today different from those in the past?

_____

4. What do you need to do before you can communicate your brand to the outside world?

_____

_____

5. What are the three steps to developing your brand identity?

_____

6. Why does Aruda suggest that it is best to have a small target audience for your brand?

_____

_____

7. What role does networking play in establishing your brand?

_____

8. What is a brand identity system?

_____

_____

9. What final piece of advice does Aruda give the reader?

_____

10. Below are the original subtitles for "Brand YOU." Try to place them on the right blanks in the article.

a) Use Your Network

b) What Makes You Compelling?

c) Live and Breathe Your Brand

d) Who Are You Targeting?

e) The Changing Workplace

■ Using the five subtitles in Question 10 as an outline, write a one-paragraph summary (100–150 words) of the reading "Brand YOU." When you have finished writing your paragraph, exchange it with a partner and **peer review** each other's work. (For more information on revision strategies, see page 204.)

Listening 4.2

NEW TRENDS IN RÉSUMÉ WRITING[2]

While the traditional paper résumé is still often used to apply for a job, many experts claim it alone is no longer sufficient to guarantee you an interview. Listen to the interview between Cégep de l'Outaouais Student Radio host Sebastien Morel and career specialist Wendy Neufeld as they discuss the new trends in résumés.

■ First, do the pre-listening discussion activity and complete the vocabulary exercise.

■ Then take time to read the comprehension questions before you listen.

PRE-LISTENING DISCUSSION

■ Discuss the following questions in groups to **activate your prior knowledge** of the subject. (For more information about listening comprehension strategies, see page 205.)

1. When was the last time you applied for a job? What kind of job were you applying for? Did you get the job?

2. Describe your résumé. What did you include on it? Did it have different sections? If so, what were they?

3. What other methods can you use to apply for a job?

PRE-LISTENING VOCABULARY

■ Guess the meaning of the following words and expressions and match them with their definitions.

WORDS/EXPRESSIONS		DEFINITIONS
1. over-the-top	____	a) way to express your thoughts and feelings
2. bullet point	____	b) improve something
3. channel	____	c) extreme or unreasonable
4. peruse	____	d) word or phrase in a list with a symbol in front of it
5. proliferation	____	e) look quickly at someone or something
6. key	____	f) stop working, usually at a certain age
7. enhance	____	g) read something, especially in a careful way
8. glance	____	h) part of a plan, action, etc., that ensures its success
9. retire	____	i) short, with no unnecessary words
10. concise	____	j) increase in the amount or number of something

---

2. This interview is based on "Resume Writing Trends." Podcast. Podfeed.net. 4 Apr. 2011. Web. 11 May 2011. <http://www.podfeed. net/episode/BEST+OF+Resume+Writing+Trends/2987182>.

COMPREHENSION

■ Answer the following questions.

1. What is the title of Wendy's most recent book?

_____

2. What is Wendy's first piece of advice for jobseekers?

_____

3. Why may some employers lose interest in long résumés?

_____

_____

FYI

In English, the word *résumé* means "curriculum vitae," not "summary."

4. How have cover letters changed? What can explain this change?

_____

_____

5. Is it better to attach your résumé to the e-mail or include it in the body of the letter that you are sending?

_____

FYI

Both a career summary and a branding statement communicate your identity and the values you offer.

6. What are the two attributes of a good résumé?

_____

_____

7. What's the difference between a career summary and an objective?

_____

_____

_____

8. What is more important—a résumé's visual appearance or its content? Explain.

_____

9. List five rules regarding a résumé's visual appearance?

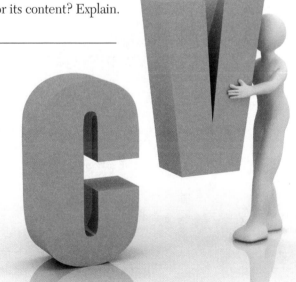

_____

_____

_____

_____

_____

10. What does Wendy mean by the "perusability factor"?

_____

_____

■ In small groups, create a checklist of dos and don'ts for résumé writing. When your list is complete, compare it to another group's list.

Dos   **Don'ts**

1. _____   1. _____
2. _____   2. _____
3. _____   3. _____
4. _____   4. _____
5. _____   5. _____

CONNECT WITH GRAMMAR

Using the Simple Past Tense

When writing your résumé, use the simple present tense to describe the duties that you currently perform. The duties that you performed at past jobs should be in the simple past tense.

How to Form the Simple Past Tense

With the exception of regular verbs ending in -e, -y or consonants preceded by a vowel, we add -ed to all regular verbs to form the simple past tense.

- If the present form of a regular verb ends in -e, we add -d to form the simple past tense.

- If the present form of a regular verb ends in -y preceded by a consonant (e.g., *apply*), we change the -y to -i and add -ed to form the simple past tense (e.g., *applied*).

- If the present form of a regular verb ends with a consonant preceded by a vowel (e.g., *plan*), we double the final consonant and add -ed to form the simple past (e.g., *planned*).

A list of irregular verb forms (verbs that do not end in -ed in the simple past tense) can be found in Appendix B of the Grammar Guide.

Part A

■ If you want your résumé to get noticed, use power verbs. Power verbs can make a dull or unimpressive résumé stand out. Put the verbs below into the simple past tense. Pay attention—there may be a few irregular verbs.

1. assist _____   8. increase _____
2. attain _____   9. lead _____
3. create _____   10. manage _____
4. develop _____   11. motivate _____
5. establish _____   12. organize _____
6. head _____   13. produce _____
7. implement _____   14. supervise _____

•••

Part B

■ Using a dictionary, write a definition for each of the fourteen verbs from Part A on a separate sheet of paper. Then choose ten of the verbs and create simple past tense sentences that illustrate the verbs' meanings.

Refer to Unit 2 of the Grammar Guide for further explanations and practice on the simple past tense.

PRONUNCIATION 🎧

Pronouncing the Simple Past Tense of Regular Verbs

The simple past tense of regular verbs (with an -*ed* ending) has three distinct pronunciations:

/əd/ as in *wanted*°   /t/ as in *walked*   /d/ as in *enjoyed*

° Pronounced as an extra syllable.

Part A

■ As you listen to the power verbs, indicate whether you hear a /əd/, /t/ or /d/ sound by writing "ed," "t" or "d" on the spaces provided.

1. attained ____	6. motivated ____	11. created ____
2. developed ____	7. implemented ____	12. established ____
3. increased ____	8. organized ____	13. assisted ____
4. produced ____	9. headed ____	14. maintained ____
5. supervised ____	10. managed ____	15. modified ____

Part B

■ Answer the following questions.

1. What rule can you establish to help you figure out when to use an /əd/ sound at the end of a regular simple past tense verb?

_____

_____

2. What rule can you establish to help you figure out when to use a /t/ sound at the end of a regular simple past tense verb?

_____

_____

3. What rule(s) can you establish to help you figure out when to use a /d/ sound at the end of a regular simple past tense verb?

_____

_____

_____

Reading 4.3

PART ONE: THE RÉSUMÉ

A common concern among new graduates who do not have a lengthy employment history is figuring out what information to put on their résumé. However, employment history is just one area that employers look at when seeking potential employees. How you present yourself on paper can say much more about who you are and what you have to offer.

- First, complete the pre-reading vocabulary exercise.

- Then read the autobiography "My Story" by Stephanie Plouffe and complete the comprehension exercise on page 97.

- Finally, exchange your book with a partner and do the discussion activity on page 97.

PRE-READING VOCABULARY

- Try to **guess the meaning** of the following words **from context** and match them with their definitions. The line numbers will help you find the words in the text.

WORDS			DEFINITIONS
1. thrive	(line 4)	____	**a)** existing before something else
2. internship	(line 5)	____	**b)** someone whose job is to carry out financial transactions in a store, shop, etc.
3. volunteer	(line 7)	____	
4. drive	(line 11)	____	**c)** period of time when one works
5. be comprised of			**d)** determination and energy to succeed
	(line 12)	____	**e)** fill a supply of something
6. prior	(line 14)	____	**f)** become very successful; grow; mature
7. cashier	(line 16)	____	**g)** unpaid job arrangement that gives a student experience
8. shift	(line 22)	____	
9. stock	(line 24)	____	**h)** consist of particular parts, groups, etc.
10. build upon	(line 28)	____	**i)** offer to do something without expecting any reward
			j) add to; increase

My Story

By Stephanie Plouffe

1   I was born in Trois-Rivières, Québec, on August 4, 1989. When I was five years old, my family moved to 1098 St. Laurent Boulevard in Montréal, Québec. I have recently graduated from the Cégep du Vieux Montréal in the Mechanical Engineering program. I thrived at the Cégep and received
5   several academic and leadership awards. I've just completed a six-week internship for Perigrine Engineering in downtown Montréal. I loved it!

2   I enjoy competitive swimming and have been volunteering for the YMCA for almost three years. In addition to swimming, I am an avid cyclist in the summers and love to snowboard in the winter.

...

3 10   My parents play an important part in my life as well as my successes. They drive me to want to excel in all I do and be a good role model for others. My life so far is comprised of a wonderful family, great friends and a small successful bicycle repair business. I started my business when I was eighteen years old. Prior to that, I worked

15   at McDonald's as a line cook for a summer, and later as a cashier for Rona.

4   Even though I only worked for a year at Rona, I really enjoyed the responsibility

20   I was given there. I had to count the cash at the beginning of my shift, and again at the end of my shift. I was responsible for helping customers, stocking inventory, and

25   I even worked in customer service for a couple of months. Having had this experience and owning and managing my own shop, I feel I am now ready to build

upon my skills as a manager and start my professional career. My ultimate

30   goal is to one day be able to own my own bike store. I believe that my future holds only what I put into it, and that life is based on hard work, education and responsibility. I hope you have enjoyed reading my autobiography.

(321 words)

FYI

In English, we say: *training* NOT *formation*; *qualifications* NOT *trainings*; *experience* NOT *experiences*; *skills* NOT *competences*; *computer* (skills) NOT *informatic*; *internship* or *on-the-job training* NOT *stage*; *high school* NOT *secondary*; *degree* NOT *diplome*.

COMPREHENSION

■ Complete Stephanie Plouffe's résumé based on the information that she provides in her autobiography. Use the template provided on page 98. Refer to some of the power verbs on page 94 to help you.

DISCUSSION

■ Exchange books with a partner and answer the following questions. Once you have answered the questions, discuss your answers with your partner.

1. Does your partner's résumé seem complete?

2. Is the impression that he or she gives of the applicant accurate? Why or why not?

3. Is all the pertinent information included on the résumé? If your answer is *no*, what important information is left out?

4. Is the applicant's educational information and work experience placed in the right order on the résumé (most recent information placed first)?

5. Would you hire the applicant? Explain your answer.

EXPANSION

■ On a separate sheet of paper, list at least five skills that you have developed in <u>each</u> of the following areas: education, work/internships and volunteer/extracurricular activities. Use power verbs (see examples on page 94) to develop one-line summaries.

• Example: *Supervised a mentoring program in my final year at the Cégep.* (Don't use *I*.)

RÉSUMÉ TEMPLATE

NAME: _____

ADDRESS: _____
_____
_____

CAREER SUMMARY: _____
_____
_____

SKILLS: _____
_____
_____

EDUCATION: _____
_____
_____

WORK EXPERIENCE: _____
_____
_____
_____
_____
_____
_____
_____
_____

ACHIEVEMENTS: _____
_____
_____

VOLUNTEER WORK: _____
_____
_____

INTERESTS: _____
_____
_____

PART TWO: THE COVER LETTER

When you send a résumé, it is important to introduce yourself first with a cover letter. Although nowadays you are most likely to apply for jobs via e-mail, the letter that you attach still requires a formal letter format. You will now read the cover letter that Stéphanie Plouffe has written responding to a job ad.

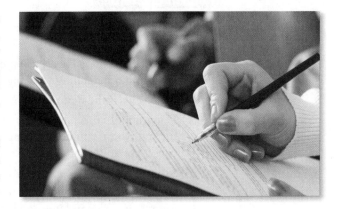

■ A cover letter generally has ten parts. Look over Stephanie's cover letter below and then focus on the letter's form by completing the comprehension exercise on page 100.

Stephanie's Cover Letter

Stephanie Plouffe
1098 St. Laurent Boulevard
Montréal, Québec
H2W 1Y4

June 17, 2011

Mr. G. Gibson
Director of Engineering
CPR Engineering Group
8268 Pie IX Boulevard
Montréal, Québec
H1Z 3T6

Dear Mr. Gibson,

I would like to apply for the position of Junior Mechanical Engineer as advertised in the June 12th edition of the *Montreal Gazette*. I feel my academic background as well as my experience relate directly to your needs.

I have recently graduated top of my class in Mechanical Engineering at Cégep du Vieux Montréal. In addition to receiving several academic achievement awards, I also received the Outstanding Leadership Award for the class of 2011.

I feel my drive to succeed and my motivation to do my best make me an ideal candidate for this job. Although my accompanying résumé illustrates my background well, I feel that a personal interview will better demonstrate my knowledge and abilities. I thank you for your consideration and hope to hear from you soon.

Sincerely,

Stephanie Plouffe
Stephanie Plouffe

Enc. Résumé

c.c. Human Resource Department

(167 words)

FYI

Ad is a common abbreviation for *advertisement*. We say "advertising" in English, not "publicity."

FYI

In an e-mail, omit the heading, address and date in the body of the cover letter and use the "From," "Sent," "To" and "Subject" lines to give your name, the date, the recipient's name and the title and/or number of the job posting.

■ Look at Stephanie's cover letter on page 99 and try to place the parts in the correct order from first to last (1–10).

a) Enclosure (enc.): This is the part of the letter where you indicate what you are including or attaching to it, e.g., a résumé. _____

b) Date: This is the day, month and year that you are sending your letter on. _____

c) Paragraph: In this paragraph, you include the title of the job that you are applying for and where you heard about the job opening; also explain why you are a good candidate and what you can bring to the organization. _____

d) Address: This is the address of the potential employer. _____

e) Paragraph: This is where you reinforce your qualifications for the job and your interest in following up the letter with an interview, and then thank the reader for his/her time. _____

f) Salutation: Don't use "Dear Sir/Madam" or "To Whom It May Concern." You can often find the name of appropriate employees in an online directory of the organization. _____

g) Heading: This is where you list your name, address, phone number and e-mail address. _____

h) Carbon copy (c.c.): This states the name(s) of anyone else in the organization to whom you are forwarding the letter. _____

i) Complimentary closing: You can close the letter with "Sincerely," "Yours truly," "Respectfully," etc. _____

j) Paragraph: In this paragraph, you should briefly describe your professional experience, specific skills and relevant accomplishments, and how they relate to the position you are applying for. You should try to use some of the keywords from the description of the position to highlight the match between the organization's needs and your qualifications. _____

DISCUSSION

■ Discuss the following questions in small groups.

1. What is the purpose of a cover letter?

2. What do you think is the most important information to include in the body of your cover letter?

3. What is the best way to make sure that your cover letter gets read?

GENERAL VOCABULARY **LIST**

My eLab
Review the vocabulary from this unit.

These are the words and phrases that you should know after completing this unit. Remind yourself of their meanings by writing down their definitions or translations.

	DEFINITIONS/TRANSLATIONS
1. boundary	
2. brand	
3. channel	
4. colleague	

5. concise _____
6. data _____
7. enhance _____
8. feedback _____
9. generation _____
10. goals _____
11. hire _____
12. internship _____
13. jobseeker _____
14. needy _____
15. network _____
16. prior _____
17. rank _____
18. recruiter _____
19. retire _____
20. shortcut _____
21. spin _____
22. stock _____
23. tagline _____
24. target (market) _____
25. volunteer _____

"Coming together is a beginning. Keeping together is progress. Working together is success." —Henry Ford

Vocabulary Assignment

■ Create a list of ten positive personality adjectives you could use to describe yourself in a cover letter or a résumé. Provide a definition for each item on your list.

Field-Specific Vocabulary List

	ENGLISH DEFINITIONS
1. _____	_____
2. _____	_____
3. _____	_____
4. _____	_____
5. _____	_____
6. _____	_____
7. _____	_____
8. _____	_____
9. _____	_____
10. _____	_____

■ Working with a partner, test each other for meanings and spelling.

FIELD WORK

Writing Assignment

■ Find a job advertisement for a position that interests you in the newspaper or on the Internet. Imagine you are applying for this job and type a cover letter and résumé for it.

Part A: Cover Letter

■ Type a 200-word cover letter for the job. Use some of the adjectives you came up with in the vocabulary assignment to describe yourself. Be sure to use correct letter-writing structure and punctuation (see page 99). (For more information on how to write a business letter, see pages 193–194.)

Part B: Résumé

■ Type your résumé. Be sure to include the following:

- A branding statement (Refer to the adjective list you created for your vocabulary assignment.)
- Power verbs (Refer to page 94.)
- The simple past tense, unless you are referring to duties that you are currently performing (For information on the simple past, refer to page 94 and to the Grammar Guide.)

Refer to

- the résumé template on page 98 to remind yourself of the résumé format;
- the list of résumé dos and don'ts on page 94; and
- the list of skills that you created for the Expansion exercise on page 97.

Speaking Assignment

Create a Brand YOU!

■ Now that you are familiar with what it takes to create a brand identity, follow the three phases that Aruda explains in the reading "Brand YOU" on page 89 to create your own brand identity.

1. Extraction Phase

Make a list of your wants, your personal and career goals and your passions. Ask yourself, "What motivates me?"

2. Express Phase

Learn about your brand community and your potential employer. This is who you will target your message to. Once you have determined your potential employer, write one sentence stating who you are.

3. Exude Phase

Create your brand identity system and a tagline. Think of the colour and style that exudes your brand.

■ Share your brand with the rest of the class in an oral presentation (3–4 minutes). (For more information on preparing an oral presentation, see page 206. If you are doing a PowerPoint presentation, refer to the PowerPoint presentation checklist on page 207.)

My eLab

My eLab Documents includes additional research assignments to help you learn more about your field of study.

Fielding Creativity

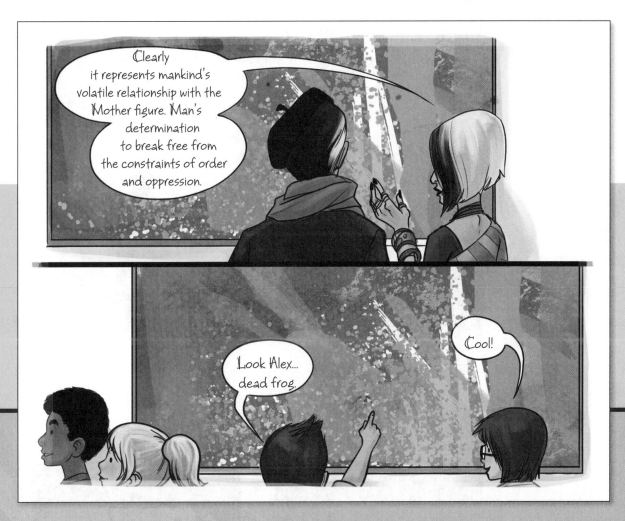

Can anatomy, math or biology be a work of art? What do digital technology and poetry have in common? These questions are among a few that you will ponder in this unit as you explore your field of study from creative, sensory and representational perspectives. You will also be asked to describe advances, processes and procedures in your field of study.

EXPLORE

In the past, botanists, anatomists and biologists meticulously drew their specimens, creating what are considered today as works of art. Sketches of inventions, maps and design plans by famed artist, scientist and Renaissance man Leonardo da Vinci command hundreds of thousands of dollars and reside in some of the world's most acclaimed museums. Clearly, an interrelationship between art and other academic disciplines and fields of study exists. Yet, where does the boundary between science and art lie?

Part A

■ Below are six images. Decide if they are scientific or artistic images. If you think they are scientific, what are they and what scientific field of study do they relate to? If you think they are art, what medium are they made of—paint, clay, plastic, etc.?

Art/Science

Image 1

Art, you see yas emmision

Image 2

Science / Art / you See the ligament.
anatomy

Image 3

Origami Art

Science it's a dynosor + bone

Image 4

Art you can see an non-real animal science Scan

Image 5   **Image 6**

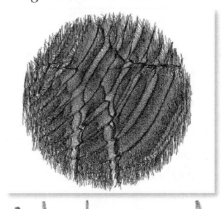

Art, blunch of color   _Art, brain of a monse_

Program math

Part B

■ Discuss the following questions in small groups.

1. What qualities or characteristics make one scientific discovery more significant than another?

2. What qualities or characteristics make one work of art more valuable than another?

3. How do art and science each benefit society?

4. What benefits do the two disciplines share?

5. What are three ways in which art interrelates with your field of study?

Reading 5.1

Look again at Image 3 in the Explore activity (page 104). This work of art, entitled "Allosaurus Skeleton" and created by origamist and engineering professor Dr. Robert J. Lang, is twenty-four inches in size and made up of sixteen squares of uncut paper. Dr. Lang is one of a handful of engineers and mathematicians who have discovered the value that traditional Japanese origami can bring to science and engineering.

■ Complete the pre-reading vocabulary exercise on page 106.

■ Then read the text and answer the comprehension questions.

FYI

Origami is the Japanese word for "paper folding." _Ori_ means "to fold" and _kami_ means "paper." Origami is the art of folding paper into the creation of paper forms, such as animals, birds, masks, geometric shapes, etc.

Part A

■ **Scan** the reading for the following words. Try to **guess the meaning** of the words **from context** and match them with the appropriate images. The line numbers will help you find the words in the text. (For more information on reading comprehension strategies, see page 189.)

1. lens	(line 53)	____	**6.** flatten	(line 25)	____
2. fortune squares	(line 31)	____	**7.** flip	(line 31)	____
3. fold	(line 5)	____	**8.** torn	(line 32)	____
4. twists	(line 20)	____	**9.** tattered	(line 32)	____
5. bends	(line 20)	____	**10.** pack	(line 5)	____

a)   b)   c)   d)

e)   f)   g)

h)   i)   j)

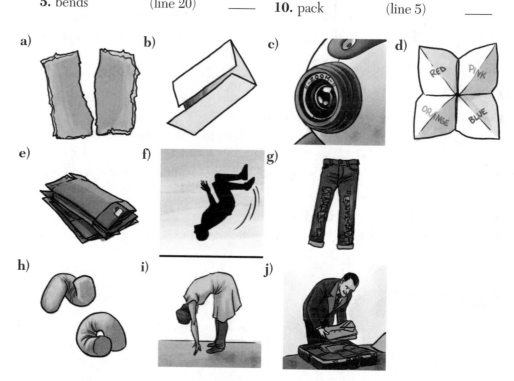

Part B

■ Answer the following questions.

1. Name three things that you flip.

_____

2. Name three body parts that you bend.

_____

3. Name three things that you pack.

_____

4. Name three things that you twist.

_____

5. Name three things that you fold.

_____

Science of Origami

Mathematicians and Artists Use Algorithms to Make Complicated Paper Sculptures

1 *September 1, 2008* — Mathematicians design new figures in a traditional art form called origami, using modern techniques. Innovations developed **in pursuit of** the art find application in multiple fields, including applied mathematics and engineering. One application [developed by Robert J. Lang] is the use of folding algorithms to pack **airbags** for the cars we drive.

2 "What first got me as a kid was the idea that you can create all these different shapes from such a simple starting material—an uncut sheet of paper," says origami artist and engineer Robert Lang, Ph.D.

3 Origami is the traditional technique of Japanese paper folding. Modern science agrees there's a lot they couldn't do without this ancient art form.

4 "Science, technology, space, automotive, medicine—all these different fields have benefited from origami," Dr. Lang says.

5 Dr. Lang is one of America's greatest origami artists. He can fold just about anything from a single sheet of paper. He's honoured that his art can also be effective for education and invention.

6 "There has been some testing that shows that after students have done origami, they have a higher appreciation or understanding of various mathematical geometric concepts," he says.

7 It's an ancient science that uses mathematics for modern-day miracles. The twists and bends in an origami turtle may just make their way into your cellphone's circuit board. And how can a paper scorpion actually save your life? The origami algorithms used to fold bugs are the same ones behind the invention of the airbags in your car.

8 "An algorithm that origami artists had **come up with** for the design of insects was the right algorithm to give the creases for flattening an airbag," Dr. Lang said. "So that has now been adopted into airbag simulation code, and **presumably** automotive engineers are now using those codes to design airbags."

9 Cal Tech says the applications are endless. From consumer programs to the space program, the options have **yet to unfold**.

10 Remember the fortune squares you flipped as a kid? That was a form of origami. So if you told fortunes through torn and tattered paper, you were actually studying science.

11 **ABOUT ORIGAMI:** Paper folded into delicate shapes may look like art, but at its foundation is a strong supporting layer of math. Beyond a basic paper airplane or simple animal shape, geometry and mathematical calculations enable the creation of astonishing shapes and designs. People have developed a way of diagramming their creations called sequenced crease patterns, which indicate where to make folds, and in what order.

12 **ORIGAMI REVEALS ANSWERS:** Algorithms developed for use in origami have been applied to several other fields. Engineers use the algorithms to design the best way to fold an airbag for optimum

---

in pursuit of: when someone tries to get, achieve or find something in a determined way

airbag: a safety device that inflates with air in an accident

come up with: discover; invent

presumably: used to say that you think something is probably true

yet to unfold: used to say that something has not happened yet

FYI

Cal Tech is an abbreviation for the California Institute of Technology.

...

deployment: use of something for a particular purpose

deployment and astronomers use them to compute the optimum configuration of space telescope lenses. In order to study galaxies and astronomical events that are far away, a large space telescope is needed. However, giant telescopes cannot be shipped into space due to the size constraints of rockets and shuttles.

13 Professional origami artist Robert Lang helped scientists at the Lawrence Livermore National Laboratory (Livermore, California) design a method for folding a space telescope so that it can be packed into a space shuttle and then easily deployed when in space. The foldable telescopic lens is called "Eyeglass."

14 In early 2002, a telescopic lens measuring over three meters in diameter was constructed. When folded origami-style, it was 1.2 meters in diameter and shaped like a cylinder. By early 2004, a five-meter prototype lens was constructed and shown to concentrate light as expected.

15 In the future, it may be possible to fold 100-meter telescope lenses into three-meter diameter cylinders and have these delivered into space—all thanks to origami.

16 **OTHER USES OF ORIGAMI:** People also use the techniques of origami to design games, puzzles and even magic tricks. Finally, the art of origami has also had applications in cartography, architecture and even biology, where it is applied to scientists' understanding of **DNA** patterns.

DNA: deoxyribonucleic acid; the genetic information in a cell

(671 words)

Sources: "Science of Origami : Mathematicians and Artists Use Algorithms to Make Complicated Paper Sculptures." *Science Daily*. 01 Sept. 2008. Web. 27 Nov. 2010. <http://www.sciencedaily.com/videos/2008/0910-science_of_origami.htm>; "Origami Science." Origami Resource Center. N.d. Web. 27 Nov. 2010. <http://www.origami-resource-center.com/origami-science.html>.

COMPREHENSION

■ Answer the following questions.

1. What first got Robert J. Lang interested in origami?

___

2. Name twelve different fields of study that have benefited from origami.

___

___

___

___

___

3. How is origami a useful tool in teaching mathematics?

___

___

4. What do an origami scorpion and an automotive airbag have in common?

___

5. How do origamists diagram their designs?

_____

6. How has origami been applied to astronomy?

_____

7. How has the design of the foldable telescope evolved and changed?

_____

_____

8. Besides its practical and scientific applications, where else has origami been utilized?

_____

9. In your opinion, is origami an art or a science? Explain.

_____

_____

EXPANSION

■ Look at the steps involved in creating the crease pattern of an origami swan and then match the instructions on page 110 with these steps.

Origami swan

Step 1	Step 2	Step 3	Step 4

Step 5	Step 6	Step 7	Step 8

 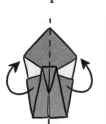  

Source: Craib, Emma. "Origami for Beginners: the Swan." Web. 27 Nov. 2010. <http://art-smart.ci.manchester. ct.us/how_to/ori_swan1.html>.

Instructions:

Step _____: Fold down the tip of the neck to make a head.

Step _____: Your paper should look like a kite.

Step _____: Fold the swan in half.

Step _____: Take a square piece of paper and fold it. Then unfold it.

Step _____: Turn the paper over and fold it again towards the centre crease as indicated in the diagram above.

Step _____: Fold the lower edges to meet at the centre crease.

Step _____: Fold up the bottom point to make a swan's neck.

Step _____: Grab the swan by its neck and pull the paper up while squeezing the paper at the base of its neck to crease it. Finally, pull the swan's head forward to make your swan.

My eLab
Try another exercise in origami.

Watching 🖥

WEATHER BECOMES ARTISTIC EXPRESSION

Like origamist Robert J. Lang, Ottawa artist Eric Sze-Lang Chan is also adept at channelling inspiration from algorithms. However, instead of creating engineering marvels, Chan creates free-form paintings by feeding Google's weather data into a computer program, which codes the data and projects it onto a canvas.

■ First, complete the pre-watching vocabulary exercise.

■ Take the time to read the comprehension questions and highlight the keywords before you watch the video.

■ While you watch the video, **listen for keyword cues** and answer the questions. (For more information on listening comprehension strategies, see page 205.)

PRE-WATCHING VOCABULARY

■ Match the following words with their correct definitions. If necessary, **look up the words** in a dictionary to help you, or work with a partner.

WORDS		DEFINITIONS
1. curator	_____	**a)** ways of communicating information and feelings, such as music, writing, painting, etc.
2. free-form	_____	**b)** produce a result, answer or piece of information
3. canvas	_____	**c)** touch something with gentle movements of your hand
4. yield	_____	**d)** continue functioning

5. stroke ____
6. impulse ____
7. medium ____
8. crossroad ____
9. elicit ____
10. run ____

e) someone who is in charge of a museum or gallery

f) piece of cloth a picture is painted on

g) succeed in getting information or a reaction from someone, especially when it is difficult to do so

h) sudden strong desire to do something without thinking about whether it is a sensible thing to do

i) without a standard structure or form

j) point where two or more things intersect

COMPREHENSION

■ Answer the following questions.

1. How does Eric Chan paint the weather?

_____

_____

_____

2. How does Eric's computer program respond when the weather changes?

_____

_____

FYI

A multicultural mosaic is a Canadian concept which celebrates and respects cultural differences.

3. According to Eric, what can result when you bring many things together into one?

_____

_____

4. What is Eric's background?

_____

5. What two crossroads does Eric's work "Intersections" represent?

_____

_____

6. How does curator Andrea Fatona describe Eric's art?

_____

_____

7. Why did Eric decide to use weather data in his artwork?

_____

_____

_____

■ Discuss the following questions in small groups.

1. In a recent interview, Eric Chan explained how his passion for computers inspired his art. Talk about something that you are passionate about and explain why it inspires you.

2. How could you incorporate your passion into your field of study?

3. Generally speaking, people have been slow to consider digital or computer-generated art as "Art." What is your opinion? Is it art or is it not? Justify your response.

CONNECT WITH GRAMMAR

Using the Future Tense (*will* and *to be* + *going to*)

Both *will* and *to be* + *going to* are used to express a prediction about the future.

> **Examples:** I think it **is going to rain**.
>
> I think it **will rain.**

Will is also used to express a future action decided upon at the moment of speaking. In other words, use *will* to express a spontaneous decision or action.

> **Examples:**
>
> Eric Chan: I can't fold this paper the right way.
>
> Robert J. Lang: Give it to me. **I'll fold** it for you.
>
> Lang's decision to fold the paper for Eric Chan is spontaneous (made at the moment of speaking).

To be + *going to* is used to express a planned future action. Your decision to do the future action was made before the moment of speaking.

> **Example:**
>
> The curator of the National Gallery of Canada said the gallery **is going to exhibit** some of Eric Chan's work next spring. (future plan)

■ Fill in the blanks using the correct future *will* or *to be* + *going to* form.

1. Robert J. Lang (display) [1] _____ some of his origami designs at the McGill University School of Engineering in the Fall. (you / go)
   [2] _____?

   Absolutely! I (make) [3] _____ an announcement about it on Facebook.

2. I'm having difficulty understanding this poem.

   Vincent and I (meet) [1] _____ with Professor Cozens tomorrow. Why don't you come?

   Thanks. I think I [2] _____.

Refer to Unit 5 of the Grammar Guide for further explanations and practice on the future tense.

Reading 5.2

Most people, when asked to explain what body art is, describe tattoos and piercings, but those who are knowledgeable on the subject might also include scarification. Few people mention cadavers and body parts—that is, until recently when an exhibition took body art to a whole new level.

FYI

Scarification involves scratching, etching or some sort of superficial cutting or incision as a permanent body modification.

■ Complete the pre-reading vocabulary exercise.

■ Then **skim** the text quickly and write down the main idea on the line below. (For more information on reading comprehension strategies, see page 189.)

Main idea: _____

_____

■ Finally, read the text and answer the comprehension questions on pages 115 and 116.

PRE-READING VOCABULARY

■ Working with a partner, look at the following definitions and fill in the missing letters of the words that they define. Paragraph numbers are given to help you find the words in context.

DEFINITIONS	WORDS
1. having no smell (paragraph 2)	_ _ o _ r _ e _ s
2. involves making new discoveries, using new methods, etc. (paragraph 2)	_ r o _ n _ _ _ r e _ _ i _ g
3. continue to behave according to a particular rule, agreement or belief (phrasal verb) (paragraph 6)	a _ _ e _ e _ o
4. thin flat piece of something (usually food) cut from a larger piece (paragraph 2)	_ l _ c _
5. very important or necessary (paragraph 3)	_ e _
6. describe or show someone or something in a particular way, according to your opinion of the person or thing (paragraph 3)	_ o _ _ _ r _ _ _
7. jump up and put the ball into the basket in basketball (paragraph 1)	_ u n _
8. small thing that you keep to remind yourself of someone or something (paragraph 6)	_ e _ e n _ _ _
9. position in which someone stands or sits, especially in a painting, photograph, etc. (paragraph 2)	_ o _ e
10. looking exactly like a real person or thing (paragraph 2)	l i _ _ _ - l _ k _

Body Art or Body Parts?

1 Have you ever watched a professional basketball player seem to float in [the] air as he or she leaps up to dunk the ball in the basket? Or maybe you [have] watched skiers and skaters competing at the Olympics, and wondered, "How did they do that?"

2 5 Gunther von Hagens' "Body Worlds: The Original Exhibition of Real Human Bodies" was developed by the German doctor and anatomist to help people understand how their bodies work by letting them look inside real human bodies. Body Worlds displays specimens preserved using Dr. Gunther von Hagens' groundbreaking invention of plastination. Plastination is a process 10 that replaces the natural fluids in the body with fluid plastics. The use of plastics for preservation means that the specimens are odourless and completely dry. Plastination allows the bodies to be fixed into life-like poses, illustrating how our bodies are structured and how they function when performing everyday activities. Each exhibition features more than 200 real human specimens, 15 including whole-body plastinates, individual organs, organ configurations and transparent body slices. The specimens on display **stem from** the body donation program that Gunther von Hagens established in 1983.

3 The Body Worlds exhibits teach a great deal about the science and anatomy of the human body. They also teach about the form and art of the 20 human body. Studies of anatomy have always been a key part of art education. Artists who know how the human body is put together, and how its muscles work, are better able to portray people in painting, sculpture and other art forms. This knowledge is important, even if artists choose to represent the human form in abstract ways rather than realistic representation. In the Body 25 Worlds exhibits, Gunther von Hagens has positioned human figures to reveal how the body is put together and how it performs different tasks. He also has presented human figures in ways that highlight different body systems.

4 By all accounts, it seems the ideal marriage between art and science, and yet the exhibit and its creator have not been exempt from criticism and 30 controversy from the general public, religious leaders and, surprisingly, the medical profession and fellow anatomists. Concerns have been **voiced** as to the accuracy of the anatomical positioning of the cadavers, whether or not the bodies have suffered an indignity, and where, in fact, these bodies have come from. Beyond all of this, one has to ask oneself: is the public display of 35 dead people art?

5 Performance artist and pop singer Lady Gaga seems to think so. Lady Gaga has requested to have plasticized corpses on stage with her during her next tour, and von Hagens is anxious to accommodate her request.

6 "As someone who practises the violin every day, I feel that music is vital to 40 our humanity and fundamental to our well-being. The **post-mortal** plastinated body, on the other hand, is a memento mori—a reminder that we must all die. To create a convergence of both these profound subjects would be an exciting challenge. To do so with an innovative and risk-taking artist like Lady Gaga would be a perfect meeting of **boundary-pushing** minds. We both 45 adhere to high aesthetic standards. As the creator of the post-mortal beauty salon, it would be a challenge for me to combine artistic performance with science in the sense of 'science-art' together with Lady Gaga," raves Dr. von Hagens.

7 This will not be the first time the anatomist has worked in collaboration with celebrities in other fields. Several plastinated cadavers, as well as von

stem from: occur as a result of

Artist and anatomist Gunther von Hagens

voice: tell people your opinions or feelings about a particular subject

post-mortal (mortem): after death

boundary-pushing: going beyond the current limits of something

50 Hagens himself, made an appearance in the 2006 James Bond movie *Casino Royale*. As well, celebrity TV chef Jamie Oliver invited von Hagens on air to perform an autopsy revealing the negative effects a poor diet can have on your body. Talk about food for thought …

(634 words)

Sources: Adapted from: Institute for Plastination. "Gunther von Hagens' Body World: The Original Exhibition of Real Human Bodies. Educators' Guide (Grades 9–12)." Web. 9 Dec. 2010. <http://www.bodyworlds.com/Downloads/englisch/Exhibition/free%20Material/Guides/BW_EduGuide_9-12.pdf>; quotation from "Anatomist Dr. Gunther von Hagens Responds to Report of Collaboration with Lady Gaga." Gunther von Hagens' Body Worlds. 24 June 2010. Web. 27 Nov. 2010. < http://www.bodyworlds.com/en/media.html>.

COMPREHENSION

■ Answer the following questions.

1. What can looking inside real bodies teach us?

_____

2. Explain how von Hagens preserves the human specimens in his exhibits.

_____

3. What are some of the features of the exhibits?

_____

_____

_____

4. Where do the bodies in von Hagens' exhibits come from?

_____

5. Why is it important for artists to have a knowledge of human anatomy?

_____

_____

6. Who are opposed to the exhibits and why are they opposed to them?

_____

_____

_____

_____

_____

7. What two subjects is von Hagens excited about having the opportunity to converge?

_____

_____

8. What do von Hagens and Lady Gaga have in common?

_____

9. Besides art galleries, where else has von Hagens' "art" been shown? Describe one of those performances.

_____

_____

_____

10. a) What is the main idea of this article?

_____

b) Now go back to page 113 and see if the main idea you decided on is correct.

DISCUSSION

■ Discuss the following questions in small groups.

1. Do you consider von Hagens' plastinates "art"? Explain your answer. How would you define the word *art*?

2. What are some reasons why people donate their bodies to science or art?

3. Would you volunteer to have your body plastinated and then put on display after you die? Why or why not?

4. Von Hagens has recently been in the news for an exhibit featuring plastinated human bodies engaged in different sexual positions. In your opinion, does this overstep the line between art and good taste? Explain.

EXPANSION

Mathematical algorithms, art generated from computers, dead bodies—years ago, few people could have conceived of such media of artistic expressions. Yet, today these media are, for the most part, mainstream. How do you think your field of study will change in the future? What unusual developments or ideas do you see becoming mainstream?

■ Write a paragraph (100–150 words) describing your vision. Be sure to use the future verb tense and to **examine** the structure of **your paragraph**.

Revision Strategy 7: Examining Paragraphs

As you revise your texts, examine your paragraphs carefully. Among other things, you should clearly identify the topic sentence and supporting ideas in each paragraph. (For more information on revision strategies, see page 204, and for more information on topic sentences and support, see page 201.)

FYI

Haiku is a Japanese form of poetry that describes the ordinary in the everyday situation. It is a brief, seventeen-syllable verse traditionally consisting of three metrical units of five, seven and five syllables.

Listening 🎧

TWAIKU POETRY

First there was e-mail, then there was Facebook, then Twitter and now ... Twitter Haiku. More commonly referred to as "Twaiku," Twitter Haiku is a fusion of seventeen-syllable haikus and 140-characters-or-less Twitter updates. Poetry merges with digital technology in this new social media art form.

- Before you listen to the report, **skim** the listening exercises quickly and write down what you think is the main idea.

  Main idea: _____

- Complete the pre-listening vocabulary exercise.

- Finally, answer the comprehension questions while listening to the report.

Listening Comprehension Strategy 4: Skimming

Carefully examining any information provided in the exercises, for example the title, introduction, comprehension questions, vocabulary words, illustrations and captions will help you get a general idea of the topic and main idea of the listening. The more you understand about the topic before you begin to listen, the easier the listening task will be. (For more information on listening comprehension strategies, see page 205.)

PRE-LISTENING VOCABULARY

- Match the following words and expressions with their definitions.

WORDS AND EXPRESSIONS		DEFINITIONS
1. stoop	_____	**a)** make an unpleasant feeling less painful or severe
2. lend itself to	_____	**b)** bend your body forward and down
3. constrained	_____	**c)** made-up adjective form of the noun *pun*, which is a humorous play on words
4. jump on the bandwagon	_____	**d)** shocking because it is easily noticed
5. assuage	_____	**e)** feel that you must do something
6. newly hip	_____	**f)** extremely unwilling to waste time, money or space
7. punny	_____	**g)** used to describe something that has become the latest fashion
8. longing	_____	**h)** adapt to; be suitable for
9. parsimonious	_____	**i)** strong feeling of wanting something or someone
10. flagrant	_____	**j)** get involved in something that has recently become very popular

COMPREHENSION

- Answer the following questions.

1. Rayat Deonandan has several different professions. What are they?

_____

_____

2. What is the most popular haiku that Rayat has Twittered?

_____

_____

3. Why did Rayat initially start using Twitter?

_____

My eLab

Answer additional questions for "Twaiku Poetry."

4. What opportunity did Rayat see in the technology of Twitter?

_____

5. Besides being on Twitter, how else are Rayat's haikus different from traditional haikus?

_____

6. What two reasons does Rayat give to explain why more people are developing an interest in writing haikus?

_____

_____

Technology meets art in a Japanese garden.

7. What did Rayat's Twaiku inspire the interviewer to do on her show?

_____

8. What is the power of haiku?

_____

9. How are words chosen when writing haikus?

_____

10. What can listeners win if they win the Twaiku contest?

_____

EXPANSION

■ Write a haiku about your field of study or anything relevant to your field of study. Remember the five-seven-five syllable rule!

PRONUNCIATION

Pronouncing *ch*

There are at least three ways to pronounce the letters *ch* in English.
- The letters *ch* can be pronounced /tʃ/ or /ch/ as in *cheese*.
- The letters *ch* can be pronounced /ʃ/ or /sh/ as in *charade*.
- The letters *ch* can be pronounced /k/ as in *Christian*.

FYI

There are always exceptions. The letters *ch* can also be silent as in *yacht* (pronounced "yot").

FYI

Other letter combinations can also produce the /ch/ sound, such as the *t* in *future*, (pronounced "f-you-cher").

Part A

■ Listen to and repeat these words in which the *ch* spelling is pronounced /ch/.

1. catch	3. charm	5. chicken	7. choice	9. kitchen
2. challenge	4. cheese	6. chip	8. choke	10. macho

■■■

Part B

■ Listen to and repeat these words in which the *ch* spelling is pronounced /sh/. Many English words that have been borrowed from French use this pronunciation.

1. champagne	6. chef
2. charade	7. Chicago
3. chateau	8. chivalry
4. chauffeur	9. cliché
5. chauvinist	10. machine

Part C

■ Listen to and repeat these words in which the *ch* spelling is pronounced /k/.

1. chaos	3. chasm	5. chemistry	7. choir	9. Christmas
2. character	4. chemical	6. chlorine	8. Christian	10. chronic

Reading 5.3

Would you prefer your dress in Merlot, Shiraz or Pinot Noir? Would you enjoy a nice brie cheese or a camembert with that dress? These questions make no sense at all—until you realize that what you are wearing is not a dress made out of an ordinary fabric, but rather a dress made out of wine.

■ Complete the pre-reading vocabulary exercise.

■ Then read the text and answer the comprehension questions on page 123.

FYI

Wine has so many organic chemical compounds that it is considered more chemically complex than human blood.

PRE-READING VOCABULARY

Part A

■ **Identify each word's part of speech** based on the context.

■ Then **guess the meaning** of the words **from context**. The line numbers will help you find the words in the text.

■ Finally, **look the words up** in the dictionary to see if your guesses were correct. (For more information on vocabulary strategies, see page 190.)

1. garment (line 3)

    part of speech: _____

    definition: _____

2. by-product (line 5)

    part of speech: _____

    definition: _____

3. collapsible (line 8)

part of speech: _____

definition: _____

4. retrieve (line 9)

part of speech: _____

definition: _____

5. face (line 17)

part of speech: _____

definition: _____

_____

6. lingering (line 25)

part of speech: _____

definition: _____

7. damp (line 28)

part of speech: _____

definition: _____

8. harden (line 28)

part of speech: _____

definition: _____

9. fabric (line 26)

part of speech: _____

definition: _____

10. mainstream (line 54)

part of speech: _____

definition: _____

_____

Part B

■ The following phrasal verbs can have more than one meaning. Look at each phrasal verb's meaning in the context of the reading and decide what its most appropriate definition is.

1. go off (line 6)   **a)** leave   **b)** go bad   **c)** explode

2. take off (line 38)   **a)** become popular   **b)** remove   **c)** deduct as a discount

3. get rid of (line 39)   **a)** discard   **b)** eliminate   **c)** abolish

When Science Met Art: Fermenting the Future of Fashion

By Lauren Day

1. Imagine if that little red dress was made from a little red wine. In a fusion of science and fashion, artist Donna Franklin and scientist Gary Cass presented their creations—garments made entirely from fermented wine—at the Ultimo Science Festival during National Science Week from August 16–24.

2. 5 The fabric is produced from the cellulose by-product created when wine "goes off" and is contaminated with bacteria, a product which is chemically similar to cotton.

3. This **sludge-like** cellulose is **moulded** onto a collapsible mannequin and left to dry. The mannequin is then removed and the dress is retrieved,
   10 its texture not unlike a **rubbery** second skin.

4. Ironically, the pair's innovation came after "a few too many glasses of red wine."

5. "We thought, 'wouldn't it be interesting if we could convert this material into a garment?'" said Cass, who **hails from** the University of Western
   15 Australia.

6. He also believes the technology could revolutionize the fashion industry as an alternative to the fabrics currently used, which face both industrial and environmental challenges in the future.

7. Conventional cotton farming, for example, uses pesticides, herbicides
   20 and chemical fertilizers and is responsible for extensive greenhouse gas emissions. British designer Katharine Hamnet has famously predicted that: "The clothing and textile industry's impact on global warming is probably larger than all of Africa." So it comes as no surprise that the wine dresses have had such a positive response.

8. 25 But like any great innovation, certain lingering problems need to be rectified before their technology can become a fabric of the future. For instance, while the material initially feels rubbery when damp, it then hardens and cracks when dried. "The dresses have to be kept wet," says Cass. Once they dry, they become like
   30 tissue paper and can easily tear if the fabric is too thin. This is because the cellulose fibres the bacteria produce are short, unlike cotton ones, which are easily **spun** into longer fibres.

9. Moreover, the material has a distinct alcohol-like, vinegar smell, which did not impress the models who were **parading** Cass
   35 and Franklin's designs.

10. One model, Sarah, doubts she could meet anyone in the pub wearing the Micro'be dress.

11. "It smells pretty bad ... the concept might take off if they get rid of the smell," she said.

12. 40 Cass, however, said the smell was left in for artistic purposes and is easily washed out.

sludge-like: similar to soft, thick mud

mould: shape a soft substance by pressing or rolling it

rubbery: looking or feeling like rubber

hail from: come from; originate from

spun: turned around and around very quickly

parade: walk around in a way that shows that you want people to notice and admire you

...

vat: very large container for storing liquids in

goon wine: Australian slang for cheap box wine

bated breath: holding your breath because you are feeling very anxious or excited

13   The good news, though, is that the garments, which take an average of two weeks to grow in the current small-scale **vats**, are relatively cost-effective.

14   "We use about ten litres of red wine to make the garments … but it's OK because it's cheap Australian **goon wine**," Cass joked at the exhibition.

15 50   Model Sarah had better ideas for the wine: "It's disappointing—we should be drinking this, not wearing it," she joked.

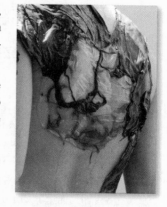

16   Nevertheless, Cass said the fashion world is waiting with [**bated**] **breath** for their fabric to become mainstream.

17 55   "The fashion industry is really pushing for this, saying 'When is it going to be commercialized? When is it going to be available?' But it's really an art project at the moment," said Cass.

18   And maybe fermented wine could be the future of fashion: "It may be Prada and Versace last year and Cab Sav Shiraz next season," Cass forecasted.

(536 words)

Voice-Generated Textile Prints

1   The continent of Australia is not only the birthplace of the Micro'be wine dress, but is also the country of origin for voice-generated fabrics and textiles called "Voiceprints." Australian electronic artist Pierre Proske created Voiceprints after developing a computer software program that measures the frequency of a person's voice. After measuring the voice frequency, the software program translates the frequency into a pattern. The frequency takes on the shape of a spiral, which the program repeats to form a pattern. Different voice frequencies create different sizes and densities of spirals, which in turn create different patterns. What does this all mean for the Australian fashion industry? Clothes really can "say a lot" about the person wearing them!

(120 words)

Sources: Day, Lauren. "When Science Met Art: Fermenting the Future of Fashion." Reportage / Online. 22 Aug. 2008. Web. 27 Nov. 2010. <http://www.reportageonline.com/2008/08/when-science-met-art-fermenting-the-future-of-fashion/>; Salleh, Anna. "Artist Makes Fabric with Voice." *News in Science*. 27 March 2006. Web. 9 Dec. 2010. <http://www.abc.net.au/science/news/stories/s1600126.htm>.

Voiceprint: Textile pattern

COMPREHENSION

■ Answer the following questions.

1. Complete the seven steps required to produce "wine" fabric in the spaces below. Some of the steps have been provided for you.

   1. wine goes off   5. *left to dry*

   2. *Bacteria*   6. *Mannequin is removed.*

   3. *Sludge-like*   7. dress is retrieved

   4. cellulose is moulded onto a collapsible mannequin

2. What were Franklin and Cass doing when they came up with the idea for a garment made of wine?
Drinking wine

3. Why would Franklin and Cass' wine fabric be a good alternative to the fabrics currently being used to make clothing?
Because that face both industrial and Environmental in the futur

4. How does the textile industry impact global warming? *Challen.*
it will help → No gas emission ✱

5. What two problems need to be resolved before the fabric can be put on the market?
the smell, and the texture (Rubbery)

6. What is the brand name of the wine dress?
Micro'be dress

7. How long does it take to produce a garment?
Two weeks

8. Why is it relatively inexpensive to produce a garment out of wine?
Because, it come from cheap australian wine *poor*

9. How is the rest of the fashion industry responding to the wine fabric?
They erecting and Asking alot of question like when it going to be available

10. What is a "voiceprint"?
it's a Software program that translate Your voice frequency in shape of spiral on the dress

DISCUSSION

■ Discuss this question with a partner or in a small group.

Designers have created clothing out of the strangest things, including human hair, meat, plastic bags and now wine and the human voice. What other things do you think could be used to create clothing?

My eLab 🖉

An additional reading is available in My eLab to help you further practise your comprehension skills.

These are the words and phrases that you should know after completing this unit. Remind yourself of their meanings by writing down their definitions or translations.

	DEFINITIONS/TRANSLATIONS
1. adhere to	
2. bend	
3. by-product	
5. canvas	
4. constrain	
6. crossroad	
7. damp	
8. elicit	
9. fabric	
10. fold	
11. garment	
12. groundbreaking	
13. harden	
14. impulse	
15. longing	
16. mainstream	
17. odourless	
18. pack	
19. portray	
20. pose	
21. raw	
22. retrieve	
23. slice	
24. twist	
25. yield	

My eLab

Review the vocabulary from this unit.

"The most beautiful experience we can have is the mysterious—the fundamental emotion which stands at the cradle of true art and true science." —Albert Einstein

Vocabulary Assignment

■ A painter needs her brushes; a chemist needs his lab coat. What are the tools of your trade? Think of ten tools or objects a person would require or need to be familiar with in order to work in your field of study. Be prepared to justify your choices.

■ Write your words in the Field-Specific Vocabulary List below and include an English definition for each. Make sure that the words you choose aren't cognates in your own language, and that you have spelled them correctly.

Field-Specific Vocabulary List

	ENGLISH DEFINITIONS
1. _____	_____
2. _____	_____
3. _____	_____
4. _____	_____
5. _____	_____
6. _____	_____
7. _____	_____
8. _____	_____
9. _____	_____
10. _____	_____

■ Exchange your list with another student and test each other on the spellings and/or meanings of the words.

Speaking Assignment

1. Representing Your Field

In this unit, you have become familiar with how artistic media can come together with scientific fields of study to create something new and exciting. In addition, you have seen how different fields of study can be represented artistically. For example, an algorithm can become a painting, and a bacterium can become a dress. However, while the science may advance and change, its representation at a given point in time remains the same. The work of art resists change and speaks to the time in which it was created. You only need to look at cave art, likely the earliest form of artistic expression, to see how art speaks to the time in which it was created.

■ Select three recent events or discoveries relevant to your field of study and represent these events or discoveries artistically. You don't need to be an artist—just a rough sketch of the events or discoveries that you will be presenting is fine.

...

- Present your art and explain what these events and/or discoveries are and how they have contributed to your field of study in a short presentation (3–4 minutes in length) to a partner, small group or the class (your teacher will decide). (For more information on presenting, see page 206.)

2. Describing a Procedure

In this unit, you have learned about how wine can become a dress; how a cadaver can be plastinated and how to create a Twaiku.

- Describe a typical technique or process (scientific, creative or otherwise) in your field of study in a short presentation (3–4 minutes in length) to a partner, small group or the class (your teacher will decide). For example, if you are in business administration, you could describe the steps taken to start a small business. If you are in dental hygiene, you could describe how to check a patient for cavities, or how to do a cleaning.

- Be sure to incorporate a minimum of five tools of the trade from the Field-Specific Vocabulary list on page 125 into your presentation. (For more information on presenting, see page 206.)

Writing Assignment

- Research a recent event or discovery relevant to your field of study. Write a 250- to 300-word basic report explaining what this event or discovery is and how it contributed to your field of study. While doing your research, ensure your secondary sources are credible, accurate, reasonable and supported by other secondary sources by using Robert Harris' CARS Checklist (see page 192). Be sure to use your own words and footnote your sources. (For more information on how to write a basic report, refer to page 195).

- Use one of the revision strategies described in this book to edit your report: *editing your work*; *emphasizing the positive*; *obtaining feedback*; *peer reviewing*; *writing a reverse plan*; *proofreading*; *examining paragraphs*. (For more information on revision strategies, see page 204.)

My eLab ⌸

My eLab Documents includes additional research assignments to help you learn more about your field of study.

© ERPI • REPRODUCTION PROHIBITED

Viral Marketing

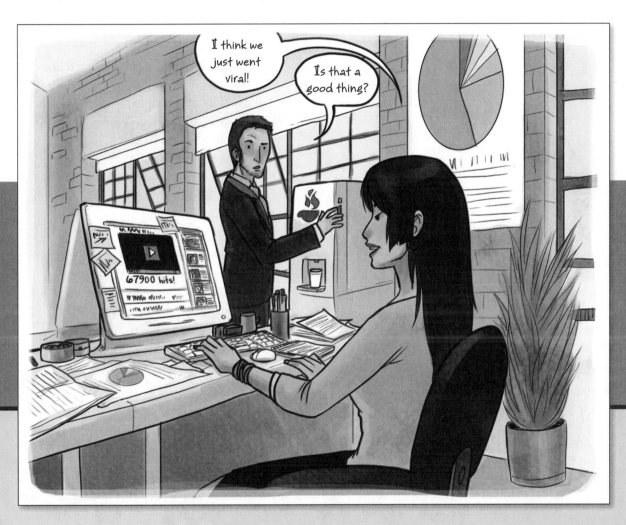

Social media is definitely on the rise. People use Twitter, Facebook, Hi5 and MSN. They search YouTube for interesting videos and they read blogs like Altitude and Mashable. They check out social sites like Bebo, MySpace, LinkedIn and Friendster. *Google* has even become a common English verb! Seen in these terms, the Internet is a vast captive market, which makes it interesting and attractive to businesses looking for new ways to position or reposition their products or services. This unit will ask you to think about and discuss how the Internet is used, and challenge you to create a viral marketing campaign and video related to your field of study.

In the "Twitterverse" (the world of Twitter users, where you tweet to tell your loyal followers what you are doing regularly in 140 characters or less), new terms are being created all the time. These Twitter terms are made by combining two or more different words.

■ Work with a partner to match the following invented Twitter terms with their definitions. Note that most of the words are made up of "tw" and parts of other words.

TERMS		DEFINITIONS
1. tweetup	＿＿	**a)** group of Twitter users interested in a common topic
2. twitt	＿＿	**b)** sweet Twitter people
3. twitterati	＿＿	**c)** organized or impromptu meeting of people who use Twitter
4. twitterature	＿＿	
5. retweet	＿＿	**d)** feeling compelled to tweet constantly about every meaningless thing you do
6. twibe	＿＿	**e)** classic literature in tweets
7. sweeple	＿＿	**f)** copying and posting another person's Twitter content
8. tweepish	＿＿	
9. tweetaholic	＿＿	**g)** person addicted to tweeting
10. twitterhea	＿＿	**h)** feeling sheepish or regretful about something you tweeted
		i) newbie (new or insignificant, bothersome person) who uses Twitter
		j) Twitter power users, whose **feeds** attract thousands of followers

feed: regular messages

Source: Adapted from: "Twitterverse." NetLingo. N.d. Web. 23 Nov. 2010. <http://www.netlingo.com/word/twitterverse.php>.

Reading 6.1

Before the Internet, how was a marketing campaign run? In the following article, you will read how the classic rock band Grateful Dead ran a very successful marketing campaign in an era before the social media networking possibilities of the Internet.

The Dead: short for "Grateful Dead"

Even though the Grateful Dead are no longer fashionable, their live act remains very profitable. In fact, the article states that **The Dead** "are becoming an unlikely case study" about consumer relationships and social media. What lessons in marketing does the article suggest can be learned from the Grateful Dead's methods?

■ **Skim** the text by reading the title and the first sentence of each paragraph, and by looking at the pictures on pages 129 and 132. Then write the main idea on the line below.

Main idea: ＿＿＿＿＿＿＿＿＿＿＿＿＿＿＿＿＿＿＿＿＿＿＿＿＿＿＿＿＿＿＿

■ Then read the comprehension questions on pages 131 to 133 before you read the text.

■ As you read the text, **take notes** on the group's methods and their marketing implications to help you answer the questions that follow. (For more information on reading comprehension strategies, see page 189.)

Marketing Lessons from the Grateful Dead

The Grateful Dead are becoming an unlikely case study in viral media

By Jordan Timm

© ERPI · REPRODUCTION PROHIBITED

The Grateful Dead formed in 1965 in San Francisco. They are best-known for their live improvisational performances, which mix elements of rock, folk, bluegrass, blues, reggae, jazz, psychedelia and country music.

1   "The Grateful Dead are a living hippie monument [...]," wrote music journalists David Dalton and Lenny Kaye. When Dalton and Kaye wrote that appraisal in 1977, punk and disco were already making The Dead, one of the few surviving institutions of 1960s west coast hippie culture, look like a
5   **museum piece**. Outside of a few brief years a decade earlier, the band had never been anywhere near the **cultural mainstream**. Fashions had come and gone without troubling them, and they wouldn't score a top-ten album or single until a **fluke** charting in 1987.

museum piece: old and outdated; unfashionable

cultural mainstream: most known and accepted aspects of a culture

fluke: lucky

2   But, fashionable or not, by the time band member Jerry Garcia
10   succumbed to a heart attack in 1995, The Dead were acknowledged as the most successful live act in music history, playing for millions and grossing millions more in three decades of hard touring. Though the band has changed shape since Garcia's passing—members have toured intermittently under different names—their fan base remains as extensive
15   and as **rabid** as ever, thanks to a relationship carefully nurtured by The Dead and their management. And as the rest of the business world **grapples** with what social media means for their relationships with consumers, The Dead are
20   becoming an unlikely case study.

The Grateful Dead on tour

3   Marketing gurus David Meerman Scott and Brian Halligan **take a crack at codifying** The Dead's non-musical innovations in *Marketing Lessons from The Grateful Dead: What Every Business Can Learn*
25   *from the Most Iconic Band in History* (Wiley). Halligan is CEO of marketing software company HubSpot, and Scott is a bestselling author with a marketing strategy company. Between them, they've seen The Dead some 150 times, and they are part of
30   the vibrant fan community the band cultivated. Here they identify **a host of** the band's innovations that correlate with emerging business principles.

4   "Freemium" may be an ugly **neologism**, but the practice of giving something away and then selling a premium version of that product has been part of The Dead's practice for decades. They were the first major act to
35   encourage fans to **tape** their concerts, even providing a special section near the soundboard for **Deadheads** who wanted to record the show. "Conventional wisdom held that if fans made their own recordings, they wouldn't need to buy records," write the authors. And while The Dead's records may never have sold in huge volume, taping encouraged a community of fans who would
40   collect and trade homemade concert recordings, obsessing over the band's ever-changing **set** lists and improvisational approach.

...

rabid: extreme and vocal

grapple: try hard to understand

take a crack at: try

codify: make sense of

a host of: many; a lot of

neologism: new word or expression

tape (v.): record

Deadhead: fan of The Grateful Dead

set: group of songs to be performed on stage

tape (n.): old-format sound recording, like today's CD or mp3

royalties: percentage of money paid to the band for each album sale

booth: table set up where you can buy or order things

burgeoning: growing

record: old-format sound recording on a vinyl disc, like today's CD or mp3

Usenet: large organization of newsgroups and news servers on the Internet

gig: performance

money order: document (like a cheque) that is safer than sending cash in the mail

newsletter: short written report containing news about a club, organization, etc., that is sent regularly to people who are interested.

mindset: way of thinking

Answer additional questions for "Marketing Lessons from the Grateful Dead."

5
45
This early form of viral marketing provided a vehicle for word-of-mouth about the band, and their extraordinary live shows spread and grew their fan base exponentially. "Each **tape** was like an **advertisement** that attracted new people to one of their concerts," write Scott and Halligan. "The more concerts [they] performed, the more tapes were in the marketplace. The more copies were made of the tapes, the more advertisements were in the marketplace pulling in new customers." By making the band's content "spreadable," concert ticket sales more than made up for any compromise of album **royalties**.

6 50
55
The Dead were also early to see the potential in communicating directly with that fan base. In 1968, the band hired somebody to run a **booth** at every concert and sign up thousands of fans for updates on the band and their tours. And they included an advertisement for their **burgeoning** newsletter service on a 1971 live album, promising to keep fans informed in exchange for a name and an address.

7
60
"At the time, it was a radical idea for a band to add a 'call to action' to an album as an overt way to build their mailing list—and by extension, their following," write Halligan and Scott. The band corresponded regularly with list members, and after a few years, The Dead were able to use their now-enormous database to ask fans to call radio stations and **record** stores when the band would release a new album. Their fans were happy to do it, because they felt they were part of a community, rather than simply being marketed to. The band has remained an early adopter of communications technologies, from **Usenet** through to iPhone apps.

8 65
70
75
The key element that's allowed for the band's success through these efforts, suggest the authors, is their authenticity. They've gone to great lengths to let their fans know that they genuinely value their relationship. When the rest of the concert industry was falling under Ticketmaster's monopoly, The Dead established their own in-house ticketing service. The best seats for every concert were reserved for those fans who knew to call the band's hotline for **gig** information and then mail in a **money order**. This way, the heart of The Dead experience was reserved for the truest believers. "We see so many organizations that do precisely the opposite," the authors write. "Instead of putting loyal customers first, they ignore them while they try to get new ones." And when the band makes mistakes, those loyal customers tend to be more forgiving.

9
80
85
Meanwhile, the openness and authenticity of communication through the band's **newsletters**, a "pre-Internet social network"—information about solo projects, wedding and birth announcements from the band's road and office crew—has helped make that fan base a real community. That community travels with the band from show to show, and over the years has established a huge part of The Dead's brand value. "Our community defines who we are. Companies cannot force a **mindset** on their customers," write Scott and Halligan. "The Grateful Dead let their audience define the ... experience. They made fans an equal partner on a journey." It's a trip that's surely been long and strange, but as Halligan and Scott remind us, it's also been profitable.

(966 words)

Source: Timm, Jordan. "Book Review: Marketing Lessons from the Grateful Dead." *Canadian Business Magazine*. 13 Sept. 2010. Web. 23 Nov. 2010. <http://www.canadianbusiness.com/after_hours/lifestyle_products/article.jsp?content=20100913_10024_10024>.

VOCABULARY

Part A

■ Match these words and expressions with their definitions. Use the line numbers provided to examine the words in context.

WORDS AND EXPRESSIONS			DEFINITIONS
1. appraisal	(line 3)	____	a) continue to be in the same state or condition
2. charting	(line 8)	____	b) help something grow or develop
3. acknowledged	(line 10)	____	c) statement or opinion judging the worth, value or condition of something
4. grossing	(line 11)	____	d) connect closely to each other
5. remain	(line 14)	____	e) ranking or rating
6. nurture	(line 16)	____	f) something in need of being examined in detail
7. case study	(line 20)	____	g) profits earned before taxes have been deducted
8. correlate	(line 31)	____	h) admitted or accepted as being true
9. marketplace	(line 46)	____	i) worth of a product
10. brand value	(line 82)	____	j) the part of business activity that is concerned with buying and selling goods in competition with other companies

Part B

■ **Look up the** following **words** in the dictionary and write their definitions.

■ **Break them up** into their roots and suffixes. Provide a definition for the suffix *-able*. What role does it play in the words' meanings? (For more information on vocabulary strategies, see page 190.)

1. fashionable: _____

2. spreadable: _____

3. profitable: _____

Definition of *-able*: _____

COMPREHENSION

■ Working with a partner, refer to your notes to answer the questions under each of the subtitles on pages 132 and 133. Note that the answers may be found throughout the text and not just in one place, and that to complete questions 3, 6, 9, 12 and 15, you may have to **infer** the answers.

Reading Comprehension Strategy 5: Inferring

Many ideas that we can understand from reading a text are not actually written in the text, but instead are inferred. Often, it is necessary to read between the lines to understand the full message of a text. (For more information on reading comprehension strategies, see page 189.)

A. Freemium

1. What did The Dead do?

_____

_____

_____

_____

2. What was the marketing strategy?

_____

_____

_____

_____

3. What Internet strategy/phenomenon does this remind you of?

_____

_____

B. Newsletter

4. What did The Dead do?

_____

_____

5. What was the marketing strategy?

_____

_____

6. What social media could replace this?

_____

C. Authenticity

7. What did The Dead do?

_____

8. What was the marketing strategy?

_____

_____

9. What Internet strategy could replace this?

_____

_____

D. In-house ticket service

10. What did The Dead do?

_____

_____

11. What was the marketing strategy?

_____

_____

12. What Internet strategy could replace this?

_____

_____

E. Brand value

13. What did The Dead do?

_____

_____

14. What was the marketing strategy?

_____

_____

15. How could this be done on the Internet?

_____

_____

DISCUSSION

■ Discuss these questions with a partner or in a small group.

1. Would the Grateful Dead still have been successful if they had not understood the powers of social networking and marketing? Explain your opinion.

2. Discuss what the Grateful Dead did right in their marketing campaign.

3. What could the Grateful Dead have done differently (to improve or simplify their campaign) if they had had access to the Internet and all the social media outlets that we have today?

EXPANSION

How could you use each of these five Grateful Dead strategies to promote your field of study on the Internet? On a separate sheet of paper, write one or two ideas for each strategy in point-form notes.

1. Freemium

2. Online newsletter, forum, Facebook, Blog or Twitter announcement

3. Authenticity

4. In-house or online ticket service

5. Brand value

Old Spice cologne

Watching 🖥️

OLD SPICE'S POPULARITY REBORN

Do you wear Old Spice cologne or do you know someone who does? Maybe you wear it because of the company's extremely creative marketing techniques. In this Global News report, you will see how Old Spice, owned by Proctor & Gamble, took a traditional advertising campaign and turned it into one of the most successful viral advertising campaigns to date using social media like Twitter, Facebook and YouTube.

■ Before you watch the video, complete the pre-watching vocabulary exercise.

■ Take the time to read the comprehension questions and highlight the keywords.

■ Then, while you watch the video, **listen for keyword cues** and answer the questions. (For more information on listening comprehension strategies, see page 205.)

PRE-WATCHING VOCABULARY

Part A

■ Match the following words and expressions with their correct definitions.

WORDS		DEFINITIONS
1. harness	____	a) spokesperson responsible for selling/pitching goods or services
2. claim	____	b) sending out radio, television or Internet content
3. pitch person	____	
4. broadcasting	____	c) improve the way that a product or service is perceived by the market
5. reposition	____	d) control and use the natural force or power of something
		e) state that something is true even though it has not been proven

EXPRESSIONS		DEFINITIONS
1. brand recognition	____	a) excessively confident
2. overflowing with bravado	____	b) so high that it can't be counted
3. off the charts	____	c) powerful formula
4. didn't cost a penny	____	d) no money needed to be paid
5. lightning in a bottle	____	e) instant knowledge of a product or service from a visual, textual or audio representation

Part B

■ Provide short answers for these questions.

1. What do you think a six-ton ego is?

_____

2. What are six-pack abs?

_____

My eLab ✎
Answer additional questions for "Old Spice's Popularity Reborn."

COMPREHENSION

■ Answer the following questions.

1. What can Old Spice claim?

_____

2. After the debut of their three traditional television commercials, the campaign "exploded online." What did TV viewers do in response to the TV commercials?

_____

3. What two things did Old Spice do next?

_____

_____

_____

4. How many viewings of the videos did they get?

_____

5. How much did it cost to broadcast all the online videos?

_____

6. Did Old Spice increase its brand recognition?

☐ Yes   ☐ No

Explain how you know.

_____

7. How does John Bell, a public relations specialist, say Old Spice managed to build trust with the public?

_____

8. What was Old Spice trying to do with this campaign?

_____

_____

_____

9. Is it easier to reposition an existing product than it is to position a new product?

☐ Yes ☐ No

Explain how you know. _____

_____

_____

10. Give the main idea of this report. This report tells us about ... _____

_____

_____

DISCUSSION

■ Discuss the following questions with a partner.

1. Do you find the Old Spice ads funny? Why or why not?

2. Do you think the ads have really changed the way people think about the cologne? Explain.

3. At the time this report aired, it was not known whether or not Old Spice sales had improved because of their viral marketing campaign. Do you think this campaign has improved sales for Old Spice? Why or why not?

4. If the Old Spice Guy is not "everyman" but "the man you want your man to be / smell like," who is Old Spice's target audience? Do you think they have defined their target audience correctly? Why or why not?

EXPANSION

In your field work writing and speaking assignments at the end of this unit, you will make a viral video as part of a viral marketing campaign to promote your field of study. To prepare for this, you should start by identifying a general audience type. Your target audience are people you think should be better informed about your field of study—high school students about to choose their program or CEGEP students in transition programs who haven't yet made up their minds about what they want to do. Or perhaps you have another group in mind.

■ Think about the age, cultural background and interests of your potential audience and prepare a general profile of the average person to whom you will attempt to promote your field of study by answering the questions on page 137. The first question is done for you as an example.

Target Audience Profile

	DESCRIPTION OF GENERAL AUDIENCE TYPE	IMPLICATIONS FOR VIRAL CAMPAIGN
1. Who should you address when you promote your field of study?	*High school and first-year CEGEP students who are deciding on their field of study*	*The message and video must be fun, fast, flashy and interesting to students.*
2. What approximate age is your target audience?		
3. Which gender do you want to target? Which gender is more likely to be interested? Is this a stereotype? Is it important to reach out to the other gender?		
4. What is the cultural background of the majority? Are there any other cultures to consider?		
5. What are the interests of people who might be considering entering your field of study?		
6. Are there other characteristics (personality traits, etc.) to consider?		

Using the Present Perfect Tense

One of the two main uses for the present perfect tense is to talk about an action that occurred in the past when it is not indicated when the action occurred.

Example:

I <u>have seen</u> the Old Spice viral marketing campaign online.

Clearly, the action happened in the past, but the speaker does not indicate when the action happened.

The present perfect is formed using the auxiliary *to have* in the present and the past participle of the main verb. The verb *have* agrees with the subject of the sentence.

Examples:

The company <u>has created</u> a viral marketing advertisement.

We <u>have seen</u> many different viral advertisements on the Internet.

■ Read the paragraph below and put the verbs in the present perfect verb tense.

Viral Marketing (become) [1]_____ a very trendy way to promote the products or services of a company or organization. It (grow) [2]_____ from a relatively unknown Internet phenomenon to a multimillion-dollar marketing tool. And big name brands such as Adidas and Old Spice (begin)[3] _____ to take notice. Both companies (create) [4]_____ viral content to put online in an attempt to increase their product sales, and (enjoy) [5]_____ tremendous financial rewards as a result. However, not all viral marketing campaigns (have) [6]_____ the success of Adidas and Old Spice. Unfortunately, some viral marketing campaigns (never / catch on) [7]_____ . And over the course of the last decade, an array of viral marketing campaigns (come) [8]_____ and (go) [9]_____, mainly because they (fail) [10]_____ to spread beyond a single Internet community. Still, it is difficult to argue with those marketing experts who see it as an excellent way for brands to interact with consumers.

Refer to Units 3 and 4 of the Grammar Guide for further explanations and practice on the present perfect tense.

Reading 6.2

advertainment:
combination of **advertising** and **entertainment** (newly coined Internet term)

That's advertainment! Brands create buzz with web videos, and gimmicks. In this reading, several successful online viral marketing campaigns are discussed and analyzed.

■ **Skim** the article on the next page by reading the title and the first sentence of each paragraph, and by looking at the pictures. Then decide what you think the main idea of the text is and write it on the line below. (For more information on reading comprehension strategies, see page 189.)

Main idea: _____

- Take time to read the comprehension questions on pages 141 and 142 before you read the text.

- Then read the text and answer the questions that follow.

The Best-Ever Social Media Campaigns

By Victoria Taylor

Isaiah Mustafa as The Old Spice guy

1 Procter & Gamble's Old Spice was just another guy brand with an entertaining **spokesman** in its TV commercials until the brand's agency, Wieden+Kennedy, put Isaiah Mustafa on the web recently and invited fans to use Twitter, Facebook and other social media outlets to
5 pose questions that he quickly answered. The questions poured in— even celebrities asked a few—and Mustafa responded in more than 180 web videos shot quickly over a few days. The real-time effort was the first of its kind, but it won't be the last.

2 Marketers are eager to find clever new ways to engage consumers
10 online with branded content and interactive advertising that is good enough to make people want to share it with their network of friends. Consider Burger King's "Subservient Chicken," who has [taken] commands on the web since the guy in the chicken suit was introduced in 2004.

3 The Old Spice effort and Burger King's order-taking chicken are among
15 the best-ever social media campaigns identified by Forbes.com and a group of experts. Forbes **tapped** three experts to rank the twenty best-ever social media campaigns. The judges—David Berkowitz of the New York City agency 360i, Brandon Evans of the social marketing agency Mr. Youth in New York City and Michael Lebowitz of Big Spaceship, a digital ad shop in
20 Brooklyn—were asked to take into account the success of the campaigns as well as the quality of the execution and creativity of each one.

4 The judges shared the same opinions on some campaigns, such as the marketing effort behind *The Blair Witch Project*, which came in as the best-ever social media campaign—and one of the first of its kind. They
25 were divided on others, such as Hotmail's decision in 1996 to promote the e-mail carrier at the bottom of each e-mail sent. One judge gave it high marks because it was the first such effort. Another gave it a big yawn.

5 30 The final list included planned, strategic social media campaigns, like Bing's partnership with the Facebook game Farmville to **lure** players to the search engine with a Farmville money reward. Others were quirky, small-
35 budget web efforts that started small and

•••

spokesman, spokeswoman or spokesperson: person who speaks officially for a company

tap: use someone for his or her knowledge and experience

lure: persuade someone into doing something

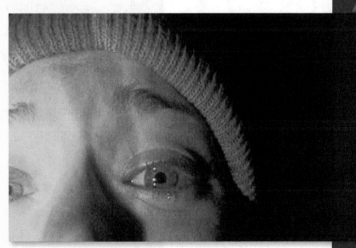

The Blair Witch Project

Blendtec: "Will It Blend?"

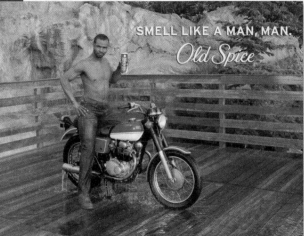

Old Spice: "Smell Like a Man, Man" campaign

vuvuzela: plastic horn you blow in to produce a loud sound

prankster: someone who plays tricks on people to make them look silly

lace: include an idea, phrase, word, etc., all through something you write or say

make a splash: do something that gets a lot of public attention

became big, such as Blendtec's "Will It Blend?" web videos. This series of fun-to-watch web videos feature company founder Tom Dickson destroying everything from a **vuvuzela** to Barbie dolls in a blender. Does it work? The
40 company says home sales of blenders have jumped 700 percent since November 2006.

6 One key to a viral campaign is a message that is compelling and interesting enough that a viewer or participant wants to share it with a friend, says Issa Sawabini,
45 a partner of the youth marketing agency Fuse. And social media is a tool that makes creating a viral or buzz-worthy campaign easier.

7 "A company can't just create a viral video, put it on YouTube and hope that people will come," he says. "You
50 need to have something that is worth talking about."

8 Some social media efforts disappoint marketers. In March 2009, Skittles redesigned its website to function as a Twitter page, with new updates for every Skittles-related tweet. **Pranksters** decided to **lace** Skittles tweets with
55 vulgar language and profanities so that they would end up on the candy's website, forcing the Mars brand to abandon the campaign.

9 The bottom line is that a successful social media campaign requires creativity and a clear message, and needs
60 to **make a splash** at the right time. A good-looking guy in a bath towel doesn't hurt either.

(585 words)

Source: Taylor, Victoria. "The Best-Ever Social Media Campaign." *Forbes.com.* 17 Aug. 2010. Web. 20 Aug. 2010. <http://www.forbes.com/2010/08/17/facebook-old-spice-farmville-pepsi-forbes-viral-marketing-cmo-network-social-media.html.>

VOCABULARY

■ **Find a** word or expression in the text that is a **synonym** for each of these adjectives/phrases. Use paragraph numbers and context clues to find the answers. (For more information on vocabulary strategies, see page 190.)

1. original (paragraphs 1 and 4): _____

2. enthusiastic (paragraph 2): _____

3. smart; intelligent (paragraph 2): _____

4. most appropriate and well done (paragraphs 3 and 4): _____

5. found something boring (paragraph 4): _____

6. peculiar; strange (paragraph 5): _____

7. worth talking about (paragraph 6): _____

8. irresistible (paragraph 6): _____

9. offensive; rude (paragraph 8): _____

10. attractive; handsome (paragraph 9): _____

COMPREHENSION

■ Answer the following questions while referring to the text.

1. What makes the Old Spice campaign original and different?

   _____

   _____

2. What were Forbes' judges hired to find?

   _____

3. What three criteria did they look for?

   _____

4. Did the judges always agree?

   ☐ Yes   ☐ No

   Explain.

   _____

   _____

5. Was Blendtec's campaign successful?

   ☐ Yes   ☐ No

   Explain.

   _____

6. Why do marketers use social media tools like Twitter, Facebook and YouTube to promote their products?

   _____

7. **a)** What important component of a viral marketing campaign does Sawabini mention and why?

   _____

   _____

   b) Why does Sawabini say that "you need to have something worth talking about"?

   _____

   _____

   _____

8. Was Skittles' campaign successful according to the text?

   ☐ Yes   ☐ No

   Explain how you know.

   _____

9. What words in the article tell you that content is important in a viral campaign?

_____

_____

_____

_____

10. **a)** What is the main idea of this article?

_____

_____

    b) Now go back to page 138 and see if the main idea you decided on in the pre-reading skimming exercise is correct.

DISCUSSION

■ Work with a partner to answer the following questions.

1. List the components that make a successful campaign, according to the article.

2. Do you know of any other successful campaigns that are using social media (other than those in this reading)? If so, what is the campaign and how is it using the media?

3. What is the most interesting viral video you have ever watched online? Describe it to your group.

EXPANSION

Sawabini says that you must have a clear message and something to say. What do you think each of the following campaigns was trying to say? In other words, what was the message behind the campaign?

1. Old Spice _____

2. Burger King _____

3. Blair Witch Project _____

4. Farmville _____

5. Blendtec _____

6. Skittles _____

Speaking

REPOSITIONING A BRAND

■ Work with a partner to reposition the Skittles brand. Decide what Skittles could have done to turn around their campaign and make it successful by discussing the following questions.

1. First, ask yourselves the questions in the chart on page 137 to identify Skittles' target audience.

2. Next, think of a short message that Skittles could use to appeal to their target audience.

3. Finally, choose one of the strategies from either the Forbes article or the Grateful Dead campaign that the Skittles campaign did not use, and discuss how they could have used it and why.

Listening 🎧

INTERVIEW WITH DAN ACKERMAN GREENBERG

Not all attempts by companies at viral ad campaigns are successful. What should a company do if they are having trouble making a successful viral marketing campaign? Is there anyone they can hire to help them? Listen to this interview on *Spark* with Dan Ackerman Greenberg, CEO (Chief Executive Officer) and co-founder of the social video marketing company Sharethrough, formerly Co-motion, and graduate of Stanford University, as he speaks about planning a viral video campaign.

■ Before you listen to the interview, complete the pre-listening vocabulary exercise.

■ **Skim** the listening introduction above, along with all of the comprehension questions on pages 144 and 145, and then write down your best guess for the main idea of the listening here.

Main idea: _____

■ Take time to read the comprehension questions and highlight the keywords.

■ Then, while you listen to the interview, **listen for keyword cues** and answer the questions. (For more information on listening comprehension strategies, see page 205.)

PRE-LISTENING VOCABULARY

Part A

■ Match the following words and expressions with their correct definitions.

WORDS		DEFINITIONS
1. embed	____	**a)** coming from those with decision-making power; planned and controlled
2. obscurity	____	**b)** state of not being known or remembered
3. engage	____	**c)** include information inside other information on the Internet so that it looks like it occurred naturally
4. top down	____	
5. bottom up	____	**d)** coming from the people; unplanned, random and uncontrolled
6. guest	____	
7. trailer	____	**e)** picture, set of words or short video intended to persuade people to buy a product or use a service
8. view/viewing	____	
9. post/posting	____	**f)** advertisement for a new film or television show
10. ad/advertisement	____	**g)** message put on the Internet for others to read
		h) instance in which a person watches a video on the Internet
		i) attract someone's attention and keep him/her interested
		j) person who is an invited visitor

EXPRESSIONS		DEFINITIONS
1. morally grey	____	a) make a process easier
2. give it legs	____	b) of questionable ethics
3. grease the wheels	____	c) momentary occurrence
4. hired guns	____	d) paid experts or consultants
5. blip in the ether	____	e) make something stronger or more viable

Part B

■ Write down the meaning of each of these words and expressions that you have seen in previous units.

1. hire:_____

2. firm:_____

3. behind the scenes: _____

Top down versus bottom up:
A top-down decision comes from the management, whereas a bottom-up decision comes from the employees or customers.

COMPREHENSION

1. According to the listening, what do average people generally do with funny videos to help the videos go viral?

_____
_____

2. How can a video get millions of hits in a short time period?

_____
_____

3. The Co-Motion Group describes itself as "viral marketing hired guns." Explain what the Co-Motion Group does. (You may need to add to your answer after listening to the entire interview.)

_____
_____
_____
_____

4. What exactly did Ackerman Greenberg do for Tech Crunch and why?

_____
_____

5. Circle the techniques that Ackerman Greenberg's company uses to help companies get their videos seen or make their videos go viral. (Circle more than one answer if necessary.)

a) Pay popular bloggers to put a link to the video on their blog

b) Post the video in forums and post comments to try to start conversations about the video

c) Create new video content for the client

d) Buy ads on blogs or forums to advertise the video

6. What does Ackerman Greenberg say

a) his company is really doing?

_____

_____

_____

b) makes people more engaged with a video?

_____

_____

_____

Dan Ackerman Greenberg

7. After listening to Ackerman Greenberg, what does it mean for people to be engaged with a video?

_____

_____

_____

8. The interviewer says that it is often hard to know if a video is an ad or simply something that someone has just posted. According to Ackerman Greenberg, is this important?

☐ Yes   ☐ No

9. a) Does Ackerman believe that what his company does is morally grey?

☐ Yes   ☐ No

b) What argument does he give that tells you his belief?

_____

_____

10. a) Give the main idea of this interview in one or two sentences.

_____

_____

_____

_____

b) Now go back to page 143 and see if the main idea you decided on is correct.

■ Discuss these questions with a partner.

Viral videos are, in theory, popular because they are supposedly real, homemade and created by average, ordinary people (bottom up). However, many videos are faked by large companies (top down) and made to look as if they are real. As a consumer, do you feel it is unethical (or morally grey) for a company to create fake online videos and market them as if they are real? Why or why not? Come up with three reasons why it is ethical and three reasons why it is unethical for companies to create fake videos and present them to Internet surfers as if they are real.

■ Now, with a different partner, each pick a different side of the issue to debate. Use your three reasons wisely to argue your side of the debate.

EXPANSION

■ Think about your field of study. Is it well-known? Well-understood? What are some of the common misperceptions that people, especially students, have about your field of study? What are some of the common stereotypes that people have about students in your field of study?

■ Now think about how you could promote your field of study to change some of these misperceptions or stereotypes. How could you promote it in a new and more attractive way to appeal to your target audience?

■ Now that you know what you wish to promote about your field of study, write a clear message for a viral video that is "compelling and interesting enough that a viewer or participant wants to share it with a friend."[1]

PRONUNCIATION

Pronouncing *h*

Many second language learners have trouble pronouncing /h/ in English. The general rule of thumb is if you see an *h*, you should pronounce it with an aspiration (a puff of air).

In this listening, you will practise pronouncing the /h/ sound when it is needed and not pronouncing /h/ when it is not needed, using words found in this unit.

Part A

■ Listen to the sentences and circle the letters of the words that you hear.

1. **a)** harnessed   **b)** our nest
2. **a)** harnessed   **b)** our nest
3. **a)** heat   **b)** eat
4. **a)** heat   **b)** eat
5. **a)** had   **b)** ad
6. **a)** had   **b)** ad

• • •

1. Taylor, Victoria. "The Best-Ever Social Media Campaign." *Forbes Magazine*. 17 Aug. 2010. Web. 20 Aug. 2010. <http://www.forbes.com/2010/08/17/facebook-old-spice-farmville-pepsi-forbes-viral-marketing-cmo-network-social-media.html.>

7. a) holidays	**b)** all the days
8. a) holidays	**b)** all the days
9. a) his hat	**b)** he's at
10. a) his hat	**b)** he's at

■ Now listen again and repeat each sentence with the correct pronunciation.

Part B

■ Listen to and repeat these words with the initial /h/ sound while placing a tissue in front of your mouth. When you say each word, the tissue should move with the pronunciation of the initial /h/.

1. hot	**6.** Hotmail	**11.** history
2. hip	**7.** hippie	**12.** highlight
3. hit	**8.** host	**13.** hype
4. help	**9.** held	**14.** hotline
5. hunt	**10.** humour	**15.** hire

Part C

■ Now listen to and repeat these words with the /h/ sound in the middle while placing a tissue in front of your mouth. When you say each word, the tissue should move with the pronunciation of the middle /h/.

1. in-house	**3.** threshold	**5.** handheld
2. behaviour	**4.** Deadheads	**6.** adhere

Reading 6.3

In "The 10 Most Annoying Online Viral Marketing Campaigns of All Time" (2009), Daniel Long states that

> there are many great viral ads that circulate the web today, though most of them are a little too obvious in promoting their brand. Typically, a successful online viral campaign is
> - short in length;
> - seen by many;
> - pretending to be user-generated content (e.g., shot on home video); and
> - elaborately composed to generate speculation and/or controversy.
>
> We especially hate the ones that lead us to think that they are real, and then proceed to annoy the heck out of us when we realize that we were **duped**.[2]

duped: fooled; tricked

Long's statement is useful to you in that you can use his criteria as a mini-checklist for a successful video as you create your own later on in this unit; however, as you do the retell activity that follows, you will notice that even if a company follows all of the criteria for success, their campaign may still be unsuccessful in the end.

2. Long, Daniel. "The 10 Most Annoying Online Viral Marketing Campaigns of All Time." PC Authority Lifestyle. 23 Jan. 2009. Web. 24 Nov. 2010. <http://www.pcauthority.com.au/Feature/135061,the-10-most-annoying-online-viral-marketing-campaigns-of-all-time.aspx>;

■ Work with a partner. After deciding who is Partner 1 and who is Partner 2, each of you will read about two viral campaigns, one that was successful and one that was not. Do not read each other's texts. Take short notes on what you read. As you read, make a logical guess about which campaign was successful and why?

■ When you are ready, cover the texts and describe what you read to your partner. Use only your notes and your own words to describe the text. Do not just reread the campaigns to your partner. See if your partner can guess which was successful and which was not from your description. Once you have finished, check with your teacher to see if you are correct in your guesses.

Partner 1

Viral Campaigns

Part A

OFFICEMAX: "ELF YOURSELF"

For its 2006 office campaign, OfficeMax encouraged web users to upload pictures of themselves. An **elf**, with the web users' faces would then dance.

5 The campaign, created by New York-based independent agency Toy and San Francisco-based EVB, led to the creation of more than 122 million elves during 10 that holiday season. It increased site traffic and generated a number of **wannabes** and **spinoffs**, driving sales 15 and brand **awareness**, according to the judges.

elf: small, imaginary person with pointed ears and magical powers (plural: elves)

wannabe: imitation of a famous and successful campaign

spinoff: another ad that copies or continues a story or theme

awareness: knowledge of

badass: biker slang meaning "very good" or "very impressive"

OfficeMax "Elf Yourself"

(65 words)

TATTOOED LEGO

Barcelona's Grey Agency has created a viral marketing campaign for Pilot Extra-Fine ball-point pens featuring LEGO people with "**badass**" tattoos drawn on their arms and faces. The purpose of the campaign was to use the 20 tattoos to show how super-thin the lines could be if drawn with a Pilot pen. These people have tattoed dedications to Harley Davidson and lots of angry skulls and seem to be taken straight out of your mother's nightmares.

(75 words)

Sources: Adapted from: "In Pictures: Best-Ever Social Media Campaigns." Forbes.com. 17 Aug. 2010. Web. 20 Aug. 2010. <http://www.forbes.com/2010/08/17/facebook-old-spice-farmville-pepsi-forbes-viral-marketing-cmo-network-social-media_slide.html>; Van Luling, Todd. "Strange but True: Tattoed LEGOS." Flavorwire.com. 22 July 2010. Web. 6 Sept. 2010. <http://flavorwire.com/106769/strange-but-true-tattoed-legos>.

Part B

MOTRIN

A viral Internet campaign for a Motrin pain medication showed a quotation from a mom describing the pain she suffered from carrying her baby in a **carrier**; underneath the quotation, an advertising message offered this advice to moms: "Take Motrin to ease the agonizing pain caused by carrying
5   your (innocent and beautiful) baby on your back all the time."

carrier: cloth wrap, sling or pack designed to hold a baby on an adult's chest or back

(59 words)

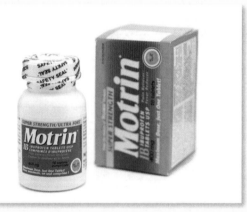

IKEA: "FACEBOOK SHOWROOM"

To promote the opening of a new store in Malmo, Sweden, IKEA had the store manager post pictures of the new showrooms on Facebook. The first people to **tag** the items **won** them. Awareness of the campaign **spread** rapidly from participants to their Facebook friends. "[This is] a great idea that
10   not only is highly viral but gets consumers engaging with actual merchandise," says Brandon Evans of the social marketing agency Mr. Youth.

tag: Internet term meaning "put your name on a picture"

win (past: won): get something as a prize

spread: become known by more and more people

(76 words)

IKEA "Facebook Showroom"

Sources: Adapted from; Barreto, Manuela. "Motrin Teaches Us the Good and the Bad Side of Viral." 77Lab news. 18 Nov. 2008. Web. 6 Sept. 2010. <http://lab.77agency.com/viral-marketing/motrin-teaches-us-the-good-and-the-bad-side-of-viral-854/>; "In Pictures: Best-Ever Social Media Campaigns." Forbes.com. 17 Aug. 2010. Web. 20 Aug. 2010. <http://www.forbes.com/2010/08/17/facebook-old-spice-farmville-pepsi-forbes-viral-marketing-cmo-network-social-media_slide.html>.

EXPANSION

■ Work with your partner to complete these exercises.

1. Look at the two successful campaigns and determine which qualities seem to be the most important for a successful campaign.

Successful campaign 1: _____

_____

Successful campaign 2: _____

_____

2. Analyze what went wrong in the two unsuccessful campaigns.

Unsuccessful campaign 1:

_____

_____

_____

Unsuccessful campaign 2:

_____

_____

_____

3. Create a new, more inspiring message for each of the two unsuccessful campaigns.

Unsuccessful campaign 1:

_____

_____

_____

Unsuccessful campaign 2:

_____

_____

_____

GENERAL VOCABULARY LIST

These are the words and phrases that you should know after completing this unit. Remind yourself of their meanings by writing down their definitions or translations.

DEFINITIONS/TRANSLATIONS

1. acknowledge
2. appraisal
3. base
4. brand recognition
5. brand value
6. broadcasting
7. buzz-worthy
8. case study
9. charting
10. claim
11. clever
12. compelling
13. correlate
14. eager
15. fashionable
16. grossing
17. harness
18. marketplace
19. nurture
20. profitable
21. quirky
22. remain
23. reposition
24. spread
25. vulgar

My eLab

Review the vocabulary from this unit.

"Not all videos go viral organically—there is a method to the madness."
—Dan Ackerman Greenberg

Vocabulary Assignment

■ Invent ten new social media terms that could be used in your field of study. Note that they should be newly coined words (neologisms), not words that you already know. Create these words by combining existing vocabulary from your field of study with concepts from the Internet, like the Twitterverse words from the Explore activity on page 128. Be creative. Make sure that the words that you use to form the new terms aren't cognates in your own language, and that you have spelled them as correctly as possible.

■ Write down a definition for each of your newly coined terms.

Field-Specific Vocabulary List

	ENGLISH DEFINITIONS
1. _____	_____
2. _____	_____
3. _____	_____
4. _____	_____
5. _____	_____
6. _____	_____
7. _____	_____
8. _____	_____
9. _____	_____
10. _____	_____

■ Ask another student if he or she can guess what your terms mean.

Writing Assignment

1. Creating a Viral Video Marketing Campaign

You are going to create a viral marketing campaign to promote your field of study on the Internet. First, refer to the detailed profile of your target audience (see the Expansion exercise on pages 136 and 137) to make sure that everything you do here appropriately targets your specific audience profile. Next, refer to the message that you created to promote your field (see the Expansion exercise on page 146); think about the concept of **virality** and about Long's criteria for a successful video (see page 147), which you should use as a mini-checklist as you create your own video.

Part A

■ Choose three of the marketing strategies mentioned in the Grateful Dead's successful marketing campaign (Reading 6.1) and/or Forbes' best-ever campaigns (Reading 6.2). Write a 100-word paragraph for each of the three strategies. In each paragraph, provide a topic sentence that explains which strategy you have chosen

virality: the factor that makes a video go viral

My eLab
Analyze the qualities of virality in online videos to discover what makes people want to share them with their friends and families.

and what you will do with it. Include support that details what exactly you intend to do with the strategy and why it will successfully promote your field of study. (For more information about writing topic sentences and support, refer to page 201.)

- Using the **paragraph examination** strategy, revise each of the three paragraphs you have written about your marketing strategies. (For information on this and other revision strategies, see page 204.)

Part B

- Write the complete dialogue for your viral video, as well as any Twitter or Facebook messages that you will use in your campaign. (Each person should write approximately 300 words in total, including video content and all messages.) Be sure to use at least five words from the General Vocabulary List on page 151 and, if possible, some of your newly created neologisms from the Field-Specific Vocabulary List on page 152 in your dialogue or messages, and highlight them. Be prepared to explain these neologisms to your teacher.

- **Proofread** your video dialogue before you record it. (For information on this and other revision strategies, see page 204.)

2. Writing a Complaint Letter

- Write a complaint letter to a company whose viral campaign irritates or offends you. Politely explain your concerns with their campaign (200 words). (For information on writing a complaint letter, see the model on page 193.)

3. Writing a Request Letter

- Write a request for more information on or samples of a product you have seen advertised on the Internet (200 words). (For information on writing a request letter, see the model on page 193.)

Speaking Assignment

1. Creating a Viral Video and Presenting Your Marketing Campaign and Your Video

Do this after completing Writing Assignment 1. Do both Parts A and B.

Part A

- Film your video with a partner or a team (Use the dialogue you wrote in Writing Assignment 1, Part B). To do this, you can borrow a video camera from your school or simply use your cellphone camera. Don't worry if it looks homemade. One of the important qualities of viral marketing videos is their real-life authenticity.

- Go viral. Put your video online at YouTube or another well-known video website and send it to as many friends and family members as possible. Place Twitter and Facebook messages online and monitor them, answering any questions and responding to any comments for at least one week. (Follow through and use your strategies from Writing Assignment 1, Part A.)

- Analyze your results. Did your video go viral? Why or why not?

Part B

■ Present your complete viral video marketing campaign (Writing Assignment 1) in a well-researched, detailed and step-by-step manner to a small group or in front of the class. Each student should speak for three to four minutes.

■ Explain all the elements of your campaign, including
  • a description of your target audience;
  • an explanation of the message you wish to promote; and
  • the strategies you decided to use and why you chose them.

■ Describe what you did online to go viral. Say whether or not your campaign was successful, and give reasons for your results.

■ Finally, show your viral video to the class.

2. Placing a Follow-Up Phone Call

Do this assignment with a partner after completing Writing Assignment 2 or 3. Ideally, your partner should read your letter before you begin this assignment.

■ With your partner, role-play a telephone call in response to the complaint or request letter you have written. Take turns being the company customer service representative and the customer. (Each of you should speak for three to four minutes.)

■ If you are the customer service representative ("rep"), ask questions about the information you have received in the letter from your "customer" to get more details. Offer an apology for the complaint or offer delivery information and coupons in answer to the request, etc.

■ If you are the customer, go into more detail about your complaint or request when you answer the rep's questions.

■ Both of you should try to use modals to ensure that your conversation is polite and formal, as well as appropriate greetings and introductions at the beginning and salutations and thanks at the end. (For information on using modals, see Unit 8 of the Grammar Guide.)

■ Your teacher may ask you to perform your phone call for another team after you have practised it a couple of times. In this case, ask your teacher if you can write a dialogue in advance, or write keywords to help you remember what you want to say.

My eLab Documents includes additional research assignments to help you learn more about your field of study.

The Pitch

Have you ever wanted to slay a dragon? Create your own product or service? Own your own business? In this unit, you will have the opportunity to do all three. The theme of this unit is based on a popular CBC television program called *Dragons' Den*. Your project is to create a product or service that fulfils a need and then pitch it to a group of venture capitalists. To do this, you will work as a team to complete five steps, drawing on knowledge that you have obtained in your field of study. Your final objective will be to write a proposal for your invention and present it in a pitch. Get ready to meet the judges!

EXPLORE

Part A

Part of making a successful pitch to **venture capitalists** is being able to describe your product or service and explain the need it will fulfil. Below are the names of ten relatively successful products that you have probably never heard of.

■ Working with a partner, take turns randomly selecting a product name from the list below. Do not let your partner know the product name you have chosen. Try to invent a product that suits the name you have selected. Then describe your invented product and explain the need that your invention fulfils to your partner.

■ Your partner should try to guess which product you are describing.

1. Windy Wonder
2. Booty Pop
3. Nappak Portasleep
4. no!no!
5. Defendius Door Chain

6. Necktie Fan
7. Bumpits
8. I.C. Can
9. The Mosquito
10. BluBlocker Solar Sparkle

Part B

Below are the real descriptions for the above products.

■ Read your assigned section. Do not read each other's sections.

■ Then in your own words, explain to your partner what you have read about each product and the real need it fulfils. Try not to look at the text when you talk. Instead, use your notes. See if your partner can guess which product you are describing.

■ With your partner, write your final guesses beside each of the product descriptions.

Partner 1

a) Tired? Need a place to catch some ZZZs? Sleep tight on a portable bed that you can quickly assemble anytime, anywhere. Take a nap on a _____3_____ .

b) This brightly coloured square of nylon has pockets sewn into the corners. When packed with sand, the weight of the pockets anchors the mat to the ground—no more rocks needed to do the job. Don't let the weather interfere with your picnic—buy a _____1_____ .

c) Here is a security device with a few twists—literally. It attaches to your door, so the door will only open once the puzzle maze has been completed. Be sure to give yourself a few extra minutes when the pizza delivery man knocks at your door! Get a _____5_____ .

d) When you want to be cool, all you have to do is wear this fashionable accessory. Can't stand the heat? Wear the USB-powered _____6_____ .

e) These self-gripping, leave-in, volumizing hair inserts give you instant volume and let you feel like you just stepped out of a salon! Look beautiful with _____7_____ .

Partner 2

f) These stylish sunglasses block 100 percent of UVA and UVB light waves—plus most of the harsh and squint-producing blue spectrum light! Keep in fashion while keeping the sun out with _____ *LO.* _____ .

g) If unwanted body hair has you screaming in frustration, turn to this hair removal beauty treatment for results. Say "Yes! Yes!" to _____ *NoNo!* _____ .

h) This device emits a high-frequency pulsing sound that can be heard by people younger than twenty and almost nobody older than thirty. The sound is designed to irritate young people, so that after a few minutes, they can't stand it and go away. Being bugged? Bite back with _____ *9* _____ .

i) This unusual container is designed with a self-cooling device to reduce the temperature of its contents by at least thirty degrees in three minutes. Be chill with the _____ .

j) Now you too can have a Hollywood backside that turns heads! No expensive surgery or overpriced trainer required. Comfortable enough to wear with every outfit! Every behind looks better with _____ .

Adapted from: Moon, Jade. "Inventors Are Seen as Crazy Dreamers. Until They Make Millions." *Hawaii Business.* 1 Aug. 1986. Web. 27 July 2010. <http://www.allbusiness.com/management/102044-1.html>; Cernansku, Rachel. "Five Curious Food Inventions You've Never Heard Of." *Planet Green Discovery.com*, 9 Mar. 2010, Web. 27 July 2010. <http://www.theshoppingchannel.com/category/tsc+tv/program+guide/24+hour+product+review.do>; Booty Bop Official Website. 27 July 2010, Web. 17 Dec. 2010. <http://www.bootypop.com>; Mosquito, Moving Sound Technology Inc. 27 July 2010. Web. 17 Dec. 2010. <http://www.mosquitogroup.com/>; HSN.Inc. 27 July 2010. Web. 17 Dec. 2010. <http://health-fitness.hsn.com/no-no_c-hf_a-5488_xc.aspx?o=!TNHF&cm_sp=TN°Wellness° nono&prev=hp!sf&sf=HF&osf=HF&ccm=QC|>; The Shopping Channel. 27 July 2010. Web. 17 Dec. 2010. <http://www.theshoppingchannel.com/product/more+from/blublocker+solar+sparkle+506582.do?&N=128153%20 128628%20100089&Ns=P_PRICE>; Funny Inventions and Weird Crazy Inventions. InventionReaction.com. 7 Apr. 2008, Web. 27 July 2010. <http://www.inventionreaction.com/weird-inventions/>.

Part C

■ Discuss the following questions in a small group or with your partner.

1. Have you ever invented something or thought about doing so? If so, what? If not, think about it now. Share an invention idea with your partner(s).

2. What invention do you think has made the greatest contribution to your field of study? Why?

Reading 7.1

Have you ever walked into a store, seen a new food product, digital device or piece of exercise equipment, and thought to yourself, "I could have invented that"? So why didn't you? In *"Where Do Good Ideas Come From?"*, author Steven Johnson outlines a list of seven ways in which old ideas become new ones. Here, *National Post*'s Kathryn Blaze Carlson looks at six of Johnson's key reasons why innovation occurs and answers the question, "Where do great ideas come from?"

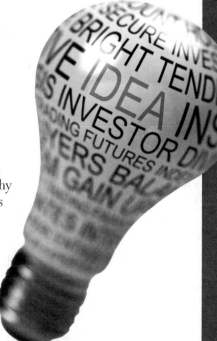

■ First, complete the pre-reading vocabulary exercise with two partners.

■ Then do the reading retell activity with your partners.

■ Finally, answer the comprehension questions on pages 161 and 162 with your partners.

PRE-READING VOCABULARY

■ Working with your partners, take turns reading these vocabulary words and their definitions. **Find an antonym** for each of the words in Part A **and a synonym** for each of the words in Part B.

Vocabulary Strategy 6: Finding Antonyms

Just as learning a variety of synonyms can strengthen and enlarge your vocabulary base, so too can learning antonyms help you to fine-tune your knowledge of English word meanings. (For more information about vocabulary strategies, see page 190.)

Part A

■ Match the words and their definitions with their antonyms. Line numbers have been included for you to see the words in context.

WORDS AND DEFINITIONS			ANTONYMS
1. chief: most important	(line 2)	_____	a) hit
2. flop: film, play, movie, product, etc., that is not successful	(line 9)	_____	b) faltering
			c) insignificant
3. idle: not working or producing anything	(line 21)	_____	d) raise
4. steady: continuing or developing gradually	(line 49)	_____	e) sprint
5. degrade: lower the character or quality of something	(line 43)	_____	f) simple
6. stroll: slow, relaxed walk	(line 68)	_____	g) busy
7. layered: complex; with many levels	(line 53)	_____	

Part B

■ Match the words and their definitions with their synonyms. Line numbers have been included here for you to see the words in context.

WORDS AND DEFINITIONS			SYNONYMS
1. breakthrough: important new discovery	(line 2)	_____	a) heap
2. hunch: intuitive feeling	(line 16)	_____	b) luck
3. accretion: gradual process by which new things are added	(line 18)	_____	c) innovation
			d) obviously
4. stack: pile of things	(line 53)	_____	e) accumulation
5. conspicuously: in a manner that is easy to notice	(line 53)	_____	f) promote
			g) premonition
			h) independently

•••

6. singlehandedly: doing
something without anyone
else's help   (line 58)   _____

7. foster: to help a skill, feeling,
idea, etc., develop over a
period of time   (line 67)   _____

8. serendipity: when a discovery
is made by accident   (line 64)   _____

READING RETELL

■ Work in a group of three. Your teacher will assign you each a different section to read. Do not read the other sections unless your teacher instructs you to.

■ **Take** point-form **notes** as you read about two of Johnson's key reasons why innovation occurs. (For more information on reading comprehension strategies, see page 189.)

■ Then, with your book closed, retell what you have read to your partners using your notes.

Partner 1

How Ideas Are Born

By Kathryn Blaze Carlson

Part A

THE ADJACENT POSSIBLE

WHAT IS IT? The adjacent possible is the notion that innovations build logically on previous breakthroughs. It is one of the chief reasons behind why several people invent the same thing at the same time—the natural next step. Mr. Johnson uses the analogy of the house to describe the concept: "You
5 begin in a room with four doors, each leading to a new room that you haven't visited yet," he said. "Those four rooms are the adjacent possible."

    EXAMPLE: YouTube, 1995. Mr. Johnson writes that had inventors Chad Hurley, Steve Chen and Jawed Karim tried to create YouTube a **decade** earlier, it would have been a "spectacular flop" because a video-sharing site
10 was not within the adjacent possible of the early World Wide Web. "For starters, the vast majority of Web users [relied on] painfully slow **dial-up connections** that could sometimes take minutes to download a small image," he writes. The average two-minute-long YouTube clip would have taken as much as an hour to download on the then-standard 14.4
15 kbps modems.

decade: ten years

dial-up connection: before high-speed connections, one modem had to telephone another modem.

THE SLOW HUNCH

WHAT IS IT? A slow hunch is an idea that develops over time. Tim Berners-Lee, inventor of the World Wide Web, described his slow hunch this way: "It was a process of accretion, not the linear solving of one problem after another."

...

© **ERPI** • REPRODUCTION PROHIBITED

20 **EXAMPLE:** The World Wide Web, 1990. "The Web came into being as a
slow hunch: from a child's exploration of a hundred-year-old encyclopedia,
to a **freelancer**'s idle **side project** designed to help him keep track of his
colleagues, to a deliberate attempt to build a new information platform that
could connect computers across the planet," Mr. Johnson writes.

(282 words)

Partner 2

Part B

EXAPTATION

WHAT IS IT? Exaptation is when an idea or hunch is cultivated and optimized
25 for one use, but then gets **hijacked** for a completely different use. It refers
to the "collisions that happen when different fields of expertise converge in
some shared physical or intellectual space," Mr. Johnson writes. "That's
where true sparks fly."

EXAMPLE: The printing press, **circa** 1400. Johannes Gutenberg is
30 credited with inventing the printing press, but each of the key elements that
comprised the world-changing machine had been
developed long before he put the parts together. Among
these key parts was the **screw press**, which had been
invented for wine-making. "He took a machine designated
35 to get people drunk and turned it into an engine for mass
communication," Mr. Johnson writes.

ERROR

WHAT IS IT? When it comes to ideas, errors are not
necessarily a bad thing, or as Mr. Johnson writes: "Error
often creates a path that leads you out of your comfortable
40 assumptions."

A screw press

EXAMPLE: Audion, 1903. Lee de Forest's Audion
—a device that could amplify audio signals without
degrading a tuner's ability to [receive] signals at
different frequencies—changed the **landscape**. The
45 Audion made radio, television and the first digital
computers possible, but it was not a deliberate invention.
"At almost every step of the way, de Forest was **flat-out**
wrong about what he was inventing," Mr. Johnson
writes. "The Audion was not so much an invention as it was a steady,
50 persistent accumulation of error."

(243 words)

Part C
PLATFORMS

WHAT IS IT? A platform is an idea or invention that allows for another idea or invention to be built on top of it. "The most generative platforms come in stacks, most conspicuously in the layered platform of the Web," Mr. Johnson writes.

55   **EXAMPLE:** The Internet, 1970. While people **tend** to use "Internet" and "Web" as synonyms, the World Wide Web is actually a system accessed via the Internet. "Tim Berners-Lee was able to singlehandedly design a new medium because he could freely build on top of the open protocols of the Internet 60 platform," Mr. Johnson writes. "He didn't have to engineer an entire system for communicating between computers spread across the planet; that problem had been solved decades before."

SERENDIPITY

WHAT IS IT? "Serendipity is built out of happy accidents, to be sure, 65 but what makes them happy is that the discovery you've made is meaningful to you," Mr. Johnson writes. The key is putting yourself in environments that foster such serendipitous connections. That could mean going for a stroll or taking a long bath—both of which allow the mind to **wander** and **stumble across** old connections. Mr. Johnson writes: "You 70 experience that delightful feeling of serendipity."

    EXAMPLE: Fuchsian functions (an influential mathematical concept), 1880s. French mathematician and physicist Henri Poincare, the father of Fuchsian functions, talks about ideas arising in **crowds**, and serendipitous moments of discovery born after getting stuck. "Disgusted with my failure," 75 he writes. "I went to spend a few days by the seaside, and thought of something else. One morning, walking on the **bluff**, the idea came to me."

(266 words)

tend: have a habit

wander: move about without a definite destination or purpose

stumble across: discover or find something by accident

crowd: large group

bluff: very steep cliff

Source: Blaze Carlson, Kathryn. "How Ideas Are Born." *National Post* 9 Oct. 2010. Web. 25 Nov. 2010. <http://news.nationalpost.com/2010/10/09/how-ideas-are-born/>.

COMPREHENSION

Part A

■ Work together with your two partners to write down the main idea of each section (in your own words) on the lines below.

The Adjacent Possible: _____

_____

The Slow Hunch: _____

_____

Exaptation: _____

_____

Error: _____

_____

Platforms: _____

_____

Serendipity: _____

_____

Part B

■ Now work together with your partners to create a sentence stating the main idea of the text as a whole.

_____

_____

EXPANSION

■ Look at all the inventions (lights, desks, etc.) in the classroom. Choose three of them and write down what need they fulfil and how you would improve upon their design to make them better fulfil this need.

Invention 1: _____

_____

Invention 2: _____

_____

Invention 3: _____

_____

■ Put a pencil on the desk in front of you. Write down four uses for the pencil. Do not include writing on your list.

_____ _____

_____ _____

■ Put two more objects on your desk. It doesn't matter what they are. Combine these two objects plus the pencil to create a new invention. Give your invention a name and a use. Describe it and the need that it fulfils.

Name of my new invention: _____

Description: _____

_____

Use: _____

_____

STEP 1: Brainstorming

Do this step and all the other steps to come with your project group. Your teacher will help you select your group and decide whether you should all have different fields of study or not. To do this step, you must carefully consider your field of study as well as the fields of study of the people in your group.

■ First, ask yourself these questions. Then share your answers with your group.

1. What do professionals in your field of study need that they currently do not have?
2. What are some products or services that professionals in your field of study could offer consumers that consumers currently do not have?

■ Next, use the following brainstorming technique called "Brain Writing" [1] to determine what product or service you will invent.

1. Individually, write your ideas on a piece of paper for two minutes. Include information related to your field of study. Then switch your paper to the left.
2. Read what the student on your right has written and then add your ideas to his or her page for two minutes. Continue like this until you have written on everyone's paper.
3. Then take turns reading all the ideas on your sheet out loud. As you listen, ask yourselves what all of your different ideas have in common. Try to create a product or service that you can all work on using knowledge from all of your fields of study.

Step 2: Describing the Product/Service Related to Your Fields of Study

■ Answer the following questions with your project group.

1. What is your product or service?
2. What need does it fulfil?
3. What does it do? How does it work?
4. Why will people buy it?
5. How is it related to each of your fields of study?
6. Describe your design (materials, dimensions, components, colour, weight, etc.).

---

1. The Personal Excellence Blog. 9 Feb. 2009. Web. 17 Dec. 2010. <http://celestinechua.com/blog/25-brainstorming-techniques>.

Listening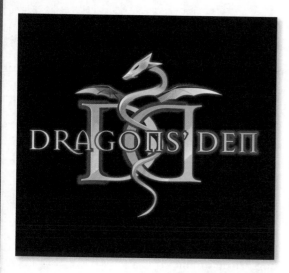

PART ONE: INSIDE THE *DRAGONS' DEN* AUDITIONS

Listen as Molly Duignan, a producer for the hit TV show *Dragons' Den*, describes the show's audition process.

■ Before you listen to the interview, complete the pre-listening vocabulary exercise.

■ Take the time to read the comprehension questions and highlight the keywords.

■ While you listen to the audition, **listen for keyword cues** and answer the questions. (For more information on listening comprehension strategies, see page 205.)

PRE-LISTENING VOCABULARY

■ Match the following words and expressions with their definitions.

WORDS		DEFINITIONS
1. no-nonsense	____	a) search; hunt
2. tycoon	____	b) very practical and direct, without wasting time on unnecessary things
3. quest	____	c) asking someone a lot of serious questions about something
4. grilling	____	d) someone who is successful in business or industry and has a lot of money and power
5. start-up	____	e) new, small company or business, especially one whose work involves computers or the Internet

EXPRESSIONS		DEFINITIONS
1. hard and fast rule	____	a) important and logical argument
2. the best and the brightest		b) top people in a field
	____	c) basic and practical details
3. nitty-gritty	____	d) directive that must be followed
4. big red flag	____	e) warning sign
5. valid pitching point	____	

COMPREHENSION

■ Answer these questions with complete sentences.

1. Why is Molly Duignan holding auditions?

_____

_____

2. Why does a pitch for the show *Dragons' Den* have to appeal to everyone from eight to 88 years old?

_____

_____

3. During a pitch, what message do the pitchers need to get across to the audience?

_____

4. Should the pitchers ask for money based on their potential for future sales?

☐ Yes   ☐ No

Explain your answer. _____

_____

5. Describe Molly Duignan's job.

_____

_____

_____

PART TWO: "GREEN OVER GREY" MAKES ITS PITCH

Now listen as Green Over Grey owners, Michael Weinmaster and Patrick Poiraud, audition for *Dragons' Den*.

■ Once again, before you listen to the interview, complete the pre-listening vocabulary exercise.

■ Take the time to read the comprehension questions on page 166 and highlight the keywords.

■ While you listen to the audition, **listen for keyword cues** and answer the questions. (For more information on listening comprehension strategies, see page 205.)

Epiphytes

PRE-LISTENING VOCABULARY

■ Match the following words and expressions with their definitions.

WORDS		DEFINITIONS
1. garden	____	**a)** earth; dirt
2. living	____	**b)** large event where companies show off their goods or services
3. soil	____	**c)** survive or tolerate something extreme, like cold weather
4. tradeshow	____	**d)** alive; not dead
5. withstand	____	**e)** area with flowers, plants and grass

EXPRESSIONS		DEFINITIONS
1. tough road	____	**a)** not located in the country
2. per square foot	____	**b)** one thousand dollars
3. a grand	____	**c)** cost for a 12-inch x 12-inch area
4. city-based	____	**d)** become more environmentally friendly
5. green up	____	**e)** hard; not easy

■ Answer these questions with complete sentences.

1. The Green Over Grey product is a living wall. What is a living wall?

_____

2. Are they a 2.5 million dollar company right now? ☐ Yes ☐ No

Explain how you know. _____

3. What does their product cost the consumer?

_____

4. What does this cost include? In other words, what does the customer get for his or her money?

_____

5. Are Mr. Weinmaster and Mr. Poiraud ambitious for their company?

☐ Yes ☐ No

Explain how you know. _____

_____

6. a) Can their product be installed outdoors? ☐ Yes ☐ No

   b) Can the product be installed in very cold climates? ☐ Yes ☐ No

   Explain how you know. _____

7. What is their approximate margin of profit during a sale?

_____

8. Where did they go to do their research for their walls?

_____

9. What kind of research did they do?

_____

_____

10. Do you think the producer will invite them to be on the show? ☐ Yes ☐ No

What makes you think so? _____

_____

Hemi-epiphytes

DISCUSSION

■ Answer these questions with a partner.

1. From what you have heard in parts 1 and 2 of this listening activity, what information is essential in a pitch?

2. Do you think that Weinmaster and Poiraud provided all of the essential information they needed to be on the show? Why or why not?

PRONUNCIATION

Pronouncing Multi-Syllabic Words

Understanding how to pronounce multi-syllabic words in English will not only help you with your pronunciation, but will also help you with your comprehension.

Part A

Recognizing and Pronouncing Stressed and Unstressed Syllables

In English, words can have one syllable (like *pitch*), two syllables (like *re-search*), three syllables (like *pro-po-sal*), four syllables (like *pre-sen-ta-tion*) or even more (like *doc-u-men-ta-tion*).

In words with two or more syllables, only one syllable is emphasized or stressed. The stress is always on a vowel, and that vowel sound is sustained longer. Also, the stressed syllable is said in a higher pitch than the unstressed syllables. For example, in the word *pro-PO-sal*, the second syllable is stressed.

■ Listen to the pronunciation of these words and underline the syllable that you hear stressed.

1. teacher
2. photography
3. analysis
4. proposal
5. presentation

6. pronunciation
7. discipline
8. notebook
9. document
10. dragon

Part B

Pronouncing Stress in Two-Syllable Nouns and Verbs

We stress the first syllable of most two-syllable nouns and adjectives, but stress the second syllable of most two-syllable verbs. For example, the noun *present* (gift) and the adjective *present* (opposite of *absent*) are pronounced "PRE-sent," whereas the verb *present* (give a presentation) is pronounced "pre-SENT."

FYI

Of course, there are exceptions, like the verbs *ANswer, PROcess* and *TRAvel.*

■ The following words have both noun and verb forms depending on the context and the way they are pronounced. You will hear the pronunciation of the verb form first and the noun form second. As you listen, repeat the pronunciation you hear for practice, and then use the rules above and what you hear to help you underline the stressed syllable in both the verb and noun forms below.

Verbs	Nouns		Verbs	Nouns
1. a) progress	b) progress		6. a) project	b) project
2. a) object	b) object		7. a) conduct	b) conduct
3. a) produce	b) produce		8. a) survey	b) survey
4. a) record	b) record		9. a) address	b) address
5. a) present	b) present		10. a) research	b) research

•••

Part C

■ Now listen to the pronunciation of the words again and check (√) whether the words you hear are in the noun or verb form.

	Verbs	Nouns		Verbs	Nouns
1. progress	_____	_____	**6.** project	_____	_____
2. object	_____	_____	**7.** conduct	_____	_____
3. produce	_____	_____	**8.** survey	_____	_____
4. record	_____	_____	**9.** address	_____	_____
5. present	_____	_____	**10.** research	_____	_____

As you become more accustomed to the way English sounds, the correct pronunciation or words will come to you more naturally. However, you can improve your pronunciation of multi-syllabic words by paying close attention to the pronunciation when you first learn a new word. You can also look in the dictionary for the stressed syllable markings if you are not sure of the pronunciation.

Root words are generally stressed, whereas prefixes and suffixes are not.

Reading 7.2

Being aware of the need that your invention or product will fulfil is of paramount importance when it comes to its design. Still, equally important is knowing whose needs are being fulfilled by your invention. For this reason, most aspiring inventors and entrepreneurs have a mental image of who they want to market their invention or product to before they draw up their design plans.

■ Complete the pre-reading vocabulary exercise.

■ Then read the comprehension questions on pages 170 and 171 before you read the text.

PRE-READING VOCABULARY

■ **Guess the meaning** of the words and expressions **from** the **context** and match them with their definitions. The line numbers will help you find the words in the text. (For more information on vocabulary strategies, see page 190.)

WORDS/EXPRESSIONS		DEFINITIONS
1. adage (line 4)	_____	**a)** type of goods or products for sale in a shop
2. case in point (line 9)	_____	**b)** used when saying the names of the people or things you are referring to
3. stumbling block (line 11)	_____	**c)** experienced something, especially problems or opposition
4. encountered (line 10)	_____	**d)** relevant example or illustration of something
5. loyalties (line 11)	_____	**e)** obstacle to someone's or something's advancement
6. launching (line 13)	_____	

•••

7. line   (line 14)   ____
8. market share (line 23)   ____
9. namely   (line 24)   ____
10. pare down   (line 39)   ____

f) percentage of the total sales for a given type of product or service

g) decrease gradually

h) desires to remain faithful to friends, principles, country, etc.

i) well-known phrase that says something wise about human experience

j) making a new product, service, etc., available for sale for the first time

Take Aim at Your Target Market

1   When designing your product, you always want to keep in mind the person you will be targeting your product/invention to. In other words, what demographic will you be trying to pitch your product to and what does this demographic value, want and need? It is a common adage among marketers that if you market your invention or product to everyone, you can **reach** no one. Nobody expressed this sentiment better than American comedian Bill Cosby. "I don't know the key to success," claimed Cosby, "but the key to failure is trying to please everybody."

2   Case in point is the story of Harley Davidson Perfume. Harley Davidson had enjoyed tremendous financial success in the late 1980s, but encountered a few stumbling blocks in the 1990s when it challenged the loyalties of its market segment, namely bikers and motorcycle enthusiasts, by launching products clearly **aimed at** a larger market segment. Harley Davidson had extended its biker brand by launching a line of biker clothing. However, ornaments, perfume and wine coolers was extending the brand too far. "Harley Davidson values are strong, masculine, very rugged values," says Charles E. Brymer, chief executive officer of the Interbrand Group, a branding consultancy based in New York. "For Harley Davidson to go into a sector that doesn't **live up to** what those values are would be disastrous."[2]

3   Brymer was right. Harley Davidson's loyal customers were **up in arms** and the company risked losing a segment of its established market share. Realizing it needed to stay true to what it did best, namely making motorcycles, Harley Davidson abandoned its attempts to increase its market share through items not designed for its core target market.

4   So what lesson did Harley Davidson learn from this business failure? Namely, that not everyone is a Harley Davidson customer. "When you study categories over a long period, you can see that adding more can weaken growth, not help it," writes Jack Trout in his book, *Differentiate or Die: Survival in Our Era of Killer Competition* (2008). "The more you add, the more you risk undermining your basic differentiating idea, which is the essence of your

2. Haig, Matt. *Brand Failures: The Truth about the 100 Biggest Branding Mistakes of All Time.* VA: Kogan Page, London and Sterling, 2003. 68. Print.

FYI

The first Harley Davidson motorcycle was built in 1903 and used a tomato can for a carburetor.

Bikers

reach: appeal to; interest; inspire

aimed at: directed toward

live up to: agree with

up in arms: angry; preparing for a fight

brand."[3] You don't want to mess with a good thing and you certainly don't want to challenge your core markets' brand loyalty because what you may in fact end up doing is **alienating** them.

5 Not everyone drives a Harley and similarly, not everyone will be a consumer of your product or service, so don't **waste** your time and money trying to sell to the **unsellable**. Instead, start with a fairly large demographic and gradually pare it down. There are many ways to **decipher** who is your target market. First of all, you likely had someone in mind when you designed your product, and you'd be wise to keep that person in mind as you start your investigation. The first step is to go out into the field and observe that "person" in their natural habitat. Like an anthropologist, you'll want to observe and record how he or she **behaves**. What does he or she value? What are his or her buying habits? This is called qualitative research and often requires patient observation over an extended period of time. The other data can be obtained more easily through questionnaires and surveys. This is the quantitative part of market research and the information you'll obtain is more readily available and easier to acquire than qualitative data. Questions about whether or not your target consumer is married or single, what his or her educational background is, where she or he lives and works can all be answered on a questionnaire and then quantifiably measured. Only once you've established who your target consumer is can you reach out to them through marketing and advertising.

6 A population segment that most of you are **well aware of**, and more than likely a member of, is the Millennials. As mentioned in Unit 4, the Millennials are presently entering the workforce and soon to become professionals in their fields of study. They are the second largest demographic in North America, and therefore have enormous buying power, something that has not been lost on Harley Davidson. Having for years targeted the predominantly white, male Baby Boomer, Harley Davidson is rethinking its marketing strategy. Their target consumer is aging, and now instead of **forking out** $12,000 to $30,000 for a motorcycle, they are saving up for retirement and a condo in Florida. The Millennials are the market Harley Davidson wants to focus on now, and the Millennials, whether they are scientists or computer technicians, will likely be the population segment you will be targeting and eventually pitching your product to at the end of this unit.

(785 words)

COMPREHENSION

1. What saying should all inventors or entrepreneurs keep in mind when pitching their product?

_____

2. What business decision almost cost Harley Davidson a portion of their market share?

_____

_____

---

3. Trout, Jack, and Steve Rivkin. *Differentiate or Die: Survival in Our Era of Killer Competition*. New York: Wiley, 2000. 192. Print.

3. What lesson can we learn from Harley Davidson's mistake?

_____

4. How should you go about determining your ideal consumer?

_____

_____

5. What is qualitative research? Give an example from the reading.

_____

_____

6. What is quantitative research? Give an example from the reading.

_____

_____

7. What can you do after you have established who your target market is?

_____

8. Why is Harley Davidson rethinking its marketing strategy?

_____

_____

9. According to the text, why would the Millennials likely be a good population segment to target your product or service to?

_____

_____

10. What is the main idea of the reading?

_____

_____

EXPANSION

■ Read the following comments made by Millennials and match each one with the corresponding statement of value on page 172. Then think of a new or existing product that could be easily marketed to Millennials based on each statement of value.

COMMENTS

1. "While driving yesterday, I saw a banana peel in the road and instinctively **swerved** to avoid it. Thanks, Mario Kart!" —*Frakin Cool* _____

2. "Nike got it right—just do it! I don't care about owning cool things—I want to do cool things!" —*Francis B.* _____

3. "Our friends are a click away on social networks such as Facebook and LinkedIn. We are the generation of collaboration and **timeliness**." —*The ZYOZY Foundation* _____

4. "When I buy something, I want it to **last**. I don't want to spend my money on something I'll have for a couple of months and then will have to **throw away**." — *Maryse* _____

swerve: make a sudden sideways movement while moving forward, usually in order to avoid hitting something (often while driving in a car)

timeliness: doing something at exactly the right time

last: continue for a particular length of time

throw away: dispose of; discard

•••

overly: more than appropriate; too

5. "I'm not wired—I'm efficient. I'm not lazy—I'm relaxed. I'm not **overly** confident—I'm self-assured." —*Millennial college student* _____

6. "We get bored easily and are tired of things not getting done. The time has come to make a change, and we are a **civic-minded** generation." —*Millennial college student* _____

civic-minded: interested or active in community affairs

STATEMENTS OF VALUES

a) Millennials are team players and enjoy doing activities in groups.

b) Millennials are price-conscious and **frugal** shoppers, but appreciate good quality.

frugal: careful to buy only what is necessary

c) Millennials crave excitement more than they crave things.

d) Millennials often view criticisms as strengths.

e) Millennials don't take themselves too seriously and are able to laugh at themselves.

f) Millennials like immediacy and don't like to wait for things to get done.

Source: Adapted from: The ZYOZY Foundation. 10 Aug. 2010. Web. 17 Dec. 2010. <http://www.facebook.com/pages/the-ZYOZY-foundation/45457906496%3E#!/pages/the-ZYOZY-foundation/45457906496>; The Millenial Mouth. 10 Aug. 2010. Web. <http://www.facebook.com/MillennialMouth2010>; Random Thoughts from People Our Age, Frakincool. 2 Dec. 2009. Web. 10 Aug., 2010. <http://www.frakincool.com/random-stuff/random-thoughts-from-people-our-age-ii/>.

Step 3: Profiling Your Target Consumer

Before you can pitch your product to a bank, a company or a venture capitalist, you will need to be able to explain who your target market consumer is. In addition, you must be able to justify why you chose to target this particular segment of the population. Being prepared to justify your choices will require you to analyze your consumer's demographic and **psychographic** background.

psychographic: looks at lifestyle, attitudes, beliefs, values, personalities, buying motives and product usage

■ Work with your project group and visualize your target consumer. Complete the chart below and answer the questions on page 173. By doing this, you will be better able to explain the design choices you have made for your product or service, and pitch your product to the Dragons at the end of this unit.

Part A: Demographic Analysis

■ Complete the following chart.

AGE	
GENDER	
GEOGRAPHIC LOCATION	
ANNUAL INCOME	
MARRIAGE/FAMILY STATUS	
EDUCATION LEVEL	
OTHER INFORMATION YOU WISH TO INCLUDE	

Part B: Psychographic Analysis

■ Answer the following questions.

1. What personal qualities or activities does your target consumer value? For example, is time spent with friends important to your target consumer? List five qualities or activities that are important to your target consumer.

_____

_____

_____

_____

_____

2. What products does your target consumer value? List five products and five product characteristics, e.g., price or convenience.

PRODUCTS	PRODUCT CHARACTERISTICS
_____	_____
_____	_____
_____	_____
_____	_____
_____	_____

3. How does your target consumer make their buying decisions? For example, does advertising influence their decision to buy a particular product? Explain.

_____

_____

_____

4. Look back at the ten inventions in the Explore section on page 156. Which of these products do you think your target consumer would or would not purchase? Choose three and justify each of your choices by referring back to the values that you wrote down in Question 1 above.

Product choice 1: _____

Justification: _____

Product choice 2: _____

Justification: _____

Product choice 3: _____

Justification: _____

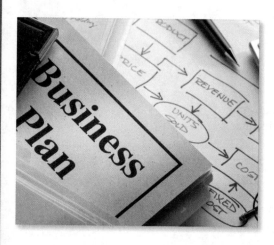

Reading 7.3

CBC's reality-TV series *Dragons' Den* turns the most high-stakes encounter in entrepreneurship—the investment pitch—into prime-time entertainment. Whether you're hunting for big investors or a small bank loan, you would do well to polish your business plan and your presentation. More than a few *Dragons' Den* contestants will wish they had followed these dos and don'ts for making a pitch.

■ Complete the pre-reading vocabulary and comprehension exercises.

■ Then read the comprehension questions on pages 178 and 179 before your read the text.

PRE-READING VOCABULARY

■ Work with a partner and **play with words**. Read the definitions below and decide which of the following words best fills each space in the crossword puzzle. If you are having trouble, use the line numbers provided to **guess the meaning** of the words **from context**. (For more information about vocabulary strategies, see page 190.)

Vocabulary Strategy 7: Playing with Words

Playing with words by combining them with others, filling in the missing letters, completing crosswords, etc., is a fun way to learn about words and word forms.

WORDS

mogul	(line 1)	network	(line 14)	hurdles	(line 58)
attire	(line 5)	validated	(line 29)	cent	(line 55)
would-be	(line 7)	capital	(line 46)	stumped	(line 61)
scolded	(line 10)	venture	(line 49)	counsel	(line 73)
lone	(line 11)	fledgling	(line 53)	undermine	(line 81)

DEFINITIONS

Across:

1. made someone feel that his or her ideas and feelings are respected and considered seriously; **2.** gradually make someone or something less strong or effective; **3.** being angrily criticized about something one (especially a child) has done; **4.** business person who has great power and influence in a particular industry; **5.** money or property, especially when it is used to start a business or produce more wealth; **6.** used to talk about the only person or thing in a place, or the only person or thing that does something; **7.** clothes

Down:

1. new business activity that involves taking risks; **2.** problems or difficulties that you must deal with before you can achieve something; **3.** a type of business or organization that has only recently been formed and is still developing; 4. group of people, organizations, etc., that are connected or work together; 5. advice; **6.** unable to find an answer or think of a reply; **7.** one penny; **8.** desiring, attempting or professing to be; hoping to become

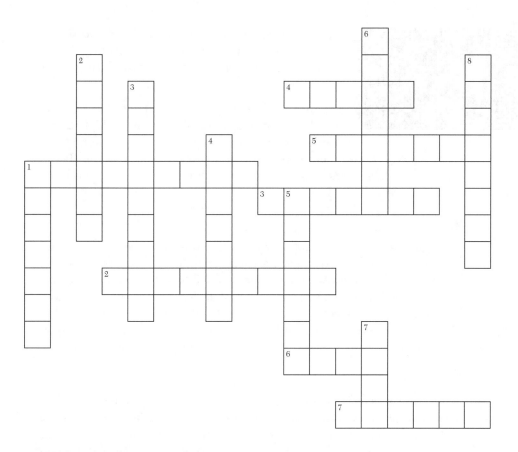

PRE-READING COMPREHENSION

■ **Skim** each section of the reading to get a general understanding of what it is about. (For more information about reading comprehension strategies, see page 189.)

■ Then try to put the correct piece of advice beginning with the word DO or the word DON'T in the space provided in each section.

a) DO: Be likeable.

b) DO: Know your market.

c) DO: Seek more than just money.

d) DO: Know your numbers.

e) DO: Supply support from others for your claim.

f) DON'T: Pitch a product.

g) DON'T: Pitch in a bikini.

h) DON'T: Forget to build barriers.

i) DON'T: Play where there is no pain.

j) DON'T: Overvalue your company.

> **My eLab** ✎
> Answer additional questions for "Lessons from *Dragons' Den*: What Dragons Want."

Lessons from *Dragons' Den*: What Dragons Want

By Sean Wise

1. _____

Sex sells. That's a fact known by the business moguls who made up the investment panel on *Dragons' Den*, and by many of the 100-plus entrepreneurs who pitched their business concepts to the Dragons. Most "pitchers" took a

conservative approach to selling with sex, dressing in
business or business-casual attire and bringing in
models to perform the task of **titillating** their
would-be investors.

But not the entrepreneur who pitched in a cowboy
hat, bikini top and cut-off shorts that would do **Daisy
Duke** proud—and was scolded by Jennifer Wood,
cattle rancher, software entrepreneur and the lone female Dragon. "If you
want to be taken seriously by professionals," Wood advised, "then act and
dress professionally."

titillating: sexually exciting

Daisy Duke: fictional
character on TV who wore very
short shorts

lend: give for a short time;
allow someone to borrow
something

leverage: influence that
you can use to make people do
what you want

2. _____

The right investor can expand your network, evolve management and **lend**
vital expertise. After investing in a young technology business that could
benefit from his expertise and resources, serial tech entrepreneur Robert
Herjavec told his fellow Dragons: "The best deals for me are the ones where
I can **leverage** my investment with my network, experience and facilities.
That way, I can increase their and my chances of making money." More than
half of the deals completed in the Den were for more than just the money.

3. _____

"Why can't I take your idea and just do it myself?" asked Herjavec of
numerous pitchers. His point: being first to market doesn't provide a
sustainable competitive advantage. Smart entrepreneurs show investors not
only how their product is great but also what difficulty others will have in
duplicating it.

sustainable: lasting;
durable

party: group of people

taping: TV show recording

4. _____

All entrepreneurs think they offer the best investment opportunity. Investors
might love your idea too—but they want to know they're not the only ones
drinking your Kool-Aid. In other words,
they see reduced risk in a business validated
by third **parties** (e.g., customers and
strategic partners) or supported by credible
market research. "I don't know anything
about software, but if Bill Gates said [your
software] was good, who would I be to
argue?" explained Jim Treliving, the
Dragon behind Boston Pizza, over drinks
after a day's **taping**.

5. _____

A large number of pitchers were unable to
explain why anyone would need their
product, sometimes due to an inability to articulate the problem it would
solve, but often because there was no such "pain" in the marketplace. Either
way, that fact didn't **sit well** with the Dragons. After listening to one
particularly **awkward** and pointless pitch, La Senza co-founder Laurence
Lewin leaned over to his fellow Dragons and said, "Trying to sell a product
that the market is not already demanding is like selling bras for [fish]."

sit well: be appreciated

awkward: not relaxed or
comfortable; embarrassing

•••

6. _____

Remember that raising capital from investors is **akin to** selling product. That product is equity, which represents a future **return**—hopefully positive—to the investor. Like any product, it must be reasonably priced.

Too many pitchers overestimated the value of their ventures. Worse, one in five had no idea how to calculate valuation, let alone justify it. "I don't have a problem with **greedy**—I have a problem with stupid greedy," investor and former software dynamo Kevin O'Leary advised one entrepreneur who'd asked for $500,000 for a 5 percent **stake** in his fledgling company. In doing so, the entrepreneur had **unwittingly** valued his business at $10 million, even though it had not yet generated a cent in sales.

7. _____

Successful pitchers in the Den knew the **driving forces** in their target markets, understood the competitive landscape and had identified the hurdles that they would have to **leap** in order to grow their businesses. More impressive were the few entrepreneurs who'd anticipated the key questions that would be asked, prepared the right answers and even provided supporting evidence. They simply could not be stumped, and this served them well against even the toughest Dragons.

8. _____

It sounds counterintuitive, but it's wrong to promote your product to investors. Sell them on your business instead. Herjavec conveyed this message to several contestants in the Den: "I invest in companies, not products. I invest in business people, not inventors. Having a great product is a start, but to be a **fundable** business you need to have **barriers to entry** [against competitors], a distribution plan that makes sense and, last but not least, a way to make money."

9. _____

This **tip** could also be phrased as "Don't bite the hand that will feed you." One pitcher challenged a Dragon's knowledge of his industry, even though the Dragon had been in that industry for years. Another pitcher told a Dragon to "keep his counsel to himself" and then proceeded to argue with the other Dragons. [...]

Investors don't want to complicate their lives by dealing with founders who are hard to work with. Prove when you pitch that you'll get along fine.

10. _____

After several contestants failed to answer basic questions about market size, gross margins, **break-even points** and their supply of goods, Treliving had seen enough. "What are these guys thinking, going in without knowing the basics?" If you can't provide potential investors with key numbers **off the top of your head**, you deprive them of required information and undermine their confidence in you.

(846 words)

akin to: the same as; equal to

return: amount of profit that you get from an investment

greedy: always wanting more

stake: investment of time or money

unwittingly: in a way that shows you do not know or realize something

driving force: energizing force behind something

leap: overcome, jump over

fundable: worth funding/ giving money to

barrier to entry: obstacle in the path of a business that makes it difficult to enter a particular market

tip: piece of advice

break-even point: point at which you will not lose money

off the top of your head: said without thinking about it first

Source: Wise, Sean. "Lessons from the *Dragon's Den*: What Dragons Want." PROFIT Magazine. Sept. 2006. Web. 7 Aug. 2010. <http://profitguide.com>.

■ Answer the following True or False questions. If the statement is false, correct it.

1. Too many entrepreneurs who pitch to the Dragons dress inappropriately.

   ☐ True ☐ False

   _____

2. Herjavec is not interested in being personally involved in the businesses he invests in.

   ☐ True ☐ False

   _____

   _____

3. Anybody can copy your idea if you don't have a patent on it.

   ☐ True ☐ False

   _____

4. The Dragons are more comfortable investing in a business or product that has a customer base or other interested investors.

   ☐ True ☐ False

   _____

   _____

5. As a pitcher, you have to be able to articulate the need your product fulfils.

   ☐ True ☐ False

   _____

   _____

6. It is important to overestimate the value of your business. It shows you are enthusiastic and enterprising.

   ☐ True ☐ False

   _____

7. Don't prepare before you enter the Den. You need to be relaxed and unrehearsed.

   ☐ True ☐ False

   _____

   _____

8. More important than having a good product is knowing how to make money with it.

   ☐ True ☐ False

   _____

9. The Dragons like to know they will be able to work well with an entrepreneur before they invest in that entrepreneur's business.

☐ True   ☐ False

10. A knowledge of your business finances and accounting practices impresses the judges.

☐ True   ☐ False

CONNECT WITH GRAMMAR

Using Modal Auxiliaries

Modal auxiliaries (modals) include: *can, could, may, might, must, should, will, would, had better* and *ought to*. Modals are always followed by the base form of a verb, no matter what the subject of the verb is.

Example:

A venture capitalist **can invest** in your business for a percentage of equity in your company.

■ Below is the list of the Dos and Don'ts that author Sean Wise writes about in Reading 7.3, "Lessons from the *Dragons' Den*: What Dragons Want." Each Do and Don't is followed by a sentence with the same meaning but containing modals. Circle the modal that best suits the meaning of the sentence. The first one is done for you as an example.

1. DON'T: Pitch in a bikini.

You can / may / (should) not pitch in a bikini.

2. DO: Seek more than just money.

You can / might / would ask for more than just money.

3. DON'T: Forget to build barriers.

You will / may / must protect your invention by getting a patent.

4. DO: Provide support from others for your claims.

You had better / would rather / could support what you are saying.

5. DON'T: Play where there is no pain.

You should / may / can want to see if there is a demand for your product in the marketplace before you invest too much time and money promoting it.

6. DON'T: Overvalue your company.

You would / should / will most likely succeed in the Den if you know what your company is really worth.

...

7. DO: Know your market.

You can / might / should always know your target market.

8. DON'T: Pitch a product.

The Dragons should / will / must be more interested in investing in a business than they will be in investing in a product.

9. DO: Be likeable.

The Dragons might / can / must like you better if you smile.

10. DO: Know your numbers.

Bring a calculator to the Den; you can / should / may need it.

Refer to Unit 8 of the Grammar Guide for further explanations and practice on modal auxiliaries.

Watching 📺

PEER FX IN THE DEN

Robert Dunlop and Florence Lea have developed an interesting new business idea. They have written the computer code and done their research, but will this be enough to convince the Dragons to invest? Watch their pitch to the Dragons on this episode of *Dragons' Den* to find out.

■ Complete the pre-listening vocabulary exercise.

■ Then read the comprehension questions on pages 181 and 182 and highlight the keywords.

■ While you watch the audition, **listen for keyword cues** and answer the questions. (For more information on listening comprehension strategies, see page 205.)

■ Match these words and expressions with their definitions.

WORDS	DEFINITIONS
1. peer _____	a) looking for; trying to get
2. seeking _____	b) idea; theory
3. rate _____	c) value
4. worth _____	d) someone who is equal to you, with the same interests, age, job level, etc.
5. each other _____	e) fixed or standard amount of money on a scale
6. fee _____	f) amount of money to be paid
7. hefty _____	g) unusually expensive; high or increased amount
8. steep _____	h) large amount
9. lazy _____	i) not willing to work hard for something
10. premise _____	j) mutually; reciprocally

EXPRESSIONS	DEFINITIONS
1. linked up _____	a) effects
2. currency exchange _____	b) system by which money from different countries is traded
3. shark _____	c) someone who is dangerous to deal with
4. hardnosed _____	d) not affected by emotions and determined to get what he or she wants
5. FX _____	e) connected together

COMPREHENSION

■ Answer the following questions.

1. What type of service have Robert and Flo created?

_____

2. What exactly are they asking the Dragons for? _____

3. What are they willing to give the Dragons in exchange for the money?

_____

4. How old are Robert and Flo?

_____

5. a) In two or three sentences, summarize exactly what Robert and Flo's service does for consumers.

_____

_____

_____

b) What percentage do Robert and Flo intend to charge their clients as a transaction fee?

_____

c) What percentage do banks usually charge?

_____

6. How much can consumers save?

_____

7. Do Robert and Flo provide any evidence that they have researched their target market?

☐ Yes   ☐ No

Explain your answer. _____

_____

_____

_____

8. What deal are they initially offered?

_____

9. What does their financial advisor recommend?

_____

_____

10. Do they take their financial advisor's advice in the end?

☐ Yes   ☐ No

Explain how you know. _____

_____

DISCUSSION

■ Discuss the following questions in a small group.

1. Do you think this is a good deal for Robert and Flo? Explain.

2. Do you think their age makes it harder for Robert and Flo to get a good deal from the Dragons? Support your answer.

3. Should Robert and Flo give up control of their business for the money? Explain your answer.

4. Robert and Flo say that they have decided to take the deal because they think they need a shark (someone who is hardnosed and knowledgeable about business methods) to help them. Do you agree or disagree? Why or why not?

5. The Dragons tell Robert and Flo at the end of their pitch that they have done a very good job. Do you agree or disagree? Why or why not?

EXPANSION

Think back on Robert and Flo's pitch and the Dragons' reactions very carefully. Three of the Dragons were interested but two were not.

■ Write down all the elements of the pitch that Robert and Flo did well.

■ Write down all the elements of the pitch that Robert and Flo could have improved on, and explain how they could have improved on each one.

STEP 4: Preparing the Pitch

■ Look back at Steps 1, 2 and 3 in this unit and re-familiarize your self with your product or service (Step 1, page 163), its description (Step 2, page 163) and your target market (Step 3, pages 172–173).

■ In preparation for pitching your product in "The Pitch" (Step 5, page 185), make sure that you answer all of these questions thoroughly with your project group. This may take some time, but any preparation work you do now will make your presentation stronger and better later.

1. What experience or qualifications do you (or your team) have that will show the venture capitalists (your judges) that you have the ability to manage the business? Prepare business backgrounds for yourselves in preparation for this role.

2. How will you make money with this product or service?

3. How much does your product or service cost to produce?

4. How much will you sell your product or service for?

5. What similar products or services exist and how will you compete with them?

6. How much money are you looking for from the judges?

7. Exactly what will you spend this money on?

8. Besides money, is there anything else you want from the judges?

9. Remember, both parties need to come to an agreement. What is your bottom line (the highest percentage share in your business that you are willing to part with)?

10. Think about the listenings with Molly Duignan and Green over Grey (pages 164–166). Is there anything else that you should add to your pitch to make it successful?

Preparing Yourself to Act as a Judge

In addition to pitching your product, you will also play the role of a venture capitalist and judge another team's pitch.

■ Prepare a background in business for yourself in preparation for this role. Ask yourself if you will be a shark (a ruthless and emotionless nose-biter), an angel (an easy-going softy) or somewhere in the middle.

■ With other judges, brainstorm the types of questions that you should ask.

These are the words and phrases that you should know after completing this unit. Remind yourself of their meanings by writing down their definitions or translations.

DEFINITIONS/TRANSLATIONS

1. capital
2. chief
3. circa
4. counsel
5. currency
6. each other
7. encounter
8. fees
9. focus
10. hurdles
11. lazy
12. loyalty
13. mogul
14. pitch
15. premise
16. rate
17. seek
18. stack
19. start-up
20. steep
21. technical
22. tycoon
23. validity
24. venture
25. worth

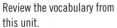

Review the vocabulary from this unit.

STEP 5: The Pitch

Part A: The Pitch (Speaking)

1. Pitching

■ Working individually, find five terms from your field of study that you will need to use in your part of the pitch. These terms should be related to some aspect of the pitch that you will contribute to. Make sure that the words you choose aren't cognates in your language, and that you have spelled them correctly.

■ With your project group, make your pitch to the judges, using information from Steps 1-4. Divide up the proposal equally among your group members and present it. (For more information about presentation strategies, see pages 206–207.) Don't forget to use visuals or props to make your proposal more stimulating. Also, make sure to incorporate your five field-of-study terms in your part of the pitch, and try to use some of the words from the General Vocabulary Lists from this and other units. You must each speak for approximately four minutes.

2. Judging

■ As you know, you will be expected to take a turn playing the role of a venture capitalist and judging another group's oral. As you listen to their oral, you will need to ask them questions throughout the presentation (see Step 4, page 183). Once their pitch is finished, you will need to take time to complete the evaluation form on page 186, and then share your feedback with the pitchers.

Part B: The Pitch (Writing)

1. Writing Your Proposal

■ Draw on the feedback you received from the judges to prepare your final written proposal.

■ Use at least five words from the General Vocabulary List on page 184, along with your five field-specific words, and underline them.

■ Working as a group, be sure that you also divide up and complete all the elements that you need to include in a proposal, such as a title page, a table of contents, an introduction, etc. (For more information about the elements that must be included in a proposal, see page 200.)

■ Each student will write an individual text of approximately 350 words to explain the elements of the pitch that he or she is responsible for.

■ With your team, choose one of the following revision strategies: *editing your work*; *emphasizing the positive*; *obtaining feedback*; *peer reviewing*; or *writing a reverse plan*. Use it to revise your written proposal. Be prepared to show both your original draft and final version (after revision). (For more information on revision strategies, see page 204.)

2. Evaluating a Pitch

■ Rate your classmates' pitch on a scale of 1 to 5 (1 being very weak and 5 being very strong).

PRODUCT					
1. Does the product or service fulfil a need related to the pitchers' fields of study?	1	2	3	4	5
2. Will lots of people be interested in buying this product?	1	2	3	4	5
3. Is the product ready for customers (or is some development still required)?	1	2	3	4	5
4. Will it be difficult for other people to copy the product?	1	2	3	4	5
MARKET					
5. Did the pitchers have a customer in mind when they invented the product or service?	1	2	3	4	5
6. Do the pitchers know how they are going to sell the product to customers?	1	2	3	4	5
7. Do the pitchers convince you that there will be a large market for the product?	1	2	3	4	5
MANAGEMENT					
8. Do you think the management team of the company has the necessary experience to run this business?	1	2	3	4	5
BUSINESS MODEL					
9. Do you think the pitchers understand the financial side of running the business well enough?	1	2	3	4	5
10. Do the pitchers have a realistic plan for the future of their business with regard to growth, sales, market penetration, etc.?	1	2	3	4	5

My eLab 🗁

My eLab Documents includes additional research assignments to help you learn more about your field of study.

Field Guide

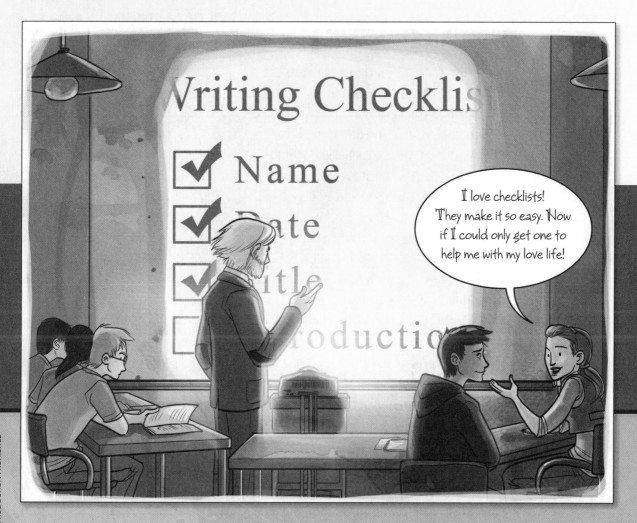

This Field Guide—with its checklists and templates—will help you develop good habits and use strategies to improve yourself in all four language skills: writing, reading, listening and speaking. It will show you how to use some very important researching and referencing techniques and will also guide you as you learn some new strategies for revising your work.

READING STRATEGIES

WRITING STRATEGIES

LISTENING STRATEGIES

SPEAKING STRATEGIES

Focusing on Comprehension

To help me understand the meaning of a reading, I can use the following strategies:

☐ **Strategy 1: Activating prior knowledge.** I reflect on and talk about what I perceive to be the subject of the reading before I read it.

☐ **Strategy 2: Visualizing.** I close my eyes and create a picture in my mind of what I am reading.

☐ **Strategy 3: Scanning.** I slowly scan the page from the top to the bottom looking for a keyword. When I find it, I read only that small part of the text more carefully.

☐ **Strategy 4: Skimming.** I look at the title, subtitles, photos and captions, graphs and charts to get a general idea of the topic and main direction of the text. Then I read the first line of every paragraph to get the main points of the text.

☐ **Strategy 5: Inferring.** I recognize that many of the ideas that I understand from reading a text are not actually written in the text, but instead inferred. When I read a text, I read between the lines to understand the full message a text provides.

READING STRATEGIES

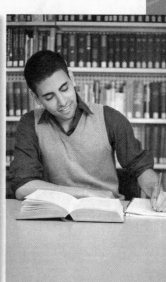

CHECKLIST 2

Focusing on Vocabulary

To help me understand the meaning of a word in a reading or listening text, I can use the following strategies:

☐ **Strategy 1: Guessing the meaning from context.** I look at the word in context and use that context to help me logically guess at its meaning.

☐ **Strategy 2: Looking up words.** I look up words up in the dictionary and use the context in the text to decide which definition is most suitable.

☐ **Strategy 3: Breaking up words.** I break up the word into its smaller parts (i.e., prefix, root word and suffix).

PREFIX	ROOT	SUFFIX

Trans ("across") – *port* ("to carry") – *er* ("someone or something that does this")

☐ **Strategy 4: Finding synonyms.** I look for the synonyms of words in order to strengthen and enlarge my vocabulary base.

☐ **Strategy 5: Identifying parts of speech.** I try to identify the part of speech of a word from its context in order to correctly define it; this also assists my overall comprehension of a text.

☐ **Strategy 6: Finding antonyms.** I look for the antonyms of words in order to strengthen and enlarge my vocabulary base. Discovering opposite meanings can improve my understanding of words.

☐ **Strategy 7: Playing with words.** I play with words by combining them with others, filling in the missing letters, completing crosswords, etc., I understand that this is a fun way to learn about words and word forms that lets me relax and experiment with the language.

CHECKLIST 3

Taking Notes

When I take notes from a reading, I ...

☐ highlight important concepts in the text;

☐ focus on facts, explanations, definitions of concepts, lists and information that is repeated;

☐ circle unfamiliar vocabulary to look up later;

☐ make connections between what I am reading and what I already know and write additional information on the topic in the margins.

Formulas That Work

When I take notes, I ...

☐ look for signals from the author that something is important.

Focusing on Research

When conducting research, I ...

☐ evaluate the sources according to the CARS checklist (see "Checklist 5: Evaluating Sources with the CARS Checklist" on page 192) and decide whether they are credible or not. I understand that evaluating a source's credibility is especially important with Internet material.

To help me evaluate my sources, I use the Wh- question words and ask the following questions:[1]

- Who wrote it? Is the person well-known and reputable in the field? A reputable source is a person who is known to be honest and does good work.

- Where is it? Is it on an institution's website, or posted in a blog?

- When was the material written? Look for a date. Is it old and out of date?

- What is the person saying? Is it something that you have heard before, or is it new?

- Why was the material written? Is it trying to sell you something? Is it political? Is it factual? Is it trying to improve the company's business sales? Is the writer impartial? A writer who has no interest in the outcome is considered impartial. However, if a company that makes plastic bags does a study showing that plastic bags aren't harmful to the environment, and publishes these results, they aren't considered impartial because these results may improve their business sales.

- How well is the material written? Is it full of grammatical, spelling and factual errors?

☐ acknowledge my sources in the text by quoting and paraphrasing (for more information about quoting and paraphrasing [and avoiding plagiarism], see page 203);

☐ document my sources in my Works Cited List using a recognized style, such as that of the Modern Language Association (see examples in "Formulas That Work" below).

Formulas That Work

To include a reference in my text according to the *MLA Handbook for Writers of Research Papers* (7th Edition),[2] I use one of the following formulas:

- Author's last name, first name. *Book title*. Ed. Editor's first name, last name. Publication city: publisher, year published. Medium [Print].

- Site title. Ed. Editor's first name, middle initial, last name. Date published (or updated) [day, month, year]. Sponsoring organization. Medium [Web]. Date accessed [day, month, year]. <URL>.

---

1. These questions were taken from Robert Harris' CARS checklist (Credibility, Accuracy, Reasonableness, Support) for choosing credible sources: Harris, Robert. "Evaluating Internet Research Sources." 17 Nov. 1997. VirtualSalt. Web. 17 Oct. 2000. <http://www.virtualsalt.com/evalu8it.htm>.
2. Gibaldi, Joseph. *MLA Handbook for Writers of Research Papers* (7th Edition). New York: The Modern Language Association of America, 2009. Print.

Evaluating Sources with the CARS Checklist

The CARS checklist, according to Robert Harris, author of the book *Webquester: A Guidebook to the Web*, is designed to help you determine the credibility, accuracy, reasonableness and support of print and online secondary sources.

Use the following checklist to determine whether or not your secondary sources pass the CARS test.

When evaluating a source for credibility, I make sure that ...

- [ ] the information provided in the source is trustworthy;
- [ ] the name and credentials of the author(s) are clearly stated;
- [ ] the author provides evidence in the form of facts, statistics, and examples to support his or her argument;
- [ ] the conclusion the author comes to is a reasonable conclusion given the evidence he or she has provided.

When evaluating a source for accuracy, I make sure that ...

- [ ] the source is up-to-date. I stay away from material that is too old or is not dated;
- [ ] assertions made are clear and detailed;
- [ ] the whole truth of an argument or position is given;
- [ ] the language is clear, and that the author avoids adverbs such as *sometimes*, *usually*, *tends to* and *seldom*, and modals such as *may*, *might*, *could*;
- [ ] the author acknowledges an opposing argument or position.

When evaluating a source for reasonableness, I make sure that ...

- [ ] the source is balanced and objective;
- [ ] the tone of the source is reasonable and balanced. In other words, the author avoids blatant criticism of an opposing argument;
- [ ] the author avoids expressions such as *every*, *all*, *always*, *never*, and other expressions that tend to exaggerate a claim;
- [ ] the author does not have a hidden agenda (conflict of interest). For example, one needs to question the validity of an argument written by a pharmaceutical company in support of a medication they produce.

When evaluating a source for support, I make sure that ...

- [ ] the source contains secondary, corroborative information that is clearly indicated in the body of the source and cited in its bibliography.
- [ ] I can triangulate the source by finding a minimum of two other sources that support the claim being made by the author(s).

Source: Adapted from: Robert Harris's CARS Checklist for Research Source Evaluation. Shelby County Board of Education. 24 Aug. 2001. Web. 26 Jan. 2011. <http://www.shelbyed.k12.al.us/schools/schs/faculty/slatham/cars.htm>.

Writing a Business Letter

When I write a business letter, I …

☐ use a correct letter format, such as the block letter format modelled in Template 1 on page 194;

☐ make sure that my verb tenses, vocabulary and spelling are correct.

A. If I am writing a **request letter**, it is because I want to ask for information, request assistance or have something sent to me by mail, so I …

☐ introduce myself (paragraph 1);

☐ explain exactly what information, assistance or object I want and why I want it (paragraph 2).

B. If I am writing a **complaint letter**, it is because I am unsatisfied with a product or service, so I …

☐ explain the problem clearly, carefully providing all the details, such as dates and amounts, and outline how the problem has affected me (paragraph 1);

☐ outline exactly and firmly what I expect the company to do about the problem (paragraph 2);

☐ warn the company about what I intend to do if they don't act (paragraph 3).

C. If I am writing a **cover letter** to send with my résumé, I …

☐ say why I am writing, what position I am applying for and how I found out about it (paragraph 1);

☐ demonstrate knowledge about the company and emphasize how my experience and credentials match up well with the requirements for the job (paragraph 2);

☐ explain that I will follow up and request an interview (paragraph 3);

☐ don't explain how I would benefit from working for the company;

☐ express my enthusiasm and confidence throughout the letter (for more information about writing a cover letter, see pages 91–92).

When I write a business e-mail message, I …

☐ follow all the same rules for writing a business letter.

Formulas That Work

> No matter what kind of business letter I am writing, I am always polite, and I make sure to use a formula to thank the recipient(s) at the end of my final paragraph:
> - Thank you for your (cooperation in/understanding in/attention to) this matter.
> - Thank you for your consideration of this request/application.

TEMPLATE 1

A Business Letter[1]

Your address:

123 Circle Lane, Apartment 2
Saint Lambert, Quebec J4A 3J1

Date:

October 3, 2011

Full name, title and address of the person you are writing to:

Mr. Alain Provist, Recruiter (Use *Mr.* for a man and *Ms.* for a woman.)
JFK School of Performing Arts
3030 Villeray Street, Suite 400
Montreal, Quebec H4B 2B1

Salutation:

Dear Mr. Provist: (Use *Dear Sir*: or *Dear Madam*: when you don't know the recipient's name.)

Body:

Paragraph 1

Paragraph 2

Paragraph 3 (Be sure to thank the person in your final sentence.)

Closing:

Sincerely, (*Sincerely* is standard—although there are other closings that you may use.)

Sign your name:

Sandra Doolittle

Type your name:

Sandra Doolittle

Enclosure:

(To enclose additional information, such as a résumé, write "Enclosure" [or "Enclosures (2)" for two enclosures.] Don't use this feature if you don't need it.)

---

1. This letter provides an example of block letter format.

Writing a Basic Technical Report[1]

A technical report is written to report research and to present findings and argument(s).

All technical reports have basic features in common; however, two types of technical reports, the field report and the survey report, require something in addition: observation and analysis, and these two reports will be explained further in Checklist 3 and Templates 3 and 4.

When I write a basic technical report, I ...

☐ think about my audience and what I want them to know;

☐ include a title page.

In the introduction, I ...

☐ say why the topic is important and provide some background information;

☐ give my purpose for writing and provide a thesis statement (see below);

☐ outline a plan or explain my scope (i.e., say what I will talk about and what I will leave out).

> A **thesis statement** is a statement on which a basic technical report is entirely based. All the paragraphs must support this sentence.
>
> Before I can write a good thesis statement, I must narrow down my topic. To do this, I take my first general idea and continue to make it more and more specific until it is precise and interesting to write about.

In the body of the report, I ...

☐ use a topic sentence in each paragraph (see below);

☐ support each main idea with evidence (e.g., facts, statistics, graphs, tables and examples);

☐ use a logical, objective and specific argument;

☐ acknowledge other authors' ideas and cite them correctly (for more information about quoting and paraphrasing, see page 203).

> A **topic sentence** is a complete sentence that supports the thesis statement and that provides the main idea for the information that follows in the paragraph.
>
> All other sentences in the paragraph should support the topic sentence. They can include examples, facts, statistics, anecdotal information, etc.

In the conclusion, I ...

☐ restate the topic and purpose.

---

1. Some Canadian universities recommend a structure that is similar to this common format.

When I write a technical report, I …

☐ include headings ("1.," "2.," etc.) and sub-headings ("1.1.," "1.2." etc.) in the report to keep my information organized and clear.

TEMPLATE 2

A Basic Technical Report

Title page (title, your name, teacher's name and date)

1. **Subtitle:** Introduction
   - **1.1.** Topic and background information
   - **1.2.** Purpose and thesis statement
   - **1.3.** Outline/scope (i.e., say what I will talk about and what I will leave out)

2. **Subtitle:** _____
   - **2.1.** Topic sentence (main argument 1)
     - **2.1.1.** Support (e.g., facts, statistics, graphs, tables and examples)
     - **2.1.2.** Support (e.g., facts, statistics, graphs, tables and examples)
   - **2.2.** Topic sentence (main argument 2)
     - **2.2.1.** Support (e.g., facts, statistics, graphs, tables and examples)
     - **2.2.2.** Support (e.g., facts, statistics, graphs, tables and examples)

3. **Subtitle:** _____
   - **3.1.** Topic sentence (main argument 1)
     - **3.1.1.** Support (e.g., facts, statistics, graphs, tables and examples)
     - **3.1.2.** Support (e.g., facts, statistics, graphs, tables and examples)
   - **3.2.** Topic sentence (main argument 2)
     - **3.2.1.** Support (e.g., facts, statistics, graphs, tables and examples)
     - **3.2.2.** Support (e.g., facts, statistics, graphs, tables and examples)

4. **Subtitle:** Conclusion
   - **4.1.** Restatement of topic and purpose
   - **4.2.** Restatement of main ideas and key arguments
   - **4.3.** Your judgment and recommendation(s)

Bibliography

Appendices (graphs, tables, charts, pictures). Appendices should be numbered and you should refer to them in your text by number, e.g., _Table 1, Graph 4._

Writing a Technical Field Report
or Technical Survey Report

A true field report is usually made by an expert in a field after he or she visits a site for a specific reason; for example, to suggest improving, building or repairing something. It is usually done when the information can't be gathered by conducting more traditional research.

A survey report is a technical report that explains and analyzes information obtained through a survey about the attitudes, opinions or behaviour of a segment of the population.

When I write a field report or survey report, I ...

☐ observe and report on a problem related to my field of study;

☐ analyze my findings and make recommendations;

☐ think about my audience and what I want them to know.

In the introduction, I ...

☐ give a description of the problem as it relates to my area of expertise;

☐ clearly state my purpose for writing;

☐ provide a hypothesis, or educated guess at what the findings will show (see below).

> A **hypothesis** is a statement on which a technical field report or a technical survey report is entirely based. All the paragraphs must support this sentence. It is an educated guess at what my findings will show and it is usually based on a research question.
>
> Before I can write a good hypothesis, I must narrow down my topic. To do this, I take my first general idea and continue to make it more and more specific until it is precise and interesting to write about.

In the body of the report, I ...

☐ use a topic sentence in each new paragraph (see below);

☐ describe the data I obtained through field or survey observations (e.g., facts, statistics, graphs, tables and examples);

☐ analyze the data logically and explain how it is relevant to my field of study;

☐ acknowledge other authors' ideas and cite them correctly (for more information about quoting and paraphrasing, see page 203).

> A **topic sentence** is a complete sentence that supports the hypothesis and that provides the main idea for the information that follows in the paragraph.
>
> All other sentences in the paragraph should support the topic sentence. They can include examples, facts, statistics, anecdotal information, etc.

In the conclusion, I ...

☐ restate my problem and purpose;

☐ restate the key findings of my analysis;

☐ draw conclusions about what to do and make recommendations using my field-of-study knowledge to help me.

Formulas That Work

To describe the data I have obtained through observation and research, I use one of the following formulas:

- This suggests that ...
- These findings indicate that ...
- The statistics show that ...

Sources: Effective Writing Program. University of Calgary website. N.d. Web. 1 Oct. 2008. <http://efwr.ucalgary.ca/efwr/reportwriting>; Engineering Communication Center. University of Toronto. N.d. Web. 4 Oct. 2008. <http://www.ecf.toronto.edu/~writing/handbook-shrtrept.html>.

TEMPLATE 3

A Technical Field Report

Title page (title, your name and field of study, teacher's name and date)

(Note: Blue writing shows the differences from a basic technical report.)

1. **Subtitle:** Introduction
    - **1.1.** Description of the problem as it relates to your field of study
    - **1.2.** Purpose
    - **1.3.** Hypothesis

2. **Subtitle:** _____
    - **2.1.** Topic sentence
    - **2.2.** Description of data obtained through observation

3. **Subtitle:** _____
    - **3.1.** Topic sentence
    - **3.2.** Logical analysis of data

4. **Subtitle:** Conclusion
    - **4.1.** Restatement of purpose and analysis
    - **4.2.** Conclusions about what to do
    - **4.3.** Recommendation(s) (using your field of study to help you)

Bibliography

Appendices (graphs, tables, charts, pictures). Appendices should be numbered and you should refer to them in your text by number, e.g., *Table 1*, *Graph 4*.

TEMPLATE 4

A Technical Survey Report

Title page (title, your name and field of study, teacher's name and date)

(Note: Green writing shows the differences from a field report.)

1. **Subtitle:** Introduction
   1.1. Topic and background information
   1.2. Purpose of survey
   1.3. Hypothesis

2. **Subtitle:** _____
   2.1. Description of survey design (what did you do?)
   2.2. Description of questionnaire (number and types of questions)
   2.3. Description of participants (number of participants, gender, age, background, etc.)

3. **Subtitle:** _____
   3.1. Description of data obtained through observation

4. **Subtitle:** _____
   4.1. Logical analysis of data

5. **Subtitle:** Conclusion
   5.1. Restatement of purpose and analysis
   5.2. Conclusions about what to do
   5.3. Recommendation(s) (using your field of study to help you)

Bibliography

Appendices (graphs, tables, charts, pictures). Appendices should be numbered and you should refer to them in your text by number, e.g., *Table 1, Graph 4.*

Writing a Proposal as a Team[1]

When working with a team, we ...

- [ ] think about our audience and what we want them to know;
- [ ] include a title page;
- [ ] provide a table of contents that states which team members contributed to which sections.

In the introduction, we ...

- [ ] give background information and explain what problem or opportunity made us think of this proposal;
- [ ] explain who we are and why we are the right people for the project, listing relevant qualifications and expertise;
- [ ] state our proposal/solution clearly.

In the body of the proposal, we ...

- [ ] explain the objective(s) of the project;
- [ ] detail the steps that we will take to meet our objectives;
- [ ] propose a time period for project completion;
- [ ] explain the benefits/impact of the proposed project;
- [ ] explain what results we need to attain in order to be successful;
- [ ] present a budget;
- [ ] use logical, objective and specific arguments throughout the proposal.

In the conclusion, we ...

- [ ] restate the proposal and repeat our strongest argument(s) for the project.

Sources: Basic Proposal Writing Tips. 4 Nov. 2006. Canada Business—Services for Entrepreneurs, Government of Canada, Quebec Aboriginal Services Network. Web. 5 Oct. 2008. <http://risa.ic.gc.ca/servlet/ContentServer?cid=1086261094490&lang=en&pagename=ABSN_QC%2Fdisplay&c=GuideInfoGuide>.

---

1. This is a simplified version of a common format that is widely used. The Government of Canada recommends a similar (if more complex) version in their text: "Basic Proposal Writing Tips" on the Government of Canada website.

CHECKLIST 5

Writing an Essay

Before I write an essay, I ...

☐ use brainstorming techniques individually or in a group. Brain writing (see page 163) is particularly useful for generating ideas;

☐ conduct research on the topic and select strong sources (for more information about focusing on research and evaluating sources, see pages 191 and 192);

☐ narrow the topic until it is specific enough to be properly covered in a 350-word essay;

☐ write a thesis statement (see below);

☐ write a plan (outline) or a rough draft (see "Template 5: An Essay Plan (Outline)" on page 202 for one possible way of preparing to write).

> A **thesis statement** is a statement on which an essay is entirely based. It is "usually a single sentence that summarizes the answer you give to the issue or question the paper addresses."[1] All the paragraphs must support this sentence.
>
> Before I can write a good thesis statement, I must narrow down my topic. To do this, I take my first general idea and continue to make it more and more specific until it is precise and interesting to write about.

In the introduction, I ...

☐ begin with a controversial or surprising statement to grab my readers' attention;

☐ provide general background information on the topic;

☐ finish with the thesis statement (see above).

In the body of the essay, I ...

☐ use a topic sentence to explain the main idea/argument at the beginning of each paragraph (see below);

☐ provide accurate and relevant support for each of the main ideas/arguments.

> A **topic sentence** is a complete sentence that supports the thesis statement and that provides the main idea for the information that follows in the paragraph.
>
> A topic sentence must contain both an obvious topic and a clear direction.
>
> **Examples:**
>
> ~~My field of study is what I will talk about.~~ (No direction: What about your field of study?)
>
> ~~It teaches useful skills for a wide variety of jobs.~~ (No topic: What teaches?)
>
> My field of study, Liberal Arts, teaches useful skills and information that prepare us for a wide variety of possible careers. (This sentence has both a topic [Liberal Arts] and a direction [teaches useful skills].)
>
> All other sentences in the paragraph should **support** the topic sentence. These sentences can include examples, facts, statistics, etc.

• • •

---

1. Fox, Tom, Johns, Julia and Keller, Sarah. *Cite It Right*. Osterville: Source Aid LLC, 2007. Print.

In the conclusion, I ...

☐ rephrase the thesis and main arguments;

☐ finish with a follow-up to the information in the first sentence of the introduction.

Before I submit the essay, I ...

☐ use revision strategies to check and improve my work. For instance, I edit my work immediately after I write and I proofread it several days later; I can also obtain feedback from a peer or write a reverse plan to ensure that the content of my essay is complete (for more information on revising, see "Focusing on Revision" on page 204).

Formulas That Work

> When I write an essay, I ...
>
> ☐ try not to use the first-person pronoun *I*;
>
> ☐ write "In conclusion," not "Finally," to introduce the conclusion. *Finally* is for a last argument, not for the conclusion.

TEMPLATE 5

An Essay Plan (Outline)

TITLE

INTRODUCTION
General opening statement
More specific details (set-up)
Thesis statement

BODY
Point 1
    Topic sentence
    Support (details, facts, examples)
Point 2
    Topic sentence
    Support (details, facts, examples)
Point 3
    Topic sentence
    Support (details, facts, examples)

CONCLUSION
Summary of all the main points discussed in the body of the text
Restatement of thesis (wrap-up)

CHECKLIST 6

Quoting and Paraphrasing (and Avoiding Plagiarism)

When I cite a source, I ...

☐ make sure that I understand the meaning of the author's idea and express it accurately;

☐ acknowledge in the text that the author expressed the idea and make sure to include the number of the page on which I found the information. Note that when referencing from the Internet, page numbers aren't required;

☐ cite my sources in the Works Cited List (for more information about documenting sources, see page 191).

When I quote, I ...

☐ always use the author's exact wording with quotation marks ("...");

☐ check my spelling and make sure that everything is accurately copied.

When I paraphrase, I ...

☐ read the passage many times to understand it well;

☐ write out the idea freely in my own words without looking at the author's words;

☐ find synonyms for key concepts;

☐ check that my paraphrase is written in a completely different way from the author's original words, but ensure that it still contains all of the original meaning.

Formulas That Work

To include a reference in my text according to the *MLA Handbook* (7th Edition), I use one of the following formulas:

- According to the author, cedar bushes should be planted every twenty-four inches (Laurence 283).

- Laurence states that "optimal spacing for cedars is twenty-four inches" (283).

- If you decide to plant a cedar hedge, you will need to keep about twenty-four inches of space between each bush (Laurence 283).

CHECKLIST 7

Writing a Summary

When I write a summary, I ...

☐ make sure that I understand the text (see "Checklist 1: Focusing on Comprehension" on page 189);

☐ take notes on the main ideas and key arguments (see "Checklist 3: Taking Notes" on page 190);

•••

- [ ] use only my own words (see "Checklist 6: Quoting and Paraphrasing (and Avoiding Plagiarism)" on page 203);
- [ ] don't give my own opinion;
- [ ] write three or four sentences; for short texts, I try to be as concise as possible and do not write more than 40 percent of the length of the original.

CHECKLIST 8

Focusing on Revision

To help improve my written work, I can use the following strategies:

- [ ] **Strategy 1: Editing my work.** Immediately after I write my text, I edit my work. I reread my text to make sure that its content is clear, well-organized and complete. I check that my paragraphs are well-structured. I look for error patterns in verb tenses and verb forms. By editing my own work I am able to notice and correct errors in spelling, grammar, structure and content.

- [ ] **Strategy 2: Emphasizing the positive.** I read my partner's text and highlight ideas I think are important to the text. Then I ask my partner to read these highlighted ideas aloud to me and explain why they are important in the text.

- [ ] **Strategy 3: Obtaining feedback.** Working in a group of three, I read aloud the text of another student in the group. The writer of the text listens carefully as I and the other student in the group comment on his or her text.

- [ ] **Strategy 4: Peer reviewing.** I exchange texts with a partner and, using a pencil, underline or circle any errors I notice in verb tense, pronouns, spelling, structure and content. etc. I then return the text to my partner and explain what I found.

- [ ] **Strategy 5: Writing a reverse plan.** After I write my text, I work backwards from the text to create a reverse plan. Then I make a short list of points that I do not have in my text that I believe I should originally have included.

- [ ] **Strategy 6: Proofreading.** After I write my text, I put it aside for a day or two. Then, I look it over carefully with a fresh perspective, checking for surface errors in grammar, spelling and punctuation.

- [ ] **Strategy 7: Examining paragraphs.** I look at the paragraph I have written and make sure it is the correct length, and that it has a topic sentence and support for the topic sentence (see page 201 for more information about topic sentences and support).

CHECKLIST 1

Focusing on Comprehension

To help me prepare for and then understand a listening text, I can use the following strategies:

☐ **Strategy 1: Listening for keyword cues.** I listen carefully for each keyword that I have highlighted in my questions. When I hear a keyword, I focus carefully on that small part of the listening text in order to hear the answer.

☐ **Strategy 2: Activating your prior knowledge.** I reflect on and talk about a subject before I listen in order to activate and remember topical information and key vocabulary that I already know about the subject.

☐ **Strategy 3: Notetaking.** As I listen, I write down key information in point form and only include details if they help to explain or clarify (for more information, see "Checklist 2: Taking Notes" below).

☐ **Strategy 4: Skimming.** I look at any information provided to me about the listening text. The title, introduction, biographical information, comprehension questions, vocabulary, photos and captions will help me get a general idea of the topic and main direction of the listening.

Most importantly, I relax!

(For strategies to understand vocabulary while listening, see "Checklist 2: Focusing on Vocabulary" on page 190.)

CHECKLIST 2

Taking Notes

When I take notes during a listening or a watching, I ...

☐ look for signals in the speaker's words or tone of voice that something is important;

☐ listen for facts, explanations, definitions of concepts, lists and information that is repeated;

☐ jot down keywords, without trying to write complete sentences. These keywords will help me remember enough of the context to write full sentences, if needed;

☐ organize my notes as I listen the first time by adding in headings and sub-headings. This will help me to understand the speaker's overall argument or direction. After my first listening, I can write down under each heading some questions that I think I should try to answer as I listen a second time. (See pages 70–71 for an example of notes that are well-organized.)

CHECKLIST 1

Preparing an Oral Presentation

Before I present my information, I ...

☐ use brainstorming techniques individually or in a group. Discussing from different perspectives (see page 17) is particularly useful for generating ideas;

☐ research my topic thoroughly to be sure that my information is accurate and relevant, and that my main ideas are well-supported (for more information, see "Checklist 3: Evaluating Sources with the CARS Checklist" on page 192);

☐ prepare a point-form outline of what I am going to say;

☐ organize my material in a similar way to the written form (for example, if I am reporting, I use the rules for writing a report on page 195 to help me structure my presentation and keep focused on what I need to say);

☐ include an introduction and conclusion;

☐ check that my grammar is accurate (especially my verb tenses);

☐ check that my use of general vocabulary and field-related words learned in the unit are correct;

☐ practise presenting it out loud using keywords that I have written on cue cards.

When I present my information, I ...

☐ speak at a normal pace without hesitation;

☐ use descriptive adjectives to make my presentation more interesting;

☐ do not use French;

☐ use visual aids to help people understand my information (without distracting them).

☐ do not read from a text, but instead use my prepared keywords on cue cards.

Formulas That Work

When I do a presentation, I ...

☐ make sure to stand up straight and keep my hands still, and I do not chew gum;

☐ speak loudly and clearly, and modulate my tone of voice;

☐ take time to look each person in the eye a few times throughout the presentation;

☐ respect my time limit.

CHECKLIST 2

Preparing a Group Presentation

Before we present our information, we ...

- [ ] follow the same instructions as in "Checklist 1: Preparing an Oral Presentation" on page 206;
- [ ] ensure that all members of the group are equally involved in the preparation stage;
- [ ] provide feedback to our teammates.

When we present our information, we ...

- [ ] ensure that each group member speaks for approximately the same length of time;
- [ ] respect our own time limits;
- [ ] help our fellow teammates if they need our assistance.

CHECKLIST 3

Preparing an Effective PowerPoint Presentation

When I prepare a PowerPoint presentation, I ...

- [ ] have a picture on every slide (a picture is worth a thousand words!);
- [ ] use a 32- to 36-point sans serif font; for example, Arial, Futura or Verdana;
- [ ] use a 44-point font for titles;
- [ ] do not have complete sentences (complete sentences are only used when you are preparing a PowerPoint presentation that will not be presented; for example, an online PowerPoint presentation);
- [ ] use point form, keywords and bullets;
- [ ] have 25 words or less per slide;
- [ ] use a dark colour text on a light background;
- [ ] use a light colour text on a dark background;
- [ ] avoid bright blue backgrounds;
- [ ] avoid fly-in effects and sound effects;
- [ ] respect copyright rules for quotations and images;
- [ ] respect the number of words permitted by the teacher.

I remember that if I can say it with a picture, I DO!

Appendix
CEGEP Programs[1]

Academic programs:

200.B0	Science
200.10	Science – International Baccalaureate
300.A0	Social Science
300.10	Social Science – International Baccalaureate
500.A1	Creative Arts, Literature and Languages
500.10	Creative Arts, Literature and Languages – International Baccalaureate
501.A0	Music
506.A0	Dance
510.A0	Fine Arts
700.A0	Arts and Sciences
700.B0	Liberal Arts

Technical programs:

110.A0	Dental Technology
110.B0	Denturology
111.A0	Dental Hygiene
112.A0	Acupuncture
120.A0	Dietetics
140.A0	Medical Electrophysiology
140.B0	Biomedical Laboratory Technology
141.A0	Respiratory and Anaesthesia Technology
142.A0	Diagnostic Imaging
142.B0	Nuclear Medicine Technology
142.C0	Radiation Oncology
144.A0	Physical Rehabilitation
144.B0	Orthotics and Prosthetics
145.A0	Animal Health Technology
145.B0	Hunting and Fishing Resource Development
145.C0	Environmental and Wildlife Management
147.A0	Natural Environment Technology
147.A0	Natural Environment Technology (Wildlife Development)
147.A0	Natural Environment Technology (Forest Resource Development)
147.A0	Natural Environment Technology (Natural Resources Development)
147.A0	Natural Environment Technology (Environmental Protection)
152.A0	Farm Management and Technology
152.A0	Farm Management and Technology (Livestock Production)
152.A0	Farm Management and Technology (Crop Production)
153.A0	Livestock Production
153.B0	Horticultural and Environmental Technology
153.B0	Horticultural and Environmental Technology (Fruit and Vegetable Crop Cultivation for Field and Greenhouse)
153.B0	Horticultural and Environmental Technology (Ornamental Plant Cultivation)
153.B0	Horticultural and Environmental Technology (Vegetable, Fruit and Industrial Crop Cultivation)

153.B0	Horticultural and Environmental Technology (Environment)
153.C0	Ornamental Horticulture Landscaping and Marketing
153.C0	Ornamental Horticulture Landscaping and Marketing (Landscaping Development)
153.C0	Ornamental Horticulture Landscaping and Marketing (Service and Product Marketing)
153.C0	Ornamental Horticulture Landscaping and Marketing (Green Spaces)
153.D0	Farm Equipment Technology
154.A0	Food Processing
155.A0	Equine Technology
155.A0	Equine Technology (Trail Horses)
155.A0	Equine Technology (Race Horses)
155.A0	Equine Technology (English Style)
155.A0	Equine Technology (Western Style)
160.A0	Optical Dispensing
160.B0	Hearing Aid Technology
171.A0	Funeral Service Technology
180.A0	Nursing
180.B0	Nursing Assistant
181.A0	Pre-hospital Emergency Care
190.A0	Forest Products Processing Technology
190.B0	Forest Technology
210.A0	Laboratory Technology
210.A0	Laboratory Technology (Analytical Chemistry)
210.A0	Laboratory Technology (Biotechnology)
210.B0	Laboratory Technology (Chemical Processes)
210.02	Chemical Engineering Technology
221.A0	Architectural Technology
221.B0	Civil Engineering Technology
221.C0	Building Systems Technology
221.D0	Realty Appraisal
221.D0	Realty Appraisal (Construction Estimating)
221.D0	Realty Appraisal (Property Evaluation)
222.A0	Urban and Regional Planning
230.A0	Geomatics
230.A0	Geomatics (Cartography)
230.A0	Geomatics (Geodetic Surveying)
231.A0	Fish Farming
231.B0	Seafood Processing
232.A0	Pulp and Paper Technology
233.B0	Furniture Making and Cabinet Making
233.B0	Furniture Making and Cabinet Making (Architectural Woodworking)
233.B0	Furniture Making and Cabinet Making (Mass Production)
235.B0	Industrial Engineering Technology
235.C0	Pharmaceutical Production Technology
241.A0	Mechanical Engineering Technology
241.C0	Composite Materials Processing
241.12	Plastics Processing
241.D0	Industrial Maintenance Technology
243.A0	Computerized Systems Technology
243.B0	Electronics Engineering Technology (Audiovisual)
243.B0	Electronics Engineering Technology (Computers and network)

---

1. For the most up-to-date information, see **www.mels.gouv.qc.ca**

243.B0	Electronics Engineering Technology
243.B0	Electronics Engineering Technology (Telecommunications)
243.C0	Industrial Electronics Technology
243.16	Electronic Design
244.A0	Applied Physics Technology
248.A0	Naval Architecture
248.B0	Navigation
248.C0	Marine Engineering Technology
251.B0	Textile Production
260.A0	Water Treatment
260.B0	Occupational Health and Safety and Environmental Protection
270.A0	Metallurgical Engineering Technology
270.A0	Metallurgical Engineering Technology (Materials Testing)
270.A0	Metallurgical Engineering Technology (Mechanized Welding)
270.A0	Metallurgical Engineering Technology (Processing Procedures)
271.A0	Mineral Technology
271.A0	Mineral Technology (Applied Geology)
271.A0	Mineral Technology (Mining)
271.A0	Mineral Technology (Mineral Processing)
280.A0	Aircraft Piloting
280.A0	Aircraft Piloting (Planes)
280.A0	Aircraft Piloting (Helicopters)
280.A0	Aircraft Piloting (Float Planes and Single Engine Planes)
280.B0	Aircraft Construction
280.C0	Aircraft Maintenance
280.D0	Avionics
310.A0	Police Technology
310.B0	Youth and Adult Correctional Intervention
310.C0	Paralegal Technology
311.A0	Fire Safety and Prevention
322.A0	Early Childhood Education
351.A0	Special Care Counselling
384.A0	Research and Survey Techniques
388.A0	Social Service
391.A0	Community Recreation Leadership Training
393.A0	Information and Library Technologies
410.A0	Transportation Logistics
410.B0	Accounting and Management Technology
410.C0	Insurance and Financial Services
410.D0	Business Management
411.A0	Medical Records Management
412.A0	Office System Technology
412.A0	Office System Technology (Micropublishing and Hypermedia)
412.A0	Office System Technology (Office Work Coordination)
414.A0	Tourism
414.A0	Tourism (Development and Promotion of Travel Products)
414.A0	Tourism (Hospitality and Tour-Guiding)
414.A0	Tourism (Tourist Product Development)
414.B0	Adventure Tourism
420.A0	Computer Science Technology
420.A0	Computer Science Technology (Administrative Data Processing)
420.A0	Computer Science Technology (Industrial Data Processing)
420.A0	Computer Science Technology (Network Management)

430.A0	Hotel Management
430.B0	Food Service and Restaurant Management
551.A0	Professional Music and Song Techniques
551.A0	Professional Music and Song Techniques (Composition and Arrangement)
551.A0	Professional Music and Song Techniques (Music Theatre Performance)
551.A0	Professional Music and Song Techniques (Performance)
561.A0	Theatre Production
561.A0	Theatre Production (Sets and Costumes)
561.A0	Theatre Production (Stage Techniques and Lighting)
561.A0	Theatre Production (Stage Techniques and Management)
561.B0	Dance-Performance
561.B0	Dance-Performance (Classical Dance)
561.B0	Dance-Performance (Contemporary Dance)
561.C0	Professional Theatre (Acting)
561.D0	Circus Arts
561.D0	Circus Arts (General Circus Performer)
561.D0	Circus Arts (Specialized Circus Performer)
570.A0	Graphic Design
570.B0	Museum Techniques
570.C0	Industrial Design Techniques
570.D0	Display Design
570.E0	Interior Design
570.F0	Photography
571.A0	Fashion Design
571.B0	Apparel Production Management
571.C0	Fashion Marketing
573.A0	Applied Arts and Crafts
573.A0	Applied Arts and Crafts (Sculpture)
573.A0	Applied Arts and Crafts (Ceramics)
573.A0	Applied Arts and Crafts (Textile Construction)
573.A0	Applied Arts and Crafts (Cabinetmaking and Millwork)
573.A0	Applied Arts and Crafts (Textile Printing)
573.A0	Applied Arts and Crafts (Jewellery)
573.A0	Applied Arts and Crafts (Violin Making)
573.A0	Applied Arts and Crafts (Leatherwork)
573.A0	Applied Arts and Crafts (Glasswork)
574.A0	Animation
574.B0	3D Animation and Image Synthesis
581.A0	Computer Graphics in Prepress Work
581.B0	Printing Techniques
581.C0	Printing Works Management
582.A1	Multimedia Integration
589.A0	Television Production and Postproduction Techniques
589.A0	Television Production and Postproduction Techniques (Production)
589.A0	Television Production and Postproduction Techniques (Postproduction)
589.B0	Media Communication Techniques
589.B0	Media Communication Techniques (Radio Hosting and Production)
589.B0	Media Communication Techniques (Advertising Coordination and Consulting)
589.B0	Media Communication Techniques (Journalism)

PHOTO CREDITS

Notes

FIELDS OF VISION: ENGLISH FOR WORK AND STUDY